Woolf Studies Annual

Volume 20, 2014

PACE UNIVERSITY PRESS • NEW YORK

Copyright © 2014 by
Pace University Press
41 Park Row, Rm. 1510
New York, NY 10038

All rights reserved
Printed in the United States of America

ISSN 1080-9317
ISBN 978-1-935625-16-2 (pbk: alk.ppr.)

Member

Council of Editors of Learned Journals

♾ Paper used in this publication meets the minimum requirements of
American National Standard for Information
Sciences–Permanence of Paper for Printed Library Materials,
ANSI Z39.48–1984

Editor

Mark Hussey — Pace University

Editorial Board

Tuzyline Jita Allan	Baruch College, CUNY
Eileen Barrett	California State University, East Bay
Morris Beja	Ohio State University
Kathryn N. Benzel	University of Nebraska-Kearney
Pamela L. Caughie	Loyola University Chicago
Wayne K. Chapman	Clemson University
Patricia Morgne Cramer	University of Connecticut, Stamford
Beth Rigel Daugherty	Otterbein College
Louise DeSalvo	Jenny Hunter Endowed Scholar for Literature and Creative Writing, Hunter College, CUNY
Anne Fernald	Fordham University
Amanda Golden	Emory University (Book Review Editor)
Sally Greene	Independent Scholar
Leslie Kathleen Hankins	Cornell College
Suzette Henke	Thruston B. Morton, Sr. Chair of Literary Studies, University of Louisville
Karen Kaivola	Augsburg College
Karen Kukil	Special Collections, William Allan Neilson Library, Smith College
Jane Lilienfeld	Curator's Distinguished Professor of English, Lincoln University
Jane Marcus	Distinguished Professor, CCNY and CUNY Graduate Center
Toni A. H. McNaron	University of Minnesota
Patricia Moran	University of Limerick
Vara Neverow	Southern Connecticut State University
Annette Oxindine	Wright State University
Beth Carole Rosenberg	University of Nevada-Las Vegas
Bonnie Kime Scott	San Diego State University
Brenda R. Silver	Dartmouth College
Susan Squier	Brill Professor of Women's Studies and English, Pennsylvania State University
Peter Stansky	Stanford University
Alex Zwerdling	University of California, Berkeley

Many thanks to readers for volume 20 (in addition to the Editorial Board): Judith Allen (Writers House, U of Pennsylvania); Sarah Cole (Columbia U); Jane de Gay (Leeds Trinity U); Brenda Helt (Independent Scholar); Georgia Johnston (St. Louis U); Emily Kopley (McGill U); Tonya Krouse (U of Kentucky); Karen Levenback (Independent Scholar); Eleanor McNees (U of Denver); Jeanette McVicker (SUNY Fredonia); Elisa Kay Sparks (Clemson U, Emerita).

Woolf Studies Annual is indexed in *Humanities International Complete, ABELL* and the *MLA Bibliography*.

Contents

Woolf Studies Annual

Volume 20, 2014

	viii	Abbreviations
Clara Jones	1	Virginia Woolf's 1931 "Cook Sketch"
Ella Ophir	25	*A Room of One's Own*, Ordinary Life-Writing, and *The Note Books of a Woman Alone*
David Bradshaw	41	"Wretched Sparrows": Protectionists, Suffragettes and the Irish
Rod C. Taylor	53	Narrow Gates and Restricted Paths: The Critical Pedagogy of Virginia Woolf

GUIDE

	83	Guide to Library Special Collections

REVIEWS

Beth Rigel Daugherty	103	*Virginia Woolf's Essayism* by Randi Saloman
Jenny McDonnell	107	*Woolf and the City* Elizabeth F. Evans and Sara Cornish, Eds.
Eleanor McNees	110	*The Years* by Virginia Woolf, Anna Snaith Ed.

Carrie J. Preston	**114**	*Social Dance and the Modernist Imagination in Interwar Britain* by Rishona Zimring
Molly Hite	**117**	*Virginia Woolf in Context* Bryony Randall and Jane Goldman, Eds.
Gayle Rogers	**121**	*Julian Bell: From Bloomsbury to the Spanish Civil War* by Peter Stansky and William Abrahams
Bruce Robbins	**124**	*The Labors of Modernism* by Mary Wilson
Michele Wick	**128**	*Virginia Woolf and Neuropsychiatry* by Maxwell Bennett
Vara Neverow	**131**	*Mapping the Modern Mind: Virginia Woolf's Parodic Approach to the Art of Fiction in* Jacob's Room by Lindy van Rooyen
Anne Dwyer	**135**	*Virginia Woolf and the Materiality of Theory: Sex, Animal, Life* by Derek Ryan
Cailin Copan-Kelly	**138**	*Virginia Woolf's Late Cultural Criticism* by Alice Wood
Sarah Terry	**142**	*Virginia Woolf's Likes & Dislikes*, Collected and Edited with an Introduction and Notes by Paula Maggio; *The Best of Blogging Woolf, Five Years On* by Paula Maggio; *Walking in the Footsteps of Michel de Montaigne* by Judith Allen; *How Should One Read a Marriage? Private Writings, Public Reading, and Leonard and Virginia Woolf* by Drew Patrick Shannon; *Virginia Woolf as a 'Cubist Writer'* by Sarah Latham Philips; *Virginia Woolf and the Spanish Civil War: Texts, Contexts & Women's Narratives* by Lolly Ockerstrom.

Elizabeth Sheehan	**150**	*The Modernist Party* Kate McLoughlin, Ed.; *Modernism, Feminism and the Culture of Boredom* by Alison Pease
Anne Donlon	**156**	*Communal Modernisms: Teaching Twentieth-Century Literature and Culture in the Twenty-First-Century Classroom* Emily Hinnov, Lauren Rosenblum, Laurel Harris, Eds.
Kristin Anderson	**159**	*Virginia Woolf and the Natural World* Kristin Czarnecki and Carrie Rohman, Eds.
Frances Spalding	**163**	*The Charleston Bulletin Supplements* by Virginia Woolf and Quentin Bell. Claudia Olk, Ed.
Justine Dymond	**165**	*Haptic Modernism: Touch and the Tactile in Modernist Writing* by Abbie Garrington
Amanda Golden	**168**	*The Boundaries of the Literary Archive: Reclamation and Representation* Carrie Smith and Lisa Stead, Eds.
Deborah Longworth	**172**	*Cambridge Companion to Literature of London* Lawrence Manley, Ed.; *Virginia Woolf, Life and London* by Jean Moorcroft Wilson
Elicia Clements	**176**	*Virginia Woolf and Classical Music: Politics, Aesthetics, Form* by Emma Sutton
Adam Parkes	**179**	*Shell Shock and the Modernist Imagination: The Death Drive in Post-World War I British Fiction* by Wyatt Bonikowski
	183	Notes on Contributors
	192	Policy

Abbreviations

AHH	*A Haunted House*
AROO	*A Room of One's Own*
BP	*Books and Portraits*
BTA	*Between the Acts*
CDB	*The Captain's Death Bed and Other Essays*
CE	*Collected Essays* (4 vols.)
CR1	*The Common Reader*
CR2	*The Common Reader, Second Series*
CSF	*The Complete Shorter Fiction*
D	*The Diary of Virginia Woolf* (5 vols.)
DM	*The Death of the Moth and Other Essays*
E	*The Essays of Virginia Woolf* (6 Vols.)
F	*Flush*
FR	*Freshwater*
GR	*Granite & Rainbow: Essays*
JR	*Jacob's Room*
L	*The Letters of Virginia Woolf* (6 Vols.)
M	*The Moment and Other Essays*
MEL	*Melymbrosia*
MOB	*Moments of Being*
MT	*Monday or Tuesday*
MD	*Mrs. Dalloway*
ND	*Night and Day*
O	*Orlando*
PA	*A Passionate Apprentice*
RF	*Roger Fry: A Biography*
TG	*Three Guineas*
TTL	*To the Lighthouse*
TW	*The Waves*
TY	*The Years*
VO	*The Voyage Out*

Virginia Woolf's 1931 "Cook Sketch"
Clara Jones

In a 1997 *Woolf Studies Annual* article Susan Dick brought to light typescript drafts of an unpublished story by Virginia Woolf entitled "The Cook" held in the Monks House Papers in Sussex University Library. Dick convincingly reads this story as evidence not only of Woolf's long-standing preoccupation with life writing but also her belief in "the importance of the unrecorded lives of domestic servants" (123).[1] According to Dick, Biddy Brien, the eponymous cook of the story, and her long years of service with the middle-class Savery family, are closely based on Virginia Woolf's own childhood cook, Sophia Farrell, who later worked for the Stephen children when they moved to Bloomsbury. Dick dates "The Cook" drafts to the late twenties or early thirties, referring to Woolf's contemporary diaries and letters to support this dating. However, she singles out the following extract from Woolf's October 1931 diary as "the only reference Woolf makes to writing something about a cook" (129):

> Dear me, I spent 20 minutes dashing off a cooks talk – so much I need random rollicking humour. Oh what a grind that [writing *The Waves*] was! It comes over me now. Literally I have a pain in my head – but my head has many pains – when I try to stretch another book – (*D*4 48)

Dick points out that: "Although the editors of the Diary assume Woolf is referring

---

[1] In her 2010 study of the interactions of class and desire in Woolf's shorter fiction, Heather Levy offers a detailed engagement with "The Cook," paying close attention to a shorter second draft of the story that Dick did not transcribe in her 1997 article. While Levy's focus on the connections between this story and other examples of Woolf's shorter fiction provides an interesting context, her reading of the relationship between Biddy Brien and Mrs. Savery as one of "self-respecting spiritual (if not economic) equal[s]" (176) with possibly lesbian undertones overlooks the way in which Biddy's devotion to Mrs. Savery is clearly characterized by Woolf as a product of late-Victorian paternalistic social relations, which demanded utter self-sacrifice and devotion from servants and benevolent care from masters. For a full transcription of the alternative, shorter draft of "The Cook" see Heather Levy, "'These Ghost Figures of Distorted Passion': Becoming Privy to Working-Class Desire in 'The Watering Place' and 'The Ladies Lavatory,'" *Modern Fiction Studies*, 50 (2004) 31-58, 31-58. Mary Wilson's recent study of the treatment of domesticity and servants in modernist fiction includes a chapter concerning the figure of the cook in Woolf's writing and an insightful reading of place, object and identity in "The Cook." Wilson addresses questions, including Woolf's approach to perspective in "The Cook," which will also concern me in my discussion of the Morgan sketch. See *Labors of Modernism: Domesticity, Servants, and Authorship in Modernist Fiction* (Farnham: Ashgate, 2013): 36-40.

in this entry to 'The Cook,' the absence [. . .] of anything approaching 'random rollicking humour' leaves this assumption open to question" (129). Susan Dick's hunch is correct since another—both lost and rollicking—"cooks talk" written by Woolf can be found in the pages of her 1931 notebook held in the Morgan Library in New York.

 Written in the same period that Dick suggests the Monks House stories were written, this unfinished, unpublished sketch, which I will refer to as the "Cook Sketch," is also concerned with a cook. However, it departs from the Monks House story in key formal and thematic ways. Most strikingly, the "Cook Sketch" is written mainly in the voice of the cook, a crucial difference from "The Cook" in which a narrator records the story of faithful Victorian cook, Biddy Brien, only at times rendering her speech within quotation marks. This article discusses the implications of Woolf's act of class ventriloquism in the sketch and suggests how it might inform our understanding of Woolf's (often vexed) attitudes towards class. The paper also contributes to the recent trend in Woolf studies, described by Anna Snaith as providing "a more nuanced and contextualized treatment of issues surrounding Woolf, class and gender" (9). I establish the literary and historical contexts for Woolf's sketch, building on Susan Dick's article in which she identifies Woolf's concurrent completion of *The Waves* and her fraught revision of the "Introductory Letter" to the Women's Co-operative Guild authored collection *Life as We Have Known It* as key contexts for "The Cook." Before moving on to these critical considerations, I will provide a brief overview of the rich and wide-ranging narrative of the "Cook Sketch," identifying some of its central motifs and characters.

I

 While "The Cook" opens with rather conventional introductions, there are no such formalities in the Morgan "Cook Sketch," which opens *in medias res*:

> Oh yes, oh yes, oh yes, certainly we will have mutton for dinner. {And} But what is the price of mutton in this neighbourhood, I said to my cook. And she said […][2]

This opening chain of distracted affirmatives and the slightly disgruntled question that follows about the price of mutton are the only words assigned to the cook's

---

[2] Letter to a Young Poet: Autograph Manuscript, 1931 Sept. 24, The Morgan Library and Museum, MA3333, f. 44. All the quotations that follow from the "Cook Sketch" will come from the transcription that accompanies this article. My thanks to the Society of Authors as the literary representative of the Estate of Virginia Woolf for permission to quote unpublished material in this article.

employer in the "Cook Sketch." The rest of the story is dedicated to the cook's prolonged and expansive response to this question.

> I think you ought to go [yourself] & speak to Mr Livestock - {Why} He has been palming us off with second rate joints ever so often lately. You can tell New Zealand by its pink [vein] They send them over by [haunches].[3] They arent what we're accustomed to. They arent what the best families have.

The cook's commentary begins with her annoyance at the "second rate" joints Mr. Livestock the butcher has been supplying and her suspicion that they are from "New Zealand." The butcher's comic name and the cook's conspiratorial reference to the mutton's colonial origins appear to confirm Woolf's characterization of the sketch as a playful and even "rollicking" writing exercise.

There is more historical context, however, to this opening gambit than might at first appear. The misrepresentation of Australasian mutton as British meat by unscrupulous butchers was a source of public outrage at the turn of the century and continued to trouble the popular imagination and feature in the pages of newspapers well into the 1930s when legislation for the compulsory labelling of the origins of meats was enacted (Higgins 164). David M. Higgins states that the "practice of 'passing-off' Australasian exports as British meat" was motivated by the substantial profit butchers could make—effectively "the difference between the wholesale price of the imported meat and its retail price as British meat" (163). As well as noting that this mis-selling tended to focus in London, Higgins highlights a contemporary inquiry that suggested that cooks of well-to-do West End families were sometimes complicit in this underhand practice: "butchers sold imported meat as home killed, but because professional cooks were aware of this and received a large commission, they would buy the imported meat under the pretense of buying English but cook the meat in such a way that it would not be detected by the household" (172). The cook's alertness to Mr. Livestock's potentially disreputable behavior, then, does not simply signal her busy-bodying character but rather registers Woolf's alert-

---

[3] The New Zealand Shipping Company developed refrigerated containers in 1882 and delivered its first cargo of frozen meat to England in September of that year. Gordon Holman, *In the Wake of Endeavour: The History of The New Zealand Shipping Company and Federal Steam Navigation Company* (London: Charles Knight & Co., 1973). An article in the *Daily Mirror* on Thursday 16 April 1931 entitled "London's 1,000 Ships" describes record "consignments of frozen lamb and mutton from Australia and New Zealand" arriving in London that month (20). Another article entitled "Putting The Case For More Home-Grown Meat" written by Lord Beaverbrook and published on Tuesday 8 October 1929 in the *Daily Express* attempts to quell fears surrounding the quality of New Zealand meat: "Mutton and lamb can come frozen all the way from New Zealand in so fine a state that only gastronomic snobbery looks down upon a leg of Canterbury lamb" (10).

ness to contemporary issues of domestic economy, showing a side of Woolf not on regular display and challenging the now declining but once popular image of Woolf as detached aesthete.[4]

As well as alluding to contemporary scandal surrounding the misrepresentation of Australasian mutton and lamb, the cook's imperious dismissal of these joints—"They arent what we're accustomed to. They arent what the best families have"—and her snooty association with "the best families" imply an attachment to the protocols of class, which appears to be challenged only lines later when, advancing on the theme of groceries, the cook's monologue turns to a more specific discussion of the current economic climate, food prices and the government's failure "to protect us working-classes."

The cook's narrative moves circuitously around the deficiencies of Prime Minister Ramsay MacDonald, tales of King George's recent illness, her own upbringing and back to the important question of what there is to eat. She remembers "when it was killing day we begged a bit off the butcher, whose son's now in hospital with a bad leg." The story of the butcher's son George and the cook's anxious disclosures about his bad leg trouble the light-hearted tone of her childhood reminiscences:

> They dont tell him, but what I'm thinking is they know for certain he wont stand again. And his hands no good to him – what use is hands to a man trained {to a} in a bacon factory where its hauling hauling hauling by day, by night corpses of pigs, & off to Smithfield

In this passage the sketch's interest in meat and its quality, which previously seems to have been deployed in the interests of authenticity and atmosphere, takes on a strange almost gruesome narrative [il]logic. Here Mr. Livestock's bad joints of mutton seem to find their peculiar double in George's "bad" legs. The reference to the "corpses" rather than the carcasses of pigs that follows humanizes the dead animals in a way that jars. Indeed, there are altogether too many joints and limbs flung about together in this passage—"hands," "hands," "bacon," "corpses of pigs." The disruptive and grisly quality of this section finds its apt resolution in

---

[4] Michèle Barrett's recent article on Woolf's meticulous research for Leonard's 1920 book *Empire and Commerce in Africa* represents an exciting contribution to this changing view of Woolf. Barrett's study of Woolf's research notes reveals her interest in empirical data and casts her as an "even slightly pedantic scholar." It seems significant, in light of this sketch's preoccupation with the international meat trade, that some of Woolf's research notes for this 1920 project concerned the increases in Argentine "frozen sheep export trade." See "Virginia Woolf's Research for *Empire and Commerce in Africa* (Leonard Woolf, 1920)," *Woolf Studies Annual* 19 (2013): 83-122 (101).

the repetition of "hauling" in the final line with its careless singsong close: "& off to Smithfield."

Even the cook's innocuous observations about the view from George's hospital window subtly gesture to the sketch's darker sub-textual concerns. The winding vista, "up the river, down the river," reminds her of when she "was a girl with my first baby: Tommy Atkins, the [bakers] son at Aldershot." That the cook's first charge shares his name with the popular slang term for an ordinary soldier[5] is significant, as is the cook's imaginative association of baby Tommy Atkins with the disabled young man in hospital. With the anxiety of the above passage in mind, this evocation of Tommy Atkins suggests that, as well as being marked by concerns about the 1931 financial depression, this sketch broods on the violent legacy of World War I.

As will be clear from the quotations so far, the cook's tone is forthright and conversational but also marked by Woolf's awkward attempts at rendering working-class speech. The cook's taste for royal gossip appears to reflect Woolf's snobbish ideas about working-class taste for trivial gossip about their "betters" (ironic given Woolf's own fascination with Royal gossip).[6] This is especially clear in the cook's keen interest in where Princess Mary buys her mutton and later her preoccupation with King George's parrot who wakes him every morning.

The "Cook Sketch" is, then, a mixture of the serious and playful and is a more revealing text than Woolf's description of it as simply humorous light relief suggests. This will become all the more evident as I consider the sketch in the context of Woolf's contemporary literary projects and the fraught British historical moment at which it was written. I will also consider the contentious question of Woolf's co-option of a working woman's voice in this sketch, positioning the ventriloquizing we encounter in the "Cook Sketch" both in relation to Woolf's failure to include working-class voices in *The Waves* and her encounter with the autobiographical writing of Guildswomen in the 1931 collection *Life as We Have Known It*.

---

[5] For the origins and history of the use of Tommy Atkins see John Laffin, *Tommy Atkins: The Story of the English Soldier* (London: Cassell & Company, 1966). See also Richard Holmes's *Tommy: The British Soldier on the Western Front*, 1914-1918 (London: Harper Perennial, 2005).

[6] Woolf's responses in her diary to the abdication crisis of 1936 are a good example. At the same time as analyzing the knee-jerk patriotism which led her to feel "perceptibly humiliated" on behalf of her country, Woolf records every tidbit of gossip she picks up: "Bergen says Timmy says he is now merely haggling for a sufficient income. K. George left him nothing; & he has lavished money & jewels on Simpson" (*D5* 40). In her 1933 review of Marie, Queen of Romania's autobiography Woolf explores the curious appeal of "Royalty" and their strange familiarity. She concludes in apparently republican spirit: "Can we go on bowing and curtseying to people who are just like ourselves?" (*E6* 55).

II

The three-page "Cook Sketch" is in a fifty-two-page autograph manuscript notebook, which is for the most part dedicated to a draft of Woolf's essay "A Letter to a Young Poet." The first page of the notebook is headed with the title "Letter to a Young Poet" and in the top left-hand corner the date "1931 Sept. 24th" is written. Unlike much of Woolf's unpublished work the precise dating of the notebook and the useful reference from Woolf's diary on 14 October 1931 allows us to be fairly clear on the dating of the "Cook Sketch." As is clear from the images reproduced here, this sketch also seems to have been dashed off in twenty minutes, as Woolf puts it in her diary. Written in Woolf's most loose and sweeping hand over just three pages, the sketch contains hardly any deletions and some words remain indecipherable—these are enclosed in square brackets in my transcription.

Woolf's "A Letter to a Young Poet," then, represents the immediate literary context for her "Cook Sketch." Not only does the sketch share the space of the 1931 notebook with this essay but it was also during a break in writing this piece that she wrote the "Cook Sketch." Published in the summer of 1932, "A Letter" critiques the "colloquial" tendencies of the emerging generation of poets including John Lehmann, to whom the letter is addressed. In it Woolf complains:

> Something has worked in which cannot be made into poetry; some foreign body, angular, sharp-edged, gritty, has refused to join in the dance. Obviously, suspicion attaches to Mrs Gape; she has asked you to make a poem of her. (*E5* 310)

Woolf has been roundly criticized for her sneering association of all that is "actual," "colloquial" and "foreign" to poetry with the charwoman, Mrs. Gape. Hermione Lee rightly locates in it "something of the priggishness of her earlier resistance to Joyce" (619).

While Woolf's figuring of Mrs. Gape in "A Letter" is clearly reflective of certain class prejudices, any dogmatism about Mrs. Gape and her place in poetry here is complicated by Woolf's concurrent experimentation with voice in the "Cook Sketch."[7] In the sketch we find an attempt to recount the, according to Woolf, "untellable" story of Mrs. Gape. In "A Letter" Woolf refers to "Mrs Gape, the charwoman, whose retort to the greengrocer gives me the keenest pleasure." (*E5* 307) In the "Cook Sketch" we find Woolf's imagined version of this "retort" in the

---

[7] Susan Dick suggests that the style and rhythm of "The Cook" was, in part, determined by Woolf's concurrent drafting of "A Letter," which was much concerned with these questions. She also suggests links between Mrs. Gape, Biddy Brien and Woolf's character Mrs. Crosby in *The Years* (130).

cook's feud with the butcher and later in her consternation at food prices:

> And the tricks they play, if ones not watching: the innards & the neck cant weigh all that: not two pounds 3 {oz} ounces which is what they charge us for: & then the backs come so high – its wicked in these days of want; when every penny counts.

Reference to the Morgan draft of "A Letter" is also suggestive in this regard. While there are frequent mentions of "your Charwoman," Mrs. Gape does not feature at all and in the Morgan draft it is the unnamed charwoman who rows with the greengrocer. It seems clear that the late appearance of the "Cook Sketch" in the course of the draft notebook (it occupies pages forty-four to forty-six of the fifty-two page notebook) and Mrs. Gape's absence from the draft and presence in the final version of the essay are linked. Woolf's voluble and assertive cook, and Mrs. Gape who is spoken for and about in "A Letter," are bound up together, anxiously, in Woolf's imagination. My intention here is not to co-opt the "Cook Sketch" as part of an apologia for "A Letter to a Young Poet" or its treatment of Mrs. Gape, but rather to suggest that the imaginative overlap and also the tension between these texts usefully exposes the complicated and contradictory way in which issues of class and voice figure in Woolf's work. This will become increasingly apparent as I now move to focus on classed voices and *The Waves*.

Returning to Woolf's diary entry of 14 October, it is clear that she conceived the "Cook Sketch" in relation to her recently completed novel *The Waves*, published on 8 October 1931. In this entry Woolf pits the "random rollicking humour" of the "Cook Sketch" against what she characterizes as the mental and physical "grind" of writing *The Waves*. I am wary of taking Woolf at her word here or accepting her implied division between *The Waves* and the "Cook Sketch" for a number of reasons.

Firstly and obviously, *The Waves*, a novel composed of the intercutting monologues of its six central characters and in which the third person narration is relegated to brief italicized interludes, is a project profoundly concerned with the narrative possibilities of voice. Drafts of *The Waves* also reveal that Woolf initially intended to include working-class voices in this polyvocal text and Gillian Beer has characterized Woolf's failure to do so in the final novel as "a loss in a book that was to be, according to the title page of the first draft, 'the life of anybody'" (89-90). The effaced working-class speech, significantly for my purposes, belongs to servants. Florrie, who leaves home to become a "kitchenmaid" (Graham 1.67), writes in a letter home that she has "'fallen into a good crib where they keep a man & three maids'" (Graham 1.108). The narrator continues, she "was now learning how to make make mashed potatoes by watching the cook; if the an awful, formidable woman…" (Graham 1.108). Florrie's report of her circumstances reminds us of the cook's account of her first employment with the Atkins of Aldershot, while the "awful, formidable" cook in this passage may be read as an embryonic version of the cook in her later sketch.

The final version of *The Waves* still offers numerous glimpses of working women who may be read as silent prototypes for the cook of Woolf's later sketch. There is "the cook [who] shoves in and out the dampers" and the "women [who] shuffle past with shopping-bags" (115) on whom Neville fixes grimly as he considers Percival's death, while later there is the old woman who "sits, arms akimbo, in an omnibus with a basket" whom Jinny points out to Neville (137). There is also, most strikingly, the totemic Mrs. Moffatt, Bernard's college "bedder," whose "sayings" he keeps noted down and who, he reassures himself throughout the novel, will "come and sweep it all up" (58, 60, 142).[8]

Beer suggests that Woolf's decision to omit working-class speech was prompted by her awareness of her limits as a writer, "[b]ecause of her uncertainty about the sounds of other kinds of voice and her fear of condescending" (89). Certainly, Woolf's attempts at ventriloquizing the speech of working people in previous projects had been edged with snobbish amusement, for instance in her 1919 short story "Kew Gardens" where the conversation of two lower-middle-class women is reduced to a chain of words concerning family and, tellingly, food: "My Bert, Sis, Bill, Grandad, the old man, sugar…" (*CSF* 93). Or else these efforts were characterized by a complete failure of understanding as in the nonsense song of the beggar woman in *Mrs. Dalloway*: "ee um fah um so/ foo swee too eem oo - " (88).[9]

The voice that we encounter in the "Cook Sketch," however, with its odd mixture of slapstick—as in the cook's anecdotes about King George's parrot— and reverie—as in her memories of "the brooch shaped like a lyre" gifted to her by her first employers in Aldershot—marks a subtle shift in Woolf's approach to working-class voices. This increased interest can be linked to her practice in *The Waves*. There we find the ordinary and the absurd—for instance Percival's nose blowing (92)—crop up repeatedly in its characters' monologues. Both Woolf's negative association of *The Waves* and the "Cook Sketch" in the diary entry quoted at the start, and the glimmers of working-class speech that were excluded from *The Waves* and, most tellingly, Bernard's keen notation of Mrs. Moffatt's speech suggest some kinship between these texts.

---

[8] In her important study of the anti-imperialist, socialist politics of *The Waves*, Jane Marcus suggests that Mrs. Moffatt is one of Woolf's "recurring" and powerfully disruptive charwomen, who serve to symbolically expose the corruption and dependency at the heart of the British class structure (81).

[9] Writing of the beggar woman's song in *Mrs. Dalloway*, Alex Zwerdling notes that the speech of the working classes is not simply rendered as "nonsense" but "a whole section of society is thus treated as *terra incognita*" (97).

While drafting *The Waves* Woolf toyed with introducing a working-class child, Albert, the son of "a cowman," whose life she might record alongside that of Roger, the son of a "civil servant." Pulling back from this plan, Woolf's later draft seems almost apologetic: "No single person could follow two/ Lives so opposite; could speak two languages so different" (Graham 1.68). Finn Fordham reads this episode as Woolf's attempt to "[seek] forgiveness" for her suppression of Albert's narrative and to "share with her reader her own problem of not being able to follow such 'opposite' lives" (257). Such an interpretation casts interesting light on Woolf's possible motivations for undertaking the "Cook Sketch." In spite of her relief at the positive reception of *The Waves*, that she continued to experiment with working-class voice in her "Cook Sketch" suggests a lingering preoccupation or perhaps even self-reproach concerning the working-class characters she omitted from *The Waves*.

Before moving on to consider the way in which the "Cook Sketch" is informed by Woolf's involvement with the Women's Co-operative Guild, I explore the significant parallels between this sketch and Woolf's "London Scene" essays, published in *Good Housekeeping* between 1931 and 1932. Written between February and April 1931, several months before the "Cook Sketch," these six essays collectively offer a tour of the sites and monuments of London—from the London Docks to Keats's House on Hampstead Heath. While appearing to be a light-hearted series written for a popular, women's interest magazine, Woolf scholars have located throughout the essays evidence of Woolf's feminist and anti-imperialist politics.[10]

Virginia Woolf's dismissive tone when describing her "London Scene" essays in her diary is the first hint of their potential connection with the "Cook Sketch":

---

[10] In an early and important reading of this series in her 1985 study of Virginia Woolf and London, Susan M. Squier suggests that "Woolf's 'London Scene' essays, informed by her feminism, encounter the city as both the center of patriarchy and the testing ground for feminist values" (52). Squier's approach to the essays, in particular her preference for what she considers the more explicit social critique of an earlier draft of "The Docks of London," has since been challenged by a number of scholars. Pamela Caughie has argued in "Purpose and Play in Woolf's *London Scene* Essays" (*Women's Studies* 5.16 [1986]: 389-408) for greater attention to be paid to Woolf's aesthetic choices and writerly strategies in these essays and the significant ways in which rhetoric and performance are bound up with Woolf's social critique in these texts. Sonita Sarker locates the "London Scene" essays in the context of contemporary debates about the legacies of the British Empire and women as citizens of the Empire, in "Locating a Native Englishness in Virginia Woolf's *The London Scene*" (*National Women's Studies Association Journal* 13.2 [2001]: 1-30). In two articles in *Woolf Studies Annual*, Jeanette McVicker harnesses poststructuralist thought to establish a new reading of the "London Scene" essays, casting them as an integral bridge between the experimental aesthetics of *The Waves* and the political vision of her essay-novel *The Pargiters*. See "'Six Essays on London Life': A History of Dispersal Part I," *Woolf Studies Annual* 9 (2003): 143-65 and "'Six Essays on London Life': A History of Dispersal Part II," *Woolf Studies Annual* 10 (2004): 141-72.

"I'm being bored to death by my London articles—pure brilliant description—six of them—and not a thought for fear of clouding the brilliancy." (*D4* 301) Woolf's 1932 characterization of the articles as fine but thoughtless descriptions—mere writerly exercises—echoes her account of the "Cook Sketch." In addition to the authorial disregard these works inspired they also share an eschewed perspective on London's sites and cultural geography.

Although the "London Scene" essays do not stick faithfully to the orthodox tour of monumental London, taking in London Docklands as well as Whitehall, Westminster and St. Paul's, the "Cook Sketch" plots an altogether different but complementary course through the city. Smithfield, London's largest meat market, features in the "Cook Sketch" and would have been the destination for some of the precious imported cargo Woolf describes in her essay "The Docks of London," the first of her series for *Good Housekeeping*. Woolf's account of the labors of the dock workers, of the "thousand ships with a thousand cargoes" that need to be "unladen" (*E5* 278), recalls the back-breaking "hauling" that workers like George perform at the other end.

In contrast to genteel Cheyne Row where the narrator of "Great Men's Houses" takes in the monumentalized home of Thomas Carlyle, the cook evokes the less salubrious south London suburb of Peckham where she was in service with "the Howls." At one point the narrators of "Great Men's Houses" and the "Cook Sketch" even seem to meet each other's gaze from opposite sides of London; the former looks out to the south from the top of Parliament Hill, while the cook, we assume viewing from the south east, admires the serpentine wind of the river and views as far as Hampstead from George's hospital window.

The companion quality of these texts becomes even more pronounced in their overlapping concerns about labor, trade, and consumption. The anxious note of responsibility that "The Docks of London" closes with and Woolf's use of bodily motifs anticipate similar preoccupations in the "Cook Sketch":

> Our body is their master. We demand shoes, furs, bags, stoves, oil, rice puddings, candles; and they are brought us. Trade watches us anxiously to see what new desires are beginning to grow in us, what new dislikes. (*E5* 280)

The masterful, collective body of the consumer here is set against the diminutive "dwarf city of workmen's houses" and the "skeleton architecture" of the crane-strewn docklands but also contrasts with the decrepit and confined figure of factory-worker George in the "Cook Sketch." Similarly, the consumer's diverse list of demands and the ease with which they are supplied finds a foil in the cook's nervous calculations of the price of modest cuts of meat—"the innards and the neck cant weight all that"—and her constant fears, "in these days of want," of being exploited as a consumer. The "Cook Sketch" offers a contrasting vision of contemporary consumerism to the "London Scene" essays where the buyer is not in a position to make leisured demands for the produce and products of empire but rather frets about potential price rises at home. Read together these texts offer up a valuable insight into Virginia Woolf's familiarity with the workings of consumer capitalism, but also her strong awareness of those who benefit and those who do not.

III

The last part of this paper will consider the ways in which the content of the sketch was informed by its contemporary historical moment. I will focus on how the sketch draws on Woolf's reading of the autobiographical writing of Guildswomen and her own experiences as a Women's Co-operative Guild branch president.

The year that Woolf wrote the "Cook Sketch" was also the year that her contentious "Introductory Letter" to a collection of autobiographical writings by Guildswomen, *Life as We Have Known It*, was published. Taking the form of a remembered account of the 1913 WCG Congress in Newcastle, in the "Introductory Letter" Woolf recalls a highly organized political meeting. However, both Woolf's admiration of the Guildswomen's political commitment and her moving celebration of their writing in this introduction are tempered by her ambivalent reflections on the limits of altruism and the struggle for cross-class identification. The "Introductory Letter" is shot through with Woolf's suspicion of her own position as a "benevolent spectator" (xxi); she critiques what she describes as her "aesthetic sympathy, the sympathy of the eye and the imagination" (xxviii).

This ambivalent introduction has generated polarized critical responses. It has been held up both as an example *par excellence* of Woolf's deeply ingrained class prejudice but also as evidence of her socialist feminist credentials.[11] I am interest-

---

[11] In an influential essay on Woolf and class Mary M. Childers emphasizes what she sees as Woolf's defensiveness of her own privilege in this equivocal introduction and is critical of Woolf's dismissive attitude towards the Guildswomen's autobiographical writing. See "Virginia Woolf on the Outside Looking Down: Reflections on the Class of Women." *Modern Fiction Studies* 38 (1992): 61-79 (62). By contrast Jane Marcus has read the "Introductory Letter" as evidence of Woolf's sincere interest in "the relations between class, sex and art" and describes the letter as "another contribution to the propaganda of hope" ("'No More Horses'" 282). Recently, scholars have turned to focus more on the ambiguities and self-reflexive qualities of this tricky essay. In a subtle reading Ben Clarke suggests the way in which the introduction "exposes some of the key problems of political engagement, revealing the multiple lines upon which commitment is defined and produced" (41). Jessica Berman is similarly alert to the ways in which Woolf "responds to the question of political solidarity" (118) in this text. Having explored the complex way in which Woolf presents the bodies of working women in her introduction (see *Virginia Woolf's Essays: Sketching*

ed in the way that this highly politicized argument over the "Introductory Letter" might be mediated by our knowledge that shortly after the publication of *Life as We Have Known It* in the Autumn of 1931, Woolf was writing her own mock autobiographical sketch by a working woman. I suggest that this demonstrates Woolf's continued preoccupation with the questions of class and identification that animated her "Introductory Letter." Perhaps the frustrating inability to achieve the kind of solidarity with the Guildswomen that she desired in the "Introductory Letter" partially motivated her act of ventriloquism in the "Cook Sketch." And perhaps her puzzling decision to speak for "us working classes" in the "Cook Sketch" may be read as a second attempt to imagine herself into the position of a Guildswoman.

Easier to confirm is the initial impression when reading the "Cook Sketch" that it must draw on Woolf's own reading of the Guildswomen's autobiographical writing. Indeed, examples of Woolf borrowing from the extracts in *Life as We Have Known It* abound in the "Cook Sketch." The cook's alertness to the unscrupulous behavior of shopkeepers seems modelled on Mrs. Layton's account of how when she was a girl of ten working in a shop she was "taught to weigh bread to the disadvantage of the customer." (22) Similarly, the view that the cook admires from George's hospital window—"up the river, down the river: & some days the nurse says you can see Hampstead Steeple"—puts us in mind of Mrs. Layton's account of going into service in Hampstead and her "confirmation at Christ Church, Hampstead." (23) The headquarters of the WCG were for many years based in Hampstead. Mrs. Layton's description of her time as a nursery maid also sheds light on Woolf's cook's reference to her "first baby: Tommy Atkins." Mrs. Layton recalls: "I felt very proud of my influence over my baby," (20) suggesting that when the cook refers to "my baby" she is referring to her charge rather than to her own child.

However, Woolf has not simply borrowed evocative details from the Guildswomen's writing to embellish her "Cook Sketch." She also draws on the Guildswomen's co-operative principles and her own experiences as a WCG member and branch president between 1916 and 1920. While the cook's preoccupation with food prices may be read as Woolf sending up hum-drum working-class conversation, I think it is also important to read this in terms of Woolf's understanding of WCG values, which were based on working women's role as consumers and promoted their "basket power."

Amidst the food shortages of World War I Woolf wrote to Margaret Llewelyn Davies, president of the WCG, saying: "We are trying to set up a Bread Shop here;

---

the Past [Basingstoke: Palgrave Macmillan, 2000]), in a recent article Elena Gualtieri gives a convincing account of the ways in which Woolf's introduction and her reading of the Guildswomen's writing may have influenced the style and argument of *Three Guineas*. See "Woolf, Economics, and Class Politics: Learning to Count," in *Virginia Woolf in Context*, ed. Bryony Randall and Jane Goldman (Cambridge: Cambridge UP, 2012): 183-92.

we held a committee meeting to decide about it, at which we all told stories about our house-hold difficulties" (*L2* 152).[12] Facing the uncertain economic situation of the summer and autumn of 1931, we can imagine that food availability and "household difficulties" must have once again preoccupied the WCG and its members.

The cook's anxiety about the economy and potential price rises can be read as informed by Woolf's experiences with the WCG. Likewise, the cook's suspicion of Ramsay MacDonald speaks of the specific disappointment felt by Labour Party supporters at his perceived betrayal during the summer of 1931: "what the government is for if its not to protect us working classes I don't know I saw Mr Macdonald once myself – a disappointment he was too." After failing to convince his Labour cabinet to accept 10 per cent cuts in unemployment benefit in order to balance the budget, MacDonald formed a National Government in coalition with the Conservatives and Liberals.

In a letter written in September 1931 Woolf describes the summer prior to drafting the "Cook Sketch" as one spent in "violent political argument" (*L4* 373); however, there are few references to the economic and political crises of these months in her letters or diaries. Another letter written to Margaret Llewelyn Davies in October, only days after she wrote the "Cook Sketch," registers the fraught character of Woolf's political engagement at this time:

> Did you see a very good review of L.'s book[13] by Laski in the Statesman? I must say I feel rather triumphant that he has come through with that book in spite of all his other occupations [. . .] I cant concieve how you politicians can go on being political. All the summer we had nothing but political arguments with Maynard and others; and finally felt it so completely silly, futile, petty, personal and unreal—all this about money—that I retired to my room and read poetry in a rage. (*L4* 392)

Coupled with Woolf's failure to interrogate the contemporary crisis in her diary, as she did the General Strike a few years earlier, and the absence of references in her letters, this rather petulant and accusatory letter seems designed to justify Woolf's flight from the "petty, personal and unreal" political world into the aesthetic realm of poetry. Woolf's "Cook Sketch" gives the lie to Woolf's account of herself in this letter and instead shows the degree to which she was absorbed in the pressing economic and political "arguments" she rejects there. Likewise,

---

[12] Woolf's references to her activities with the Richmond branch of the WCG were by no means always this enthusiastic. Indeed, at the time the bread shop idea was being mooted, Woolf complains in her diary of her sister members' taciturnity in meetings unless the discussion concerned food (*D1* 112). Woolf's own well-documented anxiety concerning food and eating is an additional context in which to read this sketch.

[13] The book was *After the Deluge*, Leonard Woolf's assessment of the legacy of the 1926 General Strike.

the at times politicized tone of the cook's voice further compromises Woolf's own presentation of this sketch as mere comic relief. This does not mitigate Woolf's often clumsy, music-hall version of a working-class voice in this sketch. It instead transforms her cook into a heterodox figure who speaks both Woolf's sensitivity to her historical moment but also her persistent anxieties about how she engaged with class in her writing.

My thanks to the Society of Authors as the Literary Representative of the Estate of Virginia Woolf for permission to include a transcription of the "Cook Sketch" and a facsimile of the manuscript.

This article emerged from research undertaken for a doctoral project on Virginia Woolf's political activism and social participation, at Queen Mary University of London, and I am grateful to Queen Mary for funding my research trip to the Morgan Library during the course of my PhD.

I am grateful to Michèle Barrett for her guidance at the early stages of this archival discovery and her continuing help, including feedback on drafts of this article. Thanks also to Brenda Silver for her advice. I am grateful to Mark Hussey for his advice on the transcription of the sketch.

I am indebted to the English Department at Queen Mary University of London for their generous financial support, which made possible the inclusion of the Morgan facsimile with this article.

Works Cited

Beer, Gillian. *Virginia Woolf: The Common Ground*. Edinburgh: Edinburgh UP, 1996. Print.

Berman, Jesssica. *Modernist Fiction, Cosmopolitanism, and the Politics of Community*. Cambridge: Cambridge UP, 2001. Print.

Clarke, Ben. "'But the barrier is impassable': Virginia Woolf and Class." *Woolfian Boundaries: Selected Papers from the Sixteenth Annual International Conference on Virginia Woolf,* Ed. Anna Burrells, Steve Ellis, Deborah Parsons and Kathryn Simpson. Clemson: Clemson U Digital P, 2007: 36-42. Print.

Dick, Susan. "Virginia Woolf's 'The Cook'." *Woolf Studies Annual* 3 (1997): 122-42. Print.

Fordham, Finn. *I do, I undo, I redo: The Textual Genesis of Modernist Selves in Hopkins, Yeats, Conrad, Forster, Joyce and Woolf*. Oxford: Oxford UP, 2010. Print.

Higgins, David M. "'Mutton Dressed as Lamb?': The Misrepresentation of Australian and New Zealand Meat in the British Market, 1890-1914." *Australian Economic History Review* 44 (2004): 161-84. Print.

Lee, Hermione. *Virginia Woolf*. London: Chatto & Windus, 1996. Print.

Levy, Heather. *The Servants of Desire in Woolf's Shorter Fiction*. New York: Peter Lang Publishing, 2010 Print.

Llewelyn Davies, Margaret. Ed. *Life as We Have Known It*. London: Virago, 1977. Print.

Marcus, Jane. "Britannia Rules *The Waves*." *Hearts of Darkness: White Women Write Race*. New Brunswick: Rutgers UP, 2003. Print.

———, "'No More Horses': Virginia Woolf on Art and Propaganda." *Women's Studies* 4 (1977): 265-90. Print.

Snaith, Anna. Ed. *Palgrave Advances in Virginia Woolf Studies*. Basingstoke: Palgrave Macmillan, 2007. Print.

Squier, Susan M. *Virginia Woolf and London. The Sexual Politics of the City*. Chapel Hill: U of North Carolina P, 1985. Print.

Woolf, Virginia. *The Complete Shorter Fiction of Virginia Woolf*. Ed. Susan Dick. London: Hogarth Press, 1989. Print.

———. *The Diary of Virginia Woolf Volume One*, 1915-1919. Ed. Anne Olivier Bell. New York: Harcourt Brace Jovanovich, 1982. Print.

———. *The Diary of Virginia Woolf Volume Four*, 1931-1935. Ed. Anne Olivier Bell. New York: Harcourt Brace Jovanovich, 1982. Print.

———. *The Diary of Virginia Woolf Volume Five*, 1936-1941. Ed. Anne Olivier Bell. New York: Harcourt Brace Jovanovich, 1984. Print.

———.*The Essays of Virginia Woolf Volume Five*, 1929-1932. Ed. Stuart N. Clarke. London: Hogarth, 2009. Print.

———.*The Essays of Virginia Woolf Volume Six*, 1933-1941. Ed. Stuart N. Clarke. London: Hogarth, 2012. Print.

———. *The Letters of Virginia Woolf Volume Two*, 1912-1922. Ed. Nigel Nicolson and Joanne Trautmann. London: Hogarth, 1976. Print.

———. *The Letters of Virginia Woolf Volume Four*, 1929-1931. Ed. Nigel Nicolson and Joanne Trautmann. London: Hogarth, 1978. Print.

———. *Mrs Dalloway*. With an introduction and notes by Elaine Showalter. London: Penguin, 1992. Print.

———. *The Waves*. With an introduction and notes by Kate Flint. London: Penguin, 1992. Print.

———. *The Waves: The Two Holograph Drafts*. Transcribed and ed. by J. W. Graham. London: Hogarth Press, 1976. Print.

Zwerdling, Alex. *Virginia Woolf and the Real World*. Berkeley: U of California P, 1986. Print.

Transcription: The "Cook Sketch"

Letter to a Young Poet: Autograph Manuscript, 1931 Sept. 24, Morgan Library and Museum (MA3333) ff. 44-46

Symbols used in transcription:

{word} cancelled word or passage
<word> interlinear or marginal revision
[word] questionable transcription
[?] illegible word

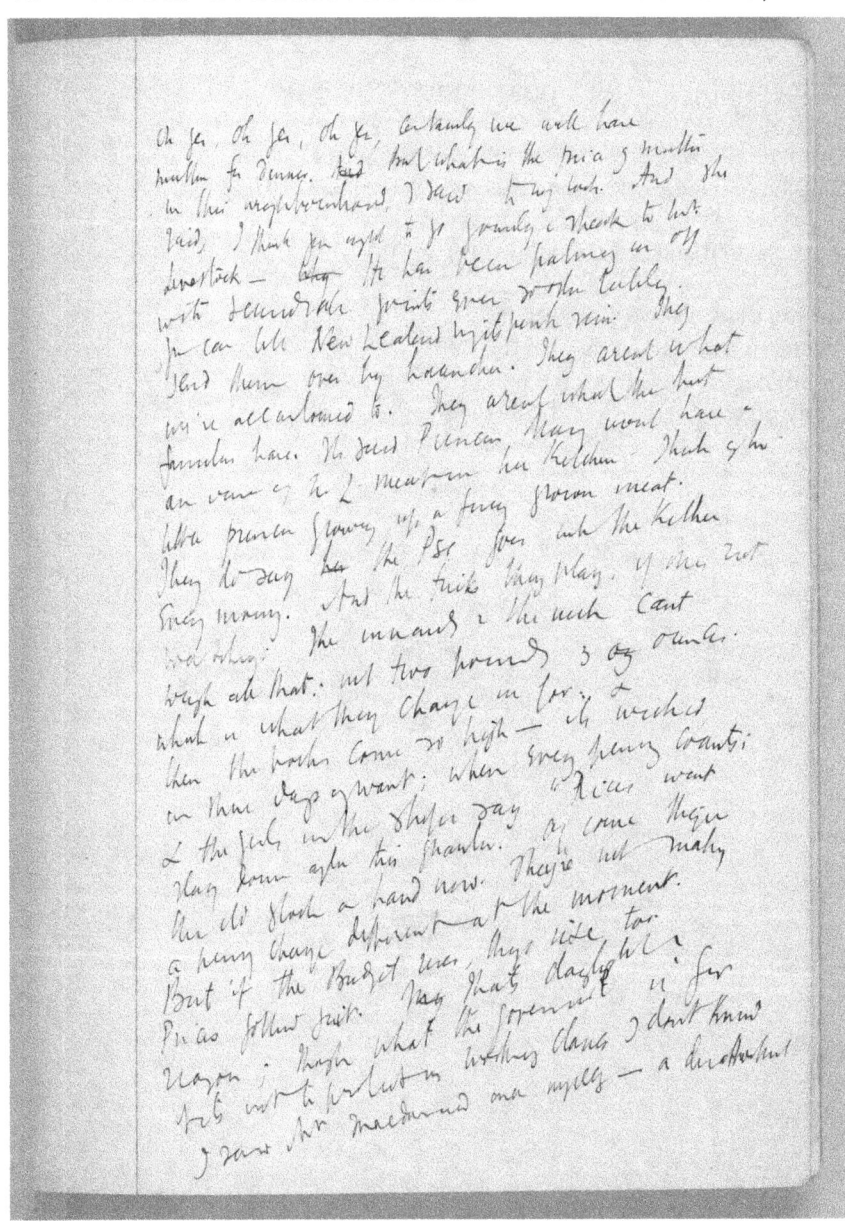

Letter to a young poet : Autograph manuscript, 1931 Sept. 24, p. 44.
The Pierpont Morgan Library, New York. MA 3333. Purchased on the Fellows Fund with the special assistance of Miss Anne S. Dayton, Mrs. Enid A. Haupt, Mrs. James H. Ripley, Mr. and Mrs. August H. Schilling, and Mr. John S. Thacher, 1979. Photographic credit: The Pierpont Morgan Library, New York.

f. 44

Oh yes, oh yes, oh yes, certainly we will have mutton for dinner. {And} But what is the price of mutton in this neighbourhood, I said to my cook. And she said, I think you ought to go [yourself] & speak to Mr Livestock - {Why} He has been palming us off with second rate joints ever so often lately. You can tell New Zealand by its pink [vein] They send them over by [haunches].[14] They arent what we're accustomed to. They arent what the best families have. Its said Princess Mary[15] wont have an ounce of Mr L. meat in her kitchen. Think of her little princes growing up on fully [grown] meat. They do say {her} the Pss goes into the kitchen every morning. And the tricks they play, if ones not watching: the innards & the neck cant weigh all that: not two pounds 3 {oz} ounces which is what they charge us for: & then the backs come so high – its wicked in these days of want; when every penny counts; & the girls in the shops say "Prices wont stay down after this [quarter]. Of course they've the old stock on hand now. They're not making a penny change different at the moment. But if the Budget rises, [they'll] rise too. Prices follow suit. {My} Thats daylight: [reason]; though what the government is for if its not to protect us working classes I don't know I saw Mr Macdonald once myself – a disappointment

[14] See note 3 above
[15] Princess Mary was given the title Princess Royal in 1931 by her father, King George V. Her mother was Queen Mary of Teck. She had two sons, George and Gerald, who were eight and seven respectively at the time Woolf wrote the "Cook Sketch."

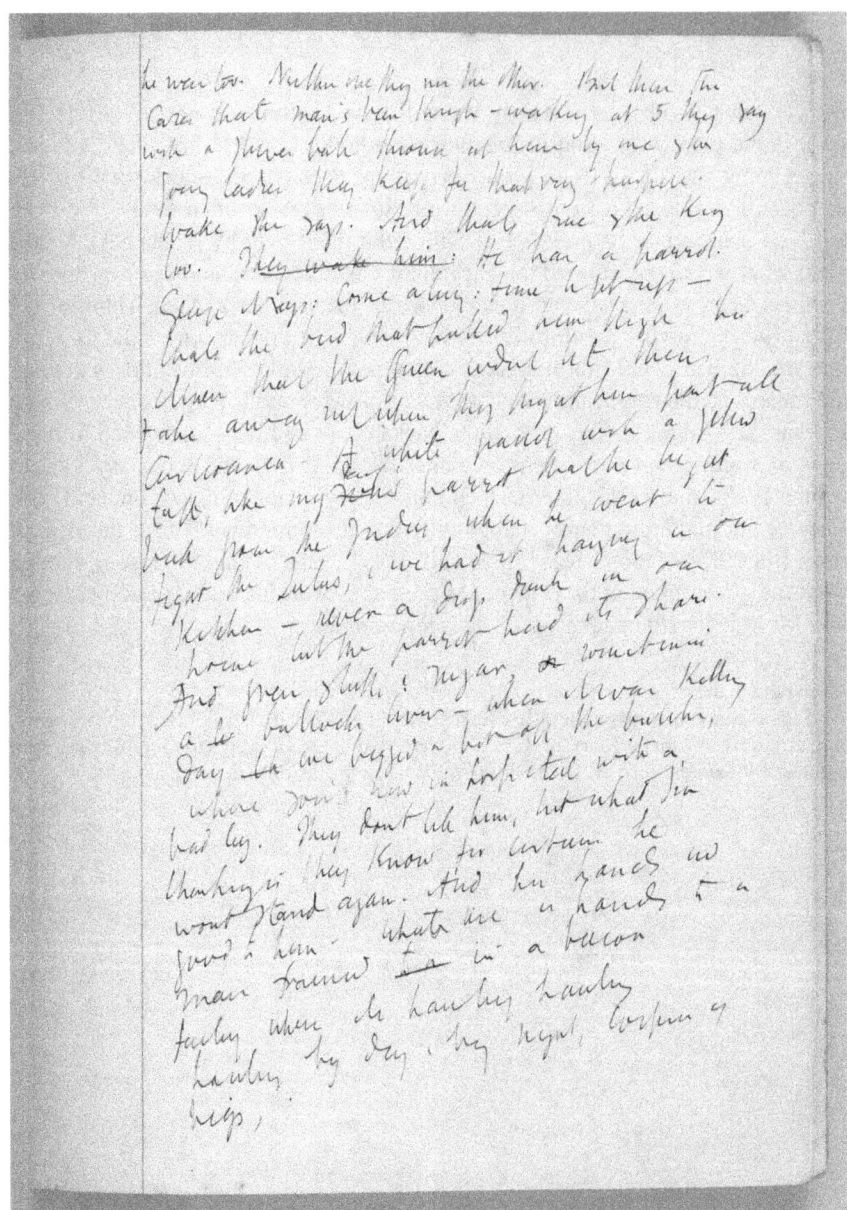

Letter to a young poet : Autograph manuscript, 1931 Sept. 24, p. 45.
The Pierpont Morgan Library, New York. MA 3333. Purchased on the Fellows Fund with the special assistance of Miss Anne S. Dayton, Mrs. Enid A. Haupt, Mrs. James H. Ripley, Mr. and Mrs. August H. Schilling, and Mr. John S. Thacher, 1979. Photographic credit: The Pierpont Morgan Library, New York.

f. 45

he was too.¹⁶ Neither one thing nor the other. But then the cares that man's been through - waking at 5 they say with a [shower] [bath]¹⁷ thrown at him by one of the young ladies they keep for that very purpose. Wake she says. And thats true of the king too. {The wake him:} He has a parrot.¹⁸ George it says: Come along: time to get up – thats the bird that pulled him through his illness that the Queen wdnt let them take away but when they bought him past all [convalescence]. A white parrot with a yellow tuft, like my {son's} <dads> parrot that he bought back from the Indies when he went to fight the Zulus,¹⁹ we had it hanging in our kitchen – never a drop drunk in our house but the parrot had its share. And [green stuff; sugar,] {&} [sometimes] a {a} bullocks liver – when it was killing day {th} we begged a bit off the butcher, whose son's now in hospital with a bad leg. They dont tell him, but what I'm thinking is they know for certain he wont stand again. And his hands no good to him – what use is hands to a man trained {to a} in a bacon factory where its hauling hauling hauling by day, by night corpses of pigs,

---

¹⁶ As my article suggests, it is likely that the cook's "disappointment" in Ramsay MacDonald is the result of his perceived betrayal of working people during the financial crisis of 1931. Shortly after forming a National Government in coalition with Liberals and Conservatives, in late September 1931, Ramsay MacDonald was expelled from the Labour Party. Austen Morgan, *J. Ramsay MacDonald* (Manchester: Manchester UP, 1987), 200.

¹⁷ While I remain uncertain about the accuracy of my reading of "shower bath" there are several features of the OED definition of this phrase that suggest it is a plausible one. Described as a "somewhat old fashioned term" used primarily before the turn of the twentieth century, it is "a bath in which water from above is poured in a shower upon the person." "shower-bath, n." OED Online. March 2013. Oxford UP. 29 April 2013. Such an antiquated and presumably inexpensive method of showering is consistent with what his biographer has identified as MacDonald's relative poverty upon moving into No. 10 Downing Street. David Marquand notes that because Prime Ministers were not paid a living allowance, MacDonald was forced to economize in various ways making life at No. 10 "the reverse of sybaritic." *Ramsay MacDonald* (London: Cape, 1977), 307. The rare figure of speech "to pull the string of the shower-bath" is also included in the OED and it is significant that one of the examples it cites is taken from *The Years*: "Why can't he flow? Why can't he pull the string of the shower bath? Why's it all locked up, refrigerated? Because he's a priest, a mystery monger."

¹⁸ King George V's pet parrot was called Charlotte and, according to his biographer Kenneth Rose, the King allowed her to "roam at will." Rose does not refer to Charlotte's therapeutic role during the King's dangerous illness of 1928 but he does mention her presence at the King's death on 20 January 1936. *King George V* (London: Weidenfeld and Nicolson, 2000), 291-92 and 402.

¹⁹ It is likely that the cook is referring to the Anglo-Zulu war of 1879. Her reference to the Indies is somewhat inexplicable. This could either be a mistake because of the speed at which Woolf drafted the sketch or a not particularly funny joke at the expense of the cook and her knowledge of world geography. The white parrot in this sketch is reminiscent of the forthright and crafty parrot (also white) in Woolf's 1920s story "The Widow and the Parrot." At the end of this story the widow refuses to sell her dead brother's parrot "saying that she would not sell the bird for all the wealth of the Indies" (*CSF* 169).

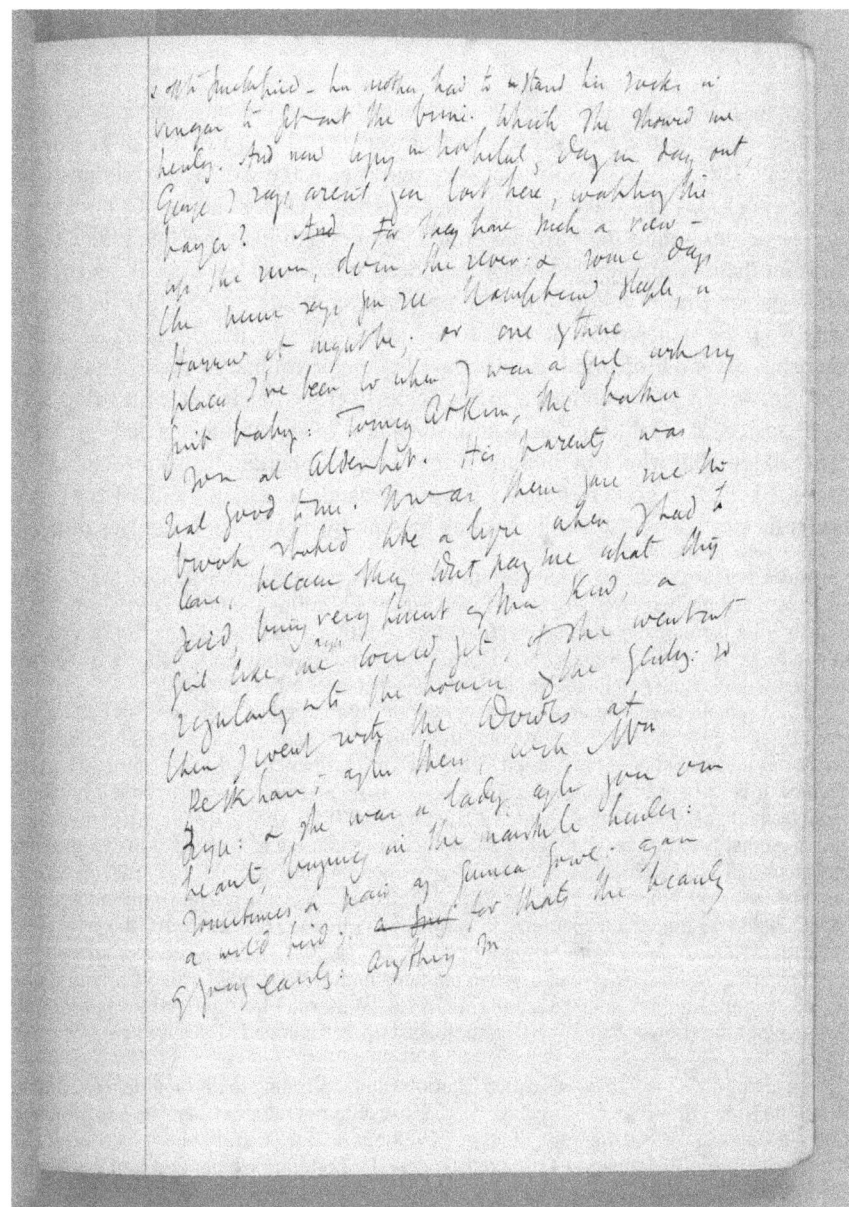

Letter to a young poet : Autograph manuscript, 1931 Sept. 24, p. 46.
The Pierpont Morgan Library, New York. MA 3333. Purchased on the Fellows Fund with the special assistance of Miss Anne S. Dayton, Mrs. Enid A. Haupt, Mrs. James H. Ripley, Mr. and Mrs. August H. Schilling, and Mr. John S. Thacher, 1979. Photographic credit: The Pierpont Morgan Library, New York.

f. 46
& off to Smithfield[20] – his mother had to {?} stand his socks in vinegar to get out the brine which she showed me [herself]. And now lying in hospital, day in day out, George I says, aren't you [lost] here, [watching this [prayer]? {And} For they have such a view – up the river, down the river: & some days the nurse says you see Hampstead Steeple, or Harrow it might be; or one of those places I've been to when I was a girl with my first baby: Tommy Atkins, the [bakers] son at Aldershot.[21] His parents was real good to me. It was them gave me the brooch shaped like a lyre when I had to leave, because they cdn't pay me what they said, being very finest of their kind, a girl like me <?> could get, if she went out regularly into the houses of the gentry: so then I went with the Howls at Peckham; after them, with Mrs Bryce: & she was a lady after your own heart, buying in the [market herself]: sometimes a pair of Guinea Fowl: [again] a wild bird; {a ?} for that's the beauty of going early: anything [m]

---

[20] Smithfield Market is London's largest wholesale meat market, located in the Smithfield area of central London. Woolf refers to Smithfield butchers in her 1934 comic prose poem "Ode Written Partly in Prose on Seeing the Name of Cutbush Above a Butcher's Shop in Pentonville" (*CSF* 237-41).

[21] Aldershot is a garrison town to the south west of London and is known for its connection with the British Army, making Woolf's choice of Tommy Atkins's name all the more pointed.

A Room of One's Own, Ordinary Life-Writing, and *The Note Books of a Woman Alone*
Ella Ophir

"And so I learnt that the one necessity for such as I am in life is one's own room." Thus wrote Evelyn Wilson, on her first night in a London bed-sitting room in 1912. She had gone to work as a live-in governess at seventeen; after ten years in other people's houses, she had retrained as a stenographer and secured, with triumph and relief, a room of her own. And with a door she could lock, she began to write. Wilson would spend the next two decades living on her own, working at "Miss de Burgh's Registry for governesses, nursery nurses, and superior maids" (Ostle vii), and keeping a record—part journal, part commonplace book—of her work, her struggles, and her reading. Not long after her death in 1934, the stack of notebooks Wilson left behind wound up in the hands of Mary Geraldine Ostle, an ordinary London working woman who had read *A Room of One's Own* with enthusiasm and gratitude. Ostle heard in Wilson's words a resounding echo of Woolf's, and grew convinced that these private notebooks had public value. After reading *A Room of One's Own* in 1929, Ostle had written to thank Woolf "from the sole[s] of my shoes." "The truth of the book lives," she declared, "& someday, let us hope, will be known." In 1938 she wrote to Woolf again, with praise for *Three Guineas*, and in this letter she identifies herself as the editor of *The Note Books of a Woman Alone*, "in which I tried to express some of the difficulties women labour under." She adds, "Your first book started it."[1]

Ostle's edition of Wilson's notebooks was published in 1935 by J. M. Dent, issued the same year in America by Dutton, and quite favorably reviewed,[2] but it was never reprinted and has remained virtually unknown. It is not referenced in the two studies of singleness in the period—Katherine Holden's *The Shadow of Marriage* and Virginia Nicholson's *Singled Out*—and it appears nowhere in the extensive scholarly work on women's life-writing. Only Thomas Mallon gives it a few pages in his survey *A Book of One's Own: People and Their Diaries* (1984); there Wilson appears in a chapter on "Prisoners," grouped, far too simply, with

---

[1] Ostle's first letter to Woolf appears in *Woolf Studies Annual* 12 (2006, edited by Beth Rigel Daugherty), her second in *Woolf Studies Annual* 6 (2000, edited by Anna Snaith). "Evelyn Wilson" (abbreviated to "Eve") is the pseudonym Ostle chose for the woman who kept the notebooks. Ostle notes that the title is Wilson's own: "I have left it as Evelyn Wilson wrote it in each of her eight fat notebooks" (xiii).
[2] Reviews of *The Note Books* appeared in *New Statesman & Nation*, *Times Literary Supplement*, *The London Mercury*, *The Fortnightly Library*, *Time and Tide*, *Boston Evening Transcript*, and *New York Times*. I discovered *The Note Books* after chancing upon *The New York Times* review.

diarists "jailed only by their own temperaments" (263). *The Note Books* then disappears again until Anna Snaith, in her work on the *Three Guineas* letters, finds Ostle's credit to *A Room of One's Own*, and briefly discusses the link in "Wide Circles" (2000), her introduction to those letters.

The Note Books is, as Snaith suggests, a concrete example of the impact and influence of *A Room of One's Own* on one of Woolf's ordinary readers. It is also, I believe, among the significant progeny of that work. The materialist argument of *A Room of One's Own*, and its examination of private life as a missing part of public history, led Ostle to read Wilson's notebooks politically, and inspired her to take on an editorial project that was daunting for someone untrained and unpracticed. It entailed "decipher[ing] curious marks and notes" (xiii) and sourcing and writing copyright requests for hundreds of quotations, many of which were copied or clipped from newspapers without identifying information. "The editor's task has been difficult" (289), she confesses in her acknowledgements, sounding relieved to be done. The result of her labor is a record rare for this era, a first-person account that reflects, and reflects upon, the shift in circumstances for increasing numbers of unmarried women: on the one hand, the opportunity for independence offered by the emergence of white-collar jobs; on the other hand, the low wages, insecurity, and isolation of what the journalist Edith Shackleton called, in her review of *The Note Books*, the "egg-and-gas-ring life."

I argue here that while Ostle's preservation of Wilson's notebooks was directly inspired by *A Room of One's Own*, the editorial presentation also sheds light on a fundamental ambivalence in Woolf's attitude toward ordinary life-writing. There is a tension in *A Room of One's Own* between Woolf's call for historiographical "reclamation work" (Highmore) on the one hand, and her investment in an ideal of literary value on the other—between a conviction about the significance of ordinary women's life-writing and a felt imperative to move contemporary women decisively beyond it.[3] There is, likewise, a distinct ambivalence in the prefatory material with which Ostle turned Wilson's notebooks over to the public. In Ostle's letter to Woolf, the political conviction behind her editorial project is clear. Her introductory "Note by the Editor," by contrast, is remarkably vague and diffident, and neither that note nor the introduction she solicited from Geraldine Waife, a former colleague of Wilson's, mentions Woolf, *A Room of One's Own*, or any of its arguments. Ostle's effacement of her political purpose may be partly a result of caution against putting off

---

[3] Ben Highmore uses the term "reclamation work" to encompass a wide range of historiographic and ethnographic efforts to salvage the records of ordinary life from "the 'condescension of history,' [which] has clearly cast much of social life into oblivion" (223). I use the term "ordinary life-writing" to refer to the diaries, notebooks, and letters of people who were not professional writers, and as distinct from memoirs and biographies which, however obscure their authors and subjects, were written for publication.

potential readers. But both her note and Waife's introduction also reflect a confusion of documentary with literary value, and a resulting ambivalence about publishing what Ostle apologetically calls "amateurish" writing (xiii). There are good reasons to follow Ostle in reading Wilson's notebooks through Woolf, but to do so most profitably we need to read beyond *A Room of One's Own*, and to navigate the tension in Woolf's thinking about ordinary life-writing and literary value. There is in Woolf's work more than Ostle found to define and illuminate the value of *The Note Books of a Woman Alone*; in equal measure, this singular, fascinating text illuminates the adaptability of Woolf's articulations of women's experience across class divisions.

As Anna Snaith has demonstrated in detail, Woolf had an abiding interest in ordinary life-writing, particularly in the role of diaries and letters in feminist historiography.[4] One early example of this is the short story "The Journal of Mistress Joan Martyn," in which a medieval historian, Rosamond Merridew, reflects on the frustrations of studying a period "more bare than any other of private records" (*CSF* 35), and tells the story (perhaps a fantasy) of discovering at an isolated country estate the intact diary of a twenty-five-year-old Joan Martyn from the year 1480.[5] The current Mr. Martyn prefers the stud books and genealogies—"Horses or Grandfathers!" (*CSF* 43)—but Merridew, thrilled at her luck, seizes upon the young woman's record. She "bypasses the books of records written by men," Snaith argues, "for the autobiographical recording of a woman's life," and the transcription of the diary in the second half of the story "reinforc[es] the importance not just of noticing, but of publishing women's accounts of their lives" ("Private Voice" 101).

A Room of One's Own echoes Miss Merridew's lament for the scarcity of private records; Woolf rues that the "average Elizabethan woman" "never writes her own life and scarcely keeps a diary," and that "there are only a handful of her letters in existence" (41). Similarly in *Three Guineas*, she wishes for the guidance that would be afforded by historical records of professional women. The regret is not just that "[t]here were no professional women, except governesses," but that "the lives of governesses . . . can be counted on the fingers of one hand" (200). She lauds the recent publication of one of these, the journal of "an obscure Miss Weeton" from the years 1807 to 1811, which seems to her to have "crept" out of hiding, its voice "reach[ing] us from the darkness" (200) of the past. Such forms of ordinary life-writing, Woolf suggests, can be a source for the missing "mass of information" (*AROO* 41) about past women's lives and, along with other kinds of

---

[4] Versions of this argument appear in "'My Poor Private Voice': Virginia Woolf and Autobiography" (2000), *Virginia Woolf: Public and Private Negotiations* (2000), and "'A View of One's Own': Writing Women's Lives and the Early Short Stories" (2004).
[5] Written in 1906, the story was first published in 1979, edited and introduced by Susan M. Squier and Louise A. DeSalvo, who also supplied the title.

records, can contribute to the "supplement to history" that she urges young female historians to create.

However, Woolf was less sure of the value of ordinary life-writing from her own time. Surveying twentieth-century women's writing in *A Room of One's Own*, she hopes that "the impulse towards autobiography may be spent" (72), that women "may be beginning to use writing as an art, not as a method of self-expression." We do find here what sounds like a call not just for historical, but also for contemporary reclamation work: she declares that she would prefer the "true history" (82) of the girl behind the shop counter to "the hundred and fiftieth life of Napoleon" (83); she conjures from the poor areas "south of the river" (80) images of the "infinitely obscure lives [that] remain to be recorded" (81). But she is not actually asking for individual testimony either written or collected; rather, she is proposing subjects for the redemptive imagination of the novelist. She is urging her fictional novelist Mary Carmichael to visit those streets and rooms, to observe and explore, and ultimately to relieve in contemplative novelistic prose "the pressure of dumbness, the accumulation of unrecorded life" that she feels hanging so heavily over the impoverished streets (81). Woolf is enjoining women novelists to break social taboos and literary proprieties and venture across urban and social terrain "in the spirit of fellowship," free of "the shoddy old fetters of class" (80). But it is novels she is after, not personal testimonies, and the distinction is significant. In the one record of Woolf's response to contemporary working-class life-writing—her "Introductory Letter" to Margaret Llewelyn Davies' *Life As We Have Known It*, a compilation of personal recollections by members of the Women's Co-Operative Guild—we find a deep ambivalence toward "infinitely obscure" women relieving "the pressure of dumbness" by publishing words of their own (*AROO* 81).

Woolf begins the "Letter" by recalling her experience at a Women's Co-Operative Guild Congress in 1913, and on one level she constructs a narrative arc in which the "impassable" (xxx) divide she felt between herself and the Guild women is diminished seventeen years later by reading their essays and letters. She weaves elements of their stories into an elegant composite account of the texture of their lives, their hardships and strength, and the transformative power of the Women's Guild. The writings, she finds, alleviate "the old curiosities and bewilderments which had made that Congress so memorable, and so thick with unanswered questions" (xxix). But she proceeds to evaluate the papers by narrowly literary standards that are, as Mary Childers puts it, "stunningly inappropriate" (69). Woolf begins the preface certain that "this book is not a book" (xvii), and in this respect she concludes where she began, constructing not an arc but a circle: "It cannot be denied that the chapters here put together do not make a book—that as literature they have many limitations" (xxix).

Woolf elaborates on this judgment in the voice of a hypothetical—and male—"literary critic," but the objecting voice merges with her own. In her own voice, Woolf frankly doubts that the women's writings will mean much to readers who cannot "supplement" them with "the memory of faces and the sound of voices" as she herself can, and the doubting literary critic shares this memory. Indeed, he anchors his judgment in his recollection of those very faces: "The writing ... lacks detachment and imaginative breadth, even as the women themselves lacked variety and play of feature" (xxix). Although Llewelyn Davies clearly presents the essays as documentary "record[s] of individual experience" contributing to the history of Co-operation (xi), Woolf cannot refrain from holding them up to the ideal of wholeness and transcendence that she articulated so powerfully two years earlier in *A Room of One's Own*: the creative mind "incandescent and undivided" (89) that can "build up out of the fleeting and the personal the lasting edifice which remains unthrown" (84).[6] Toward the end of the "Letter" Woolf declines to judge what is and is not literature (xxxxi), but she cannot wholly resist the question, relinquish the category, or suppress her judgment. Literature, the "Letter" suggests, is what real books are made of, and real books are things that do not "need shoring up" by introductions (xvii) or supplementing by direct experience of their authors. Against that aesthetic ideal, the Women's Guild testimonies are judged to be merely "fragments" and their voices, particularly unfairly, only "half articulate" (xxxxi).

Woolf's ambivalence toward the Women's Guild narratives sheds light on the submerged tension in *A Room of One's Own* between her desire for records that tell something "perfectly true and substantial" (41) about ordinary women's lives, and the question of how that truth will best be told. According to Woolf's "Letter," it was Davies herself who initially doubted the value of the women's papers, hesitating to share them with Woolf on the grounds that "they were very fragmentary and ungrammatical" and that "[i]t might be that their crudity would only perplex, that the writing of people who do not know how to write—" (xxxi). In Woolf's telling, she does not allow Davies to finish that sentence, but cuts her off to insist that "[i]n the first place, every Englishwoman knows how to write; in

---

[6] *A Room of One's Own* does critique literary canonization and even ridicules the complacent claims to universality—"sonorous phrases about 'elemental feelings', the 'common stuff of humanity'" (83)—with which it was so often defended. Melba Cuddy-Keane notes how forcefully Woolf exposes "the infiltration of socially gendered values into literary judgments" (330), and outlines the diversity of Woolf's "evaluative practice" which was certainly not "limited to 'high modernist' principles" (232). As a reader, editor, and reviewer Woolf did of course recognize the different values of different kinds of writing. But the highest value remains that of genius, defined by a "freedom and fullness of expression" (*AROO* 70) and a capturing of "reality" (*AROO* 99). The latter is an amorphous quality, but one that "fixes and makes permanent"; communicated in writing it is "what is left of past time and our loves and hates."

the second, even if she does not she has only to take her own life for subject and write the truth about that and not fiction or poetry for our interest to be so keenly roused that—that in short we cannot wait but must read the packet [of papers] at once" (xxxii-iii). Perhaps so, but when Woolf is faced with presenting those same papers to the public she feels compelled to point out that "[p]oetry and fiction seem far beyond their horizon" (xxix). Her initial conviction of the intrinsic value of personal testimony gets dampened down with reservations and qualifications, as the aesthetic ideal articulated in *A Room of One's Own* presses back in.

It is telling that in "The Journal of Mistress Joan Martyn," that great fantasy of reclamation work, the discovered voice of an "ordinary" medieval woman turns out to be a delicately sensitive, lyrical one, with the imaginative instincts of a novelist. "If I ever write again," Joan concludes, "it shall not be of Norfolk and myself, but of Knights and Ladies and of adventures in strange lands" (*CSF* 62). Joan Martyn is an earlier incarnation of Judith Shakespeare, a writer whose "genius" "never got itself onto paper" (*AROO* 44), a "poet who never wrote a word" (*AROO* 102). These figures of lost genius suggest that Woolf's ambivalence toward ordinary life-writing arises in part from the pressure of the question to which *A Room of One's Own* is a response: "the perennial puzzle why no woman wrote a word of that extraordinary literature" of the past (*AROO* 38), the challenge of the patriarchal voice that declared it "impossible for any woman, past, present, or to come, to have the genius of Shakespeare" (42). For all its intrinsic human interest and its documentary and political value, the unpolished voice and rough shape of ordinary women's life-writing trails with it the long history of oppression and frustration and often the embarrassment of poverty. It drags against the will to full liberation and incontrovertible refutation of that prating male voice.

Ostle's presentation of *The Note Books of a Woman Alone* reveals a similar tension between conviction about the value of Wilson's writing as personal testimony and documentary evidence, and misgivings about its appearance as a "work" of women's writing. As an expression of "the difficulties that women labour under," Wilson's notebooks are, as Ostle recognized, rich and multi-faceted. Wilson's journal entries record not just the circumstances of her own life, but also, on occasion, those of the clients of Miss de Burgh's Registry, women in the upper levels of domestic service. Wilson's work went far beyond the stenography for which she had been trained: she dealt directly with women applying for jobs, parents seeking positions for daughters, and women seeking household help; sometimes she had to mediate disputes between employers and employees. She brought to the work an acute sympathy born of her own experiences, as a governess, of exploitation, homelessness, and confinement. She notes sometimes paying out of her own meager earnings the registration fees of the poorest job-seekers—"my candidates," she calls them (32), or "my unemployed" (33)—and within her limited powers she advocated for the most vulnerable. Without a child of her own, Wilson took the part of a mother toward "these girls who come to me and own that they have no one behind them at all. I am a woman," she wrote, "and all women are responsible for all children" (96). One of the longest journal entries tells the hair-raising story of her efforts to get a laid-off nurse, traumatized from being torn away from the children she had raised, from infancy, for seven years, out of the abysmal workhouse infirmary to which she had been sent, in her doctor's words, "to pull herself together" (49).

At the same time Wilson's notebooks form the record of the central purpose they served for her: the intertwined projects of self-reflection and self-education, through which she strove to understand herself and her circumstances in social, psychological, and spiritual terms. In addition to the periodic journal entries, the notebooks include autobiographical recollections, a short dramatic sketch, and, comprising the bulk of the text, extensive quotations copied from her readings, often followed by her comments. Toward the end of her life, Wilson attempted to work the accumulated material of twenty years into a comprehensive conceptual order: she cut up her pages and arranged the entries into titled sections, mapping the concerns that defined her life. Among these are "Women: Their Work; Their Homes"; "Children and Family Life"; "Money"; and "Vision and Bewilderment." Thus the journal entries do not appear in chronological order, but the arc of Wilson's life emerges nonetheless: a middle-class but unhappy childhood, marked by maltreatment; the loss of her parents in young adulthood; her exclusion from the family money, as her father's business and assets went to her brothers; her precarious but cherished independence through work; social insecurity and estrangement from her family; and the fear, ultimately realized, of losing her position. At the age of forty-eight or forty-nine Wilson was laid off, with the rest of the staff, after Miss de Burgh died and the agency was sold. *The Note Books* concludes with a grim, brave final chapter in which Wilson records her resolve to hasten the course of a terminal illness so as not to outlive her small remaining savings: "I saw the doctor, played the fool, and so got the information I wanted," she writes. "I now have to keep in mind and do all he tells me not to do! . . . To be condemned to live when I lack the means is senseless" (287).

Ostle was better educated and better off than Wilson: she was a certified teacher and worked for the Froebel Society in various capacities, including registrar, secretary, and librarian.[7] Her 1938 letter to Woolf notes that she had a "one-room

---

[7] In her 1938 letter to Woolf, Ostle says that when she wrote in 1929 she was "Registrar and Secretary" of the Froebel Society, which she describes as a "women's educational society" (Snaith, "*Three Guineas* Letters" 18). The letterhead of the 1929 letter gives "The Froebel Society and Junior Schools Association" as a "Scholastic Agency for Teachers and Govern-

flat" and could afford the occasional luxury. But she too was "a woman alone"—unmarried and self-supporting—and she recognized in her own life as well as in Wilson's the historical and systemic oppression of women as a sex that Woolf had anatomized in *A Room of One's Own*. Ostle's political reading of Wilson's writing is, as I have said, clear in her letter to Woolf. It is also explicit in a "Note by the editor" that Ostle felt compelled to insert into Wilson's text. Following a series of passages Wilson copied from *Villette*, Ostle adds, "If any reader laughs at, or thinks it is out of date to quote from Charlotte Brontë concerning the difficulties of women, I suggest they beg, borrow or steal one, or all, of the following books" (187). The ensuing list includes *A Room of One's Own*.[8] But Ostle's prefatory note to *The Note Books* avoids any mention of "the difficulties of women" in general. She offers the book vaguely as "an account of a woman's mental life in varying moods" (xiii). Her very brief indication of her editorial process suggests that in terms of genre she is positioning it among collections of quotations: she explains that she "generally omitted [Wilson's] quotations from the classics because they are to be found in other anthologies" (xiii). This rationale implies a reader who would be turning to the book for aphorisms and distillations of wisdom, and that its value will be in its selection of these, rather than in the life and conditions it portrays. But framed thus, the documentary and autobiographical value of *The Note Books* is diminished. Ostle is left apologizing for it being "somewhat amateurish, even very much so at times" (xiii), and doubting its coherence: "[Eve's] comments . . . about life are here," she writes; "they illumine the book, account for the selections [of quotations], I think. I cannot know" (xiv). She repeats, "I cannot know," and concludes with a dramatic but obscuring flourish: "Eve has gone. I might not have known her even had I met her every day. For are not all souls, especially those who pity, unknowable, incalculable, alone?" (xiv). The question is perhaps intended to create an air of tantalizing mystery around a vanished soul. But in light of Ostle's statement to Woolf, it seems a dismaying retreat from the claims of documentary and autobiographical value that could so easily have been made for this book.

    Wilson's notebooks had come to Ostle through her friend Geraldine Waife, a former colleague of Wilson's who had received them, to her "great surprise" (ix), from Wilson's brother, along with word of Wilson's death.[9] The publication was

---

esses" and identifies Ostle as "Secretary and Librarian" and holder of an "N.F.U. Teacher's Cert. and Trainer's Diploma" (Daugherty, "Letters from Readers" 63). Further information on Ostle is scarce. She published two articles in the Froebel Society journal *Child Life* (1927 and 1934) and *Sharing Makes a Feast: A Christmas Play for Children and Adults* in 1934. A *London Times* obituary gives her death as May 29, 1950.

[8] The other books listed are *Poor Caroline* by Winifred Holtby, *Poor Women* by Nora Hoult, *The Rector's Daughter* by F. M. Mayor, *A Clergyman's Daughter* by George Orwell, *The Old Ladies* by Hugh Walpole, and *Miss Mole* by E. H. Young.

[9] Waife does not indicate why Wilson's brother, from whom Wilson was estranged, made her

Ostle's initiative, but she solicited an introduction from Waife, who could offer some biographical details and a personal account of the woman she knew. Like Ostle, Waife was better educated than Wilson. She seems to have worked at the agency only for a short time, and she went on to marry and have children. But she remained attuned to the challenges faced by working women, and by single women in particular: in 1923 she had published a novel about a women's teacher training college, titled *Colleagues: A Novel without a Man* and dedicated "to the million 'superfluous women' with profound respect." Waife pays tribute to Wilson as one who, though "uneducated," "made use of every incident, every book, every person encountered in her way through life, and who could therefore see and think for herself" (viii), but she too is uncertain about the purpose of publishing the book. She ends up offering *The Note Books* as a kind of inspirational or self-help work, on the grounds that "Wilson made out of her thoughts a philosophy that really stood by her in her loneliness and isolation" (x). In this way she credits the aspiration to conceptual order reflected in *The Note Books*, without apologizing for amateurishness. However, she ends up qualifying the book's value as much as Ostle does, by restricting it to readers in Wilson's own social and economic position:

> If Miss Ostle can make a book out of these note-books that will help others placed as Eve was, it will be a good thing. It will certainly not be a book for those who can get easily all the physical, mental, and spiritual help they need. It will be a book for those, like Eve, who have little time for reading, who read in a shaky bus, or hanging from a strap in the tube, or in a restaurant. There may be no other Eves, and then this book can get nowhere. But I think there may be some who need its mental shelter. (x)

"Maybe," she concludes, "some will find in it more than I, or the editor, can" (xi). This disavowal of the book's value for herself (and Ostle) seems to be a defensive marking of her own superior social position. But the restrictive assignment of its readership is also a way of dealing with *The Note Books* as a publication with a genre problem. If it could not be offered up to stand by *Bartlett's Familiar Quotations* or with the works of philosophers or theologians, what was it? "What is this book then, if it is not a book?" they seem to be asking, as Woolf did of Davies' collection (xvii). Although Woolf had asked for the "true history" of a shop girl, neither Ostle nor Waife was able to assert the value of *The Note Books* in documentary terms.

Thus it seems that Ostle and Waife ultimately read Wilson's notebooks as a demonstration of the central thesis of *A Room of One's Own*: as dramatizing how

---

the recipient of his sister's notebooks. Wilson mentions Waife as a valued friend in a few of her entries; possibly she left instructions for the notebooks to be sent to her.

financial independence and creative and intellectual achievement are interrelated, how poverty and oppression left women writers hobbled. Read this way *The Note Books* helps to answer the objection Woolf anticipates in closing *A Room of One's Own*, that she has "made too much of the importance of material things" (96). But to read *The Note Books* as a vindication of that aspect of Woolf's materialist argument is also to read Wilson's life as instructive mainly in its failure, as Waife does. She pays tribute to Eve's devotion to self-education, but follows with the pronouncement, "And yet Eve failed. She failed to make a living that would provide for her old age. . . . She was just a worn-out woman when she left Miss de Burgh's Agency, and was unable to find any work at all" (viii). And it is to read Wilson's writing likewise as an earnest but rather poor example of an established genre—the anthology of quotations, or the work of popular philosophy—much like the multitudes of failed "women's novels" that Woolf sees lying "scattered, like small pock-marked apples in an orchard, about the second-hand book shops of London" (*AROO* 67).

    The documentary and political significance of *The Note Books* was nonetheless clear at least to Edith Shackleton, who reviewed the book for the feminist weekly *Time and Time* and saw it as representing a turning point in the history of working women, and of singleness, as well as a "reproach . . . to our common sense as a community." "This is the era of the Lonely Woman," Shackleton declares: "The penniless spinster no longer pines in the irritable bosom of her family, but has fled or been hustled out to earn a living." On the one hand, this woman's living was likely to be meager, and her life solitary; on the other hand, "to the governesses and poor relations of yesterday," the modern single woman's "independence, her room of her own, would have been imagined as heavenly bliss. For this reason *The Notebooks* [sic] *of a Woman Alone* has interest." Though Shackleton's review does not mention Woolf, it appears under the title "A Room of One's Own," and the historical interest of *The Note Books*, clearer to us now than it could have been to her, also lies in its direct and indirect connections to Woolf's feminism: its place in the reception history of *A Room of One's Own*, and its parallel mapping, "from below," of Woolf's arguments about the systemic poverty of women, the politics of domestic space, and, perhaps above all, about self-education through reading.

    Given the apparent echo of *A Room of One's Own* in Wilson's assertion of the necessity of private space, and the appearance among her quotations of the final paragraph of "How Should One Read a Book?" Snaith in "Wide Circles" takes *The Note Books* as "proof that [Woolf's] work was being read by ordinary women" and that "[h]er imperfect education was offering inspiration and support to women like Evelyn Wilson" (9). In terms of reception history, however, *The Note Books* is primarily a record of Ostle's reading of Woolf, not of Wilson's. Wilson may have read

"How Should One Read a Book?" in the second volume of *The Common Reader*, which was published in 1932, two years before her death, but she may well have encountered the passage excerpted elsewhere.[10] There is no evidence that Wilson read *A Room of One's Own*. As I have noted, her testament to the necessity of her own room was written when she began working at the registry, about fifteen years before *A Room of One's Own* was published. It is hard not to think that Wilson would have seized upon a book titled *A Room of One's Own* if she had encountered it, and some of its trenchant and aphoristic lines would certainly have been copied into her notebooks, or at least have been approximated "from memory" as some of her quotations are. For Wilson was keenly attuned to analyses of the condition of women in everything she read. She gratefully copied out long passages on the subject from women writers and activists such as Winifred Holtby, E. H. Young, Ethel Mannin, and V. H. Friedlander,[11] and even from rather improbable sources, such as Joseph Conrad.

The direct connection of *The Note Books* to *A Room of One's Own*, then, is through Ostle. But even if Ostle's credit to *A Room of One's Own* had not been preserved in her letter to Woolf about *Three Guineas*, Wilson's own emphasis on the issues of power and privacy within domestic space would have invited dialogue with it. The connection was made, as I have noted, in the title of Shackleton's review, and the *New York Times* review opens by citing Woolf directly: "A room of her own and £500 a year Virginia Woolf said a woman should have if she was going to write creatively." Against that figure of the woman writer the reviewer presents Wilson, "a woman who never had more than £3 a week[12] and who never knew either success nor any sort of creation," but whose "room of her own" was nonetheless "a stronghold, symbol, and literal blessing and comfort in a hard life." The reviewer is right that Wilson's room was a "stronghold," a structure of defense: she defiantly defined "home" as "any room across the door of which I can draw the bolt" (26). But it was for her, also, as much as for any aspiring novelist with a legacy, a space of freedom and of creativity. That bolt meant she could read undisturbed and write free from prying eyes. Her notebooks were her creation.

Wilson's notebooks further testify to the need of private space for all who

---

[10] Wilson's excerpt is the final paragraph of the essay, in full, in which Woolf imagines "the Almighty," on the Day of Judgment, concluding of those who arrive with their books under their arms, "Look, these need no reward. We have nothing to given them here. They have loved reading" (*CR*2, 270; *Note Books* 210).

[11] E. H. (Emily Hilda) Young was a suffragist and popular novelist. Ethel Mannin was a leftist feminist and prolific writer of novels and non-fiction. V. H. Friedlander was a poet, novelist, and active member of the Women's Social and Political Union.

[12] According to Waife's introduction, when Wilson began working at the agency she earned about thirty shillings a week; after twenty-one years of ten-hour days she made £3 a week—perhaps £150 a year, allowing for two weeks unpaid holiday.

must live where they work, whether or not they will ever write a word. "How can I explain to these mothers, these employers of home-workers," she asks herself, "that a room alone, a warmed one to which the employee can go, is a necessity?" (1). The psychological importance of privacy goes deeper than its enabling of reflection and creation; Wilson saw it as essential to a worker's sense of integrity and dignity to have what she herself had finally attained: a space "where I may be myself, and neither apologize for nor justify my presence" (7). Tellingly, later journal entries recognize that though her room has a lock, it is still less than her own, and her presence may still be felt as an imposition: "No landlady likes you forever" (90), she observes at one point, and records at another how she is subject to hostility, and a particularly sparse meal, when she chooses not to go out on a Bank Holiday (102).

The Note Books of a Woman Alone also provides, as Snaith observes, "confirmation of so many of [Woolf's] ideas about the importance of access to books and libraries for working women" ("Wide Circles" 9). Waife remembers that Wilson "read and re-read books from free libraries" and "went without meals to buy a few more" (viii). Books were "mental food" (39), and at times more important than physical sustenance. They were also Wilson's means of access to broader horizons, compensating in some degree for her limited physical space. This mental space too was restricted by poverty, as Waife notes, and its limits are to some extent reflected in Wilson's quotations, which are heavy on classic and popular novelists such as George Eliot, Thomas Hardy, and George Gissing, whose works would have been readily available at circulating libraries and in cheap editions. Wilson is herself aware of the constraints. She is conscious of being "unlearned" (133); even in the privacy of her notebooks, behind her bolted door, she cannot entirely shut out the voice of the "well-educated man [who] would jeer at my ill-stocked mind" (42). Woolf of course knew this jeering voice. And it is the affirmation of the liberating possibilities of self-education with which she answered it that can help us read *The Note Books* as more than a document and a product of deprivation. *The Note Books* is also an exemplification of the intellectual resourcefulness and independence that Woolf celebrated in her conception of the "common reader"—solitary, idiosyncratic, unprofessional, and unbowed.

In "The Common Reader," her preface to the first volume of that collection, Woolf takes up Samuel Johnson's vision of "all those rooms, too humble to be called libraries, yet full of books, where the pursuit of reading is carried on by private people" (19). The sketch is imprinted with Woolf's (and Johnson's) class: Wilson could hardly dream of a room "full of books"; hers were few and mostly borrowed, and her single rented room was all the space she would ever call home. But Wilson was as much an exemplar of this figure as was Woolf herself: voracious and "[a]bove all guided by an instinct to create for [her]self, out of whatever odds and ends [s]he can come by, some kind of whole" (*CR*1 1). Wilson's process was cumulative, and constructive. It was also, as in Woolf's account of the common reader's, "[h]asty, inaccurate," a matter of "snatching now this poem, now that scrap of old furniture, without caring where he finds it or of what nature it may be so long as it serves his purpose and rounds his structure." Wilson gives the source of one of her quotations as "a book-marker" (213); another was copied from a Christmas card (231). She "read as a child does," Waife remembers, "everything, looking for gold" (Ostle x). Classics, the Bible, eminent nineteenth-century novelists, contemporary psychologists, sermons, journalism, letters, poems printed in newspapers, ephemera—out of such heterogeneous materials Wilson pieced together an intellectual edifice of her own. As Lily Briscoe is able to say at the end of *To the Lighthouse*, "I have had my vision" (226), so Wilson, near the end of her life, asserts, "I have lived my own life, thought my own thoughts, not those of others . . . . Hence I claim that my life has been worth living" (42).

Given the intersections of Wilson's and Woolf's themes and concerns, it is hard not to regret that Wilson never read *A Room of One's Own*, and tempting to imagine how Woolf would have responded to *The Note Books*. Woolf, however, appears not to have sought out what her "first book started." Snaith finds that Woolf mentions Ostle's second letter in her diary shortly after *Three Guineas* was published ("Wide Circles" 9). In this entry, Woolf makes note of a negative review, then follows it with "Miss Osler or some such name writes to thank & praise—my grand work &c &c" (*D*5 145). There is a note of dismissiveness in this rendering of Ostle's enthusiasm and gratitude, rather than of consolation or interest; there is no further mention of Ostle in the diary, and no record of a reply. Given Woolf's introductory "Letter" to Davies' collection of the Women's Co-Operative Guild pieces, it seems to me likely that Woolf would have responded to *The Note Books of a Woman Alone* with the same mixture of fascination and resistance: turning the pages eagerly—the "true history" of an employment agency clerk, after all, the record of a life about as "obscure" as she could wish for—and yet saying to herself as she did of that one, "this book is not a book" (xvii). As a novelist and a feminist Woolf was fascinated by the records of obscure women's lives, but she preferred them distanced by time. As with the imagined journal of Joan Martyn, or the real one of Miss Weeton, governess, these are imbued with value by their scarcity and with mystique by their almost uncanny survival. And they belong, reassuringly, to a history of oppression, not to a present in which increased opportunity brought not just the possibility but, as Woolf felt it, the imperative of demonstrating women's intellectual and creative equality. At the end of *A Room of One's Own*, Woolf's sights are fixed on the ideal of literary genius in the figure of the spirit of Judith Shakespeare, whose "opportunity to walk among us in the flesh" (102) she projects, rather pessimistically, a hundred years hence. And yet at the same time, in this final "fiction" (102) she defines a crucial cultural role for the writings of a woman like Wilson and, no less, for the work of a woman like Ostle, whose editing of Wilson was her own means of expression. Woolf urges women to cultivate "the habit of freedom and the courage to write exactly what we think" (102), for only such individual efforts, she maintains, will collectively, eventually, make it possible for "the dead poet who was Shakespeare's sister" to be born and "find it possible to live and write her poetry" (103).

In the first version of the essay "Lives of the Obscure," Woolf proposed that the memoirs of the obscure provide "that background, atmosphere and standing of common earth which nourish people of greater importance" (*E4* 140).[13] She defends the value of these "trivial and ephemeral" books on the grounds that they are essential to ordinary readers and therefore to "good" books: they provide the "gradations of merit" that ease the approach to the "sublime and precipitous"; they are replete with the rich sense of ordinary life that readers need to bring to the "splendid pinnacles" of literature. The conclusion of *A Room of One's Own* significantly revises this account of the vital service of lesser books to great ones. Like the first account, it has a rhetorical doubleness. On the one hand it insists on the necessity of the former; on the other hand it implies a rather dramatic subordination in which perhaps a century's worth of women's writing appears as so much compost for the rare flowering of genius. Women seem urged to write for a century in the service of Judith Shakespeare; their effort is called upon in "preparation," almost messianically, for her "coming" (103). This figure of transcendent female genius hovering over the end of *A Room of One's Own* cannot have eased Ostle's self-consciousness in the face of what seemed "amateurish" in Wilson's writing and in her own editorial work. On the other hand, the power that Woolf invests in the writing of "exactly what we think" is no less than the power to change the culture so fundamentally that it will in time be able to accommodate, perhaps even nourish, what it would once have destroyed. It would be hard to leave *A Room of One's Own* with the impression that such change is to be brought about more for the sake of genius than for the sake of justice: in Woolf's vision here, the two causes are ultimately one. Woolf's urging of women to work for Judith Shakespeare had, among its more immediate results, the publication of *The Note Books of a Woman Alone*, as it sanctioned not only the writing and publishing of "exactly what we think" but also affirmed that to do so "even in poverty and obscurity, is worth while" (103).

---

[13] The two paragraphs that opened the first version of "Lives of the Obscure" (published in *The London Mercury* and in *The Dial*) were cut and replaced by a new introduction in *The Common Reader*; the earlier one is reprinted in Andrew McNeillie's notes to the essay in *Essays of Virginia Woolf* Vol. 4. See also Jane Marcus's analysis of it in "Invincible Mediocrity: The Private Selves of Public Women" (*The Private Self: Theory and Practice of Women's Autobiographical Writings*. Ed. Shari Benstock. Chapel Hill: U of North Carolina P, 1988. 114-46. Print).

Works Cited

"A Woman Alone." Rev. of *The Note Books of a Woman Alone*. *New York Times* 18 Oct. 1936: BR9. ProQuest Historical Newspapers: *The New York Times* (1851-2007).

Childers, Mary M. "Virginia Woolf on the Outside Looking Down." *Modern Fiction Studies* 38.1 (1992). 61-79. Print.

Cuddy-Keane, Melba. "'A Standard of One's Own': Virginia Woolf and the Question of Literary Value." *Virginia Woolf: Turning the Centuries: Selected Papers from the 9th Annual Conference on Virginia Woolf*. Ed. Ann Ardis and Bonnie Kime Scott. New York: Pace UP, 2000. 230-36. Print.

Daugherty, Beth Rigel, ed. "Letters from Readers to Virginia Woolf." *Woolf Studies Annual* 12 (2006). 25-212.

Highmore, Ben, ed. *The Everyday Life Reader*. London: Routledge, 2002. Print.

Holden, Katherine. *The Shadow of Marriage: Singleness in England 1914-1960*. Manchester: Manchester UP, 2007.

Ostle, M.G., ed. *The Note Books of a Woman Alone*. London: J. M. Dent, 1935. Print.

Shackleton, Edith. "A Room of One's Own." Rev. of *The Note Books* [sic] *of a Woman Alone*, ed. M.G. Ostle. *Time and Tide* 18 Jan. 1936. WH/7/7.34/01/12a. Hull History Centre, Hull.

Snaith, Anna. "'A View of One's Own': Writing Women's Lives and the Early Short Stories." *Trespassing Boundaries: Virginia Woolf's Short Fiction*. Ed. Kathryn N. Benzel and Ruth Hoberman. New York: Palgrave Macmillan, 2004. 125-138. Print.

——. "'My Poor Private Voice': Virginia Woolf and Auto/Biography." *Representing Lives: Women and Autobiography*. Ed. Alison Donnell and Pauline Polkey. Houndsmills: Macmillan, 2000. 96-104. Print.

——, ed. "*Three Guineas* Letters." *Woolf Studies Annual* 6 (2000). 17-168. Print.

——. *Virginia Woolf: Public and Private Negotiations*. Houndsmills: Macmillan, 2000. Print.

——. "Wide Circles: The *Three Guineas* Letters." *Woolf Studies Annual* 6 (2000). 1-12. Print.

Nicholson, Virginia. *Singled Out: How Two Million British Women Survived Without Men After the First World War*. New York: Viking, 2007. Print.

Waife, Geraldine. Colleagues: *A Novel Without a Man*. London: Chapman & Hall, 1923.

Woolf, Virginia. *The Common Reader, Volume I*. Ed. Andrew McNeillie. London: Vintage, 2003. Print.

——. *The Common Reader, Volume II*. Ed. Andrew McNeillie. London: Vintage, 2003. Print.

——. *The Complete Shorter Fiction of Virginia Woolf*. 2nd ed. Ed. Susan Dick. San Diego: Harcourt, 1989. Print.
——. *The Diary of Virginia Woolf*. Vol. 5. Ed. Anne Olivier Bell. London: Hogarth, 1984. Print.
——. *The Essays of Virginia Woolf*. Vol. 4. Ed. Andrew McNeillie. London: Hogarth, 1994. Print.
——. "Introductory Letter to Margaret Llewelyn Davies." *Life As We Have Known It: By Co-Operative Working Women*. Ed. Margaret Llewelyn Davies. London: Virago, 1977. xvii-xxxxi. Print.
——. *A Room of One's Own / Three Guineas*. Ed. Michèle Barrett. London: Penguin, 2000. Print.
——. *To the Lighthouse*. Ed. Stella McNichol. London: Penguin, 1992. Print.

"Wretched Sparrows": Protectionists, Suffragettes and the Irish
David Bradshaw

Although Edward Lear's "Mr and Mrs Spikky Sparrow" return from their visit to London "galloobious and genteel" in their newly-acquired headwear and apparel, from the mid-sixteenth century onwards England's towns, cities and countryside had been, in reality, rather less welcoming of *Passer domesticus*. Widely condemned as a verminous pest that ravaged cornfields, gardens and grain supplies, the house sparrow's alleged predilection for strident, unruly and even murderous behavior was also held against it, and this longstanding notoriety is enshrined, for example, in the opening stanza of "Who Killed Cock Robin?":

> Who killed Cock Robin?
> I, said the Sparrow,
> with my bow and arrow,
> I killed Cock Robin.

In turn, it was the sparrow's status as a despised outcast that led to it being championed by the likes of Clare and Keats, yet even Thomas Bewick, another of its Romantic supporters, had to concede that "it follows society, and lives at its expence; granaries, barns, court-yards, pigeon-houses, and in short all places where grain is scattered, are its favourite resorts." Nevertheless, Bewick goes on to observe without pause, "It is surely saying too much of this poor proscribed species to sum up its character in the words of the Count de Buffon: —'It is extremely destructive, its plumage is entirely useless, its flesh indifferent food, its notes grating to the ear, and its familiarity and petulance disgusting'" ("The House Sparrow" 155).

Bewick proceeds to draw attention to the benefits arising from the sparrow's insatiable appetite for caterpillars and to locate the bird within a less anthropocentric scheme of abundance, but this more exalted view of the sparrow did not hold sway in the eighteenth, nineteenth and early twentieth centuries, when "most parishes had sparrow clubs, which dispensed money for dead birds and eggs" (Clark, "Irishmen of Birds," 16). Millions of sparrows were killed in Britain during this period, and the number of sparrow clubs increased rapidly in the 1880s and 1890s as the nation's burgeoning demand for food only intensified calls for the bird's extermination, while Ian Blyth, as part of his analysis of connections between *Night and Day* and the various Defence of the Realm Acts of 1914-18, notes the revival of such clubs during the First World War (Blyth 281-282). One late-Victorian proponent of eradication, a Colonel C. Russell, in his guise as "A Friend of the Farmers," argued that "we can do as well without sparrows as without rats and cockroaches" (Gurney, Russell and Coues 44), while the same volume in which his comments were published also contains an essay entitled "A Ruffian in Feathers" by Olive Thorne Miller, offering an American perspective on a bird that had been deliberately introduced into the United States from the United Kingdom with disastrous consequences. "The harshest cries of our native American birds, if not always musical in themselves, seem at least to accord in some way with sounds of nature," Miller begins. "The house-sparrow alone is entirely discordant—the one bird without a pleasing note, whose very love-song is an unmusical squeak. Nor is his appearance more interesting than his voice, and on looking into his manners and customs we discover most unlovely characteristics" (Gurney, Russell and Coues 63). Miller goes on to "chronicle the ruffian's monstrous deeds," accusing the sparrow, among other things, of brawling, "forcible divorce, and persecution of the unfortunate," infanticide, spousal brutality, disreputable morals, impudence, theft, autocracy and inveterate criminality (Gurney, Russell and Coues 63). But it was also around this time that the sparrow began to acquire a dedicated band of supporters, and this led to the so-called "Sparrow Question" (Gurney, Russell and Coues vi) being debated with no little rancor between those who advocated the bird's complete annihilation, and protectionists, often of a religious persuasion, who condemned its slaughter as both unnecessary and ungodly.

The campaign against the sparrow was led by W. B. Tegetmeier and Eleanor Ormerod. In a letter to the *The Times* of 13 January 1885, Ormerod, "*de facto* government entomologist for Britain, called for the extermination of the house sparrow" (Clark, "Irishmen of Birds," 17) and, along with Tegetmeier, she went on to bring out a pamphlet with the avowed aim of saving "the bread of the people from these feathered robbers" (Tegetmeier 90). In the run-up to its publication, Ormerod told Tegetmeier, "If we could rout *P. domesticus* it would be a national benefit" (Wallace 162), though she told another correspondent that she was intensely aware that she was addressing "things that involve discussion unbecoming in a lady writer" (Wallace 273). A prominent defender of the sparrow was the Reverend F. O. Morris, and he and his fellow, generally male, protectionists tended to dwell, as Ormerod feared they would, on her perceived deviation from the customary norms of maidenly conduct. Following the publication of her sparrow pamphlet, for example, the Reverend J. E. Walker publicly "entreated Ormerod not to 'steel' her 'compassionate, womanly heart' with her scientific studies. Instead, he suggested, she should devote herself to philanthropic works, and fulfil her duty as a woman" (Clark, "Eleanor Ormerod," 450), while Morris produced a short book called *The Sparrow Shooter* (1886), in which he ventured that "Miss Ormerod would have employed her time and her feminine talents much better if she had confined herself to the use of her needle in working for some charitable object or other" (Morris 4). Ormerod's most vocal opponent, however, was Edith Carrington, author of *Spare the Sparrow* (1897) and *The Farmer and the Birds* (1898), whose protectionist fervor epitomised the late-Victorian and early twentieth-century effort "to extend woman's role as moral guardian into the public realm" (Clark, "Eleanor Ormerod," 450). It is likely that Woolf has someone very like Carrington in mind in the "1914" chapter of *The Years* when Martin and Sara Pargiter encounter an "old lady" at Hyde Park's Speakers' Corner: her "audience was extremely small. Her voice was hardly audible. She held a little book in her hand and she was saying something about sparrows. But her voice tapered off into a thin frail pipe. A chorus of little boys imitated her" (*TY* 217). This woman is almost certainly a protectionist rather than an exterminator, and it is significant (given the connections between sparrows, the dispossessed and the Irish on which *The Years* may well draw and which I shall address below) that her words are indistinct, mocked and unheeded (a little further on Sara refers to her as "the poor old lady whom nobody listened to" [*TY* 218]).

As Christina Alt has helped to explain, it was Ormerod's resistance to the rigid gender stereotyping of such opponents as Morris, Walker and Carrington, rather than her zeal to kill sparrows, that accounts for Woolf's impassioned support of the entomologist in her "Miss Ormerod" essay of 1924 (*E3* 465; *E4* 131-140, 144-145). In Alt's words, Woolf represents Ormerod as "almost against her will and certainly against the conditions of her upbringing, challenging received values by means of her science" (Alt 139). Yet there is some evidence that as a young woman Woolf did share Ormerod's view of the sparrow as an avian pest. One day in June 1897, for example, Woolf helped her father plant seeds in the garden of 22 Hyde Park Gate in order "to produce grass—but whether the sparrows will have left any is a question. As soon as we had left the garden, the horrid little creatures swooped down twittering & made off with the oats etc" (*PA* 96). A week later, however, she was able to record in her journal that the grass was "already sprouting! Very thin & weakly indeed, but it is a comfort to think that the wretched sparrows did not get it all" (*PA* 100). Similarly, it is the sparrow's reputation as a greedy predator that Woolf seems to have in mind when, in 1926, she tells Edward Sackville-West that she "cannot write an elegant sentence when a flock of sparrows set on my thoughts directly they fall to the ground and peck them out on the keyboard" (*L3* 295), just as a passage in the fifth chapter of *Orlando*, where the mid-nineteenth century is characterized as a time when, among other things, "Rat and sparrow clubs were inaugurated," indicates that Woolf was conversant with this widespread means of suppressing the bird (*O* 177).

On the other hand, there is a far more copious and compelling body of evidence to suggest that Woolf was more typically inclined to sympathize with the "wretched sparrow" and to align herself with Romantic representations of it as a "poor proscribed species," while at the same time mobilizing the bird's negative associations as part of her struggle against patriarchal and imperialist oppression. Bonnie Kime Scott has argued that "Woolf uses animals politically to comment upon inequalities of class, gender, nation, and perhaps even race" (Scott 156), and she draws our attention to material in the *Hyde Park Gate News* that seems to indicate that, despite Virginia's "wretched sparrows" remark, the Stephen family were firmly of the protectionist persuasion. One 1892 entry, for example, detailing a boat trip to the Godrevy Lighthouse, records how "Miss Virginia Stephen saw a small and dilapidated bird standing on one leg on the light-house. Mrs Hunt called the man and asked him how it had got there. He said that it had been blown there and they then saw that it's [sic] eyes had been picked out" (*HPGN* 109; quoted Scott 50). Scott also reminds us that when Thoby Stephen, a keen naturalist, encountered nests containing eggs he was not tempted to take them away or destroy them, "as is consistent with the children's ethics in the *Hyde Park Gate News*" (Scott 57; see *HPGN* 59). Far more poignantly, in the weeks after Thoby died on 20 November 1906, Virginia dispatched a series of bulletins about his supposed recuperation to Violet Dickinson which must have been pure agony for her to concoct. In one of these, she introduces her imaginary account of the improving Thoby by excusing it as "an inarticulate scrawl, like the twitter of some frozen sparrow in the graveyard behind your house" (*L*1 264). It is almost as if Woolf envisages herself as the forlorn and moribund subject of one of Bewick's plaintive tail-pieces,[1] just as the quasi-passerine "Sparroy," of course, was one of the "menagerie of aliases" (*L*1 xviii) Virginia Stephen chose for herself when signing her many abject (and sometimes erotic) letters to Dickinson.

In her groundbreaking study Alt also discusses Woolf's 1920 essay on "The Plumage Bill" and how this polemic only reinforces Woolf's credentials as a protectionist (Alt 132-135). So it is worth noting in passing that it is not just this essay but also *Mrs. Dalloway* that contains striking evidence of Woolf's protectionist leanings. By means of "The Plumage Bill," Woolf "put herself right in the middle of the controversy surrounding the bird preservation movement and conservationist concerns as they had developed throughout the nineteenth century and as they existed in 1920" (Abbott 266), and during the course of her fourth novel Woolf draws together her strident opposition to the persecution of exotic birds and her passionate concern for the victims of shell-shock and other forms of patriarchal coercion. With her powerful denunciation of the cruelties of the plumage trade before us, and especially her condemnation of the "murder and torture" (*E*3 243) it routinely involved, it is highly significant that Sir William Bradshaw has a portrait of "Lady Bradshaw in ostrich feathers" (*MD* 86) hanging above his consulting-room

---

[1] "It is quite true that I still know all my beasts from their pictures in Bewick which we were shown before we could listen to reading aloud" (*L*1 165).

mantelpiece. Beneath this grotesque image, some of Sir William's patients "weakly broke down; sobbed, submitted" (*MD* 86), while others, "Naked, defenceless ... exhausted...received the impress of Sir William's will" (*MD* 86) in circumstances that are clearly less hideous but hardly less abhorrent than Woolf's description of how egrets and other birds were being trapped and tormented for their plumage amidst the "blazing South American landscape" (*E3* 242). Earlier in the novel, such ill-gotten plumes had also added to the disturbing intensity of one of Septimus's visions. On this occasion, Rezia had had to restrain him in Regent's Park, "or the excitement of the elm trees rising and falling, rising and falling with all their leaves alight and the colour thinning and thickening from blue to the green of a hollow wave, like plumes on horses' heads, *feathers on ladies*', so proudly they rose and fell, so superbly, would have sent him mad" (*MD* 19; italics added).

As Buffon had remarked with contempt, the plumage of the sparrow was "entirely useless," but at least two of Woolf's novels contain scenes that are made all the more resonant when they are read against the broader background of the "Sparrow Question," the various ways in which the sparrow was persecuted, and the negative associations this bird had acquired by the early twentieth century. In Chapter 13 of *Night and Day*, for example, we learn that Ralph Denham spends a great deal of every lunch-hour in Lincoln's Inn Fields, where the sparrows have come to expect "their daily scattering of bread-crumbs" (*ND* 163). One winter's day he is joined by the suffragist Mary Datchet:

> "I've never seen sparrows so tame," Mary observed, by way of saying something.
> "No," said Ralph. "The sparrows in Hyde Park aren't as tame as this. If we keep perfectly still, I'll get one to settle on my arm."
> Mary felt that she could have forgone this display of animal good temper, but seeing that Ralph, for some curious reason, took a pride in the sparrows, she bet him sixpence that he would not succeed.
> "Done!" he said; and his eye, which had been gloomy, showed a spark of light. His conversation was now addressed entirely to a bald cock-sparrow, who seemed bolder than the rest. (*ND* 164)

As Alt has observed, "Denham's benign interest in nature sets him in opposition to William Rodney, who is notable for his participation in the hunt and his unkindness to monkeys at the Zoo ... Even the simple act of feeding the sparrows in Lincoln's Inn Fields identifies Denham as belonging to the new generation of bird-lovers raised on protectionist principles" (Alt 155). Alt goes on to note that Denham's sheltering of an injured rook provides further evidence of his protectionist leanings, and, later on in the novel, Woolf may even have had in mind the event recorded in the *Hyde Park Gate News* quoted above as she reached for words to describe Ralph's wider social sympathies. "The unhappy voice afflicted Ralph," we are told of an elderly drunk he encounters on the Embankment in Chapter 28, "but it also angered him. And when the elderly man refused to listen and mumbled on, an odd image came to his mind of a lighthouse besieged by the flying bodies of lost birds, who were dashed senseless, by the gale, against the glass. He had a strange sensation that he was both lighthouse and bird; he was steadfast and brilliant; and at the same time he was whirled, with all other things, senseless against the glass" (*ND* 414).

Blyth, too, has brought intriguing contextual light to bear on Ralph's "interest in, and ... affinity with, London's sparrows" (Blyth 281), but there is even more to say, perhaps, than either he or Alt have suggested. Mary's lunchtime encounter with Ralph and his sparrows makes quite an impression on her, and in Chapter 14, for instance, we are told not only that Mary cannot concentrate on the facts and figures that have been tabled at a committee meeting, but that "her mind floated to Lincoln's Inn Fields and the fluttering wings of innumerable sparrows. Was Ralph still enticing the bald-headed cock-sparrow to sit upon his hand?" (*ND* 170). Mary is so distracted, in fact, that she even doodles a "bald-headed cock-sparrow" on her blotting paper. "She looked at Mr Clacton; yes, he was bald and so are cock-sparrows. Never was a secretary tormented by so many unsuitable suggestions ... The thought of what she might say made her bite her lips, as if her lips would protect her" (*ND* 170-171). Woolf seeks in *Night and Day*, as ever, to destabilize and interrogate conventional notions of decency and propriety, and it could be that we are simply meant to register Mary's doodle and the improper thoughts it provokes as tokens of the emotional disturbance her sudden "deep flood of desires" (*ND* 176) for Ralph has un-sluiced. But Mary returns to these sparrows more than once, and in ways that suggest that Woolf may also or alternatively have in mind more specific connections between sparrows and suffragettes. Later that day, having regained her composure, Mary returns to Lincoln's Inn Fields to find it deserted "and the sparrows silent in the bare trees" (*ND* 176), but in Chapter 20, which begins with her grievous disappointment "that by some obscure Parliamentary manoeuvre the vote had once more slipped beyond the attainment of women" (*ND* 266), Mary recalls this earlier afternoon when "she had spent the whole of a committee meeting in thinking about sparrows and colours" (*ND* 268). At one point in Chapter 14 Mary had found herself "looking out of the window, and thinking of the colour of the sky, and of the decorations on the Imperial Hotel" (*ND* 171), and it could be that these are the "colours," six chapters further on, she remembers musing about. But it is also possible that the colours Mary had in mind (in conjunction with sparrows), and has brought to mind once more, are the Women's Social and Political Union's purple, white and green. Jane Goldman has discussed both Woolf's "manipulation of these colours" in her fiction and their broader prominence in the Edwardian period, and it is tempting to read this chain of events in *Night and Day* as another "feminist gesture" (Goldman 68-75; quotes from 68) on Woolf's part. Sylvia Pankhurst recalled that in 1908 the "violence of the [anti-suffragist] rowdies met with little rebuke from political leader writers and under the heading, 'Sparrows for Suffragettes,' the *Westminster Gazette* stated, 'Essex has just provided two amusing Suffragist Incidents,' and described in the same spirit the letting loose of a flight of sparrows inside a hall where the women were speaking and the breaking up of a Suffragist meeting by boys who had rushed the speakers, and cast carbide on the wet roads" (Pankhurst 350). In the minds of the disrupters, it seems, the sparrow nuisance and the noxiousness of suffragettes were indistinguishable, and it is possible that such a connection (but without its negative connotations, of course) was also in play as Mary daydreamed of "sparrows and colours" during her suffragist committee. Significantly, the target reader of the *Westminster Gazette* at this time "was a gentleman relaxing in his club between work and the night's social events" ("Westminster Gazette") so it cannot be entirely coincidental, surely, that Woolf opens the very next chapter, Chapter 21, which is set around 1908, with a pointed jab at the intellectual content of this particular newspaper. The chapter begins with Mary travelling home from work by Tube rather than on foot and so reaching her apartment "in an incredibly short space of time, just so much, indeed, as was needed for the intelligent understanding of the news of the world as the *Westminster Gazette* reported it" (*ND* 279).

In *The Waves*, Bernard recalls that when he went for a walk in London the morning after learning of Percival's death "the sparrows were like toys dangled from a string by a child" (*TW* 211), which might seem a merely fanciful, even awkward turn of phrase until we realize that at the time that section of *The Waves* is set, "children might have parted with a penny or halfpenny to purchase a sparrow-on-a-string as a living kite" (Clark, "The Irishmen of Birds," 16). Furthermore, around the time such a "toy" reached the height of its popularity, the shrillness and supposed feistiness of sparrows led to them being linked with the Irish clamor for independence. In *An Old Woman's Outlook in a Hampshire Village* (1892), for example, the popular novelist Charlotte M. Yonge described sparrows as "poor despised creatures, whom someone has well named the Irishmen of birds, with their noise and their squabbles, their boldness and their ubiquity" (Yonge 16; partly quoted in Clark, "The Irishmen of Birds," 18). While I have been unable to trace the "someone" to whom Yonge refers, both as a child and a young woman Woolf had been a qualified admirer of Yonge's writings[2] and had read *The Heir of Redclyffe* (1853) on her honeymoon (*L2* 2, 6), so even though in 'Two Women' (1927) she quotes Yonge's declaration of her "full belief in the inferiority of women" (*E4* 420) without a trace of approval, it is perfectly possible that she encountered Yonge's

---

[2] 'Y for Miss Yonge/ Who Manythings can tell', "An Easy Alphabet for Infants" (*HPGN* 8).

comment about sparrows being the "Irishmen of birds" at first hand. Furthermore, the same association almost certainly underpins Yeats's "The Sorrow of Love," where "The brawling of a sparrow in the eaves" and "clamorous eaves" lend tumultuous voice to the poet's antipathy for populist militant republicanism. "The Sorrow of Love" is one of Yeats's earliest iterations of his despair at his beloved Maud Gonne becoming, as he saw it, so catastrophically embroiled in the raucous and incendiary grassroots struggle for Irish independence. Although he made a number of changes to this poem between composing it in October 1891—when it featured both "The quarrel of the sparrows in the eaves" and "the angry sparrows in the eaves"—its first publication in *The Countess Kathleen and Various Legends and Lyrics* (1892)— where the "angry sparrows" of his manuscript had been transformed into "warring sparrows"—and its appearance in its final form in 1925—where "The quarrel of the sparrows" was changed to "The brawling of a sparrow"—at no point, it seems, did Yeats consider dislodging his fractious Irish sparrow(s) from its rowdy Irish eaves (Stallworthy 47-48).

It is possible that Irish nationalists and London's sparrows are linked in exactly the same way in *The Years*. As Anna Snaith has remarked, "Ireland frames the published novel, from Delia's daydreams about Parnell to her marriage to Anglo-Irish Patrick" (*TY* lxv), and as she watches the earth fall into her mother's grave at the end of the "1880" chapter, Delia hears both "the sparrows chirp quicker and quicker" and "life [coming] closer and closer" (*TY* 77). The excited sparrows herald not only Delia's imminent emancipation from Abercorn Terrace, but also the greater commitment she will be able to make toward the struggle for Irish self-determination once she herself has been liberated. Given the novel's pronounced Irish strand, therefore, is it entirely coincidental that in the "1891" chapter, just after we hear newspaper vendors proclaiming the death of Parnell, we are also told that "the shrill chatter of the birds on the eaves was silenced" (*TY* 104)? From a matter-of-fact perspective, of course, this silencing of the sparrows is simply explained by their commotion having been drowned out by "the general churn and uproar" (*TY* 102) of the London traffic; but could the muffling of their "shrill chatter … on the eaves" be more resonantly an act of "Irish" homage marking the passing of a great leader? Rather than being silenced perforce, have these "Irishmen of birds" (who were surely familiar to Woolf through "The Sorrow of Love," if not through her reading of Charlotte M. Yonge) been "silenced" out of shock, respect and grief? It is more than possible, I would argue, just as when, near the beginning of the "1914" chapter, we read that Martin Pargiter believes it "must need some pluck ... to write 'God is love' on the gates of Apsley House" (*TY* 204), are we are not asked to reflect not only on the Duke of Wellington's Ascendancy roots and his imposing London home, but more specifically on the carnage of Cromwell's Siege of Drogheda in 1649, the slaughterous engagement that turned out to be the opening act of his conquest of Ireland? As the Citizen asks: "What about sanctimonious Cromwell and his ironsides that put the women and children of Drogheda to the sword with the bible text *God is love* pasted round the mouth of his cannon?" (Joyce 273-274). The annotators of *Ulysses* comment that this motto "is apparently apocryphal but an apt caricature" (Gifford 365), but whether Woolf's source for this passage is the "Cyclops" episode of *Ulysses* or an unidentified history book or the Bible (1 John 4:8; 1 John 4:16), it is important to note that immediately following it a flock of sparrows is sighted outside St. Paul's and an old man arrives to feed them:

> Soon he was haloed by a circle of fluttering wings. Sparrows perched on his head and his hands ... Then there was a ripple in the air. The great clock, all the clocks of the city, seemed to be gathering their forces together; they seemed to be whirring a preliminary warning. Then the stroke struck. "One" blared out. All the sparrows fluttered up into the air; even the pigeons were frightened; some of them made a little flight round the head of Queen Anne. (*TY* 204-205)

The old man's concern for the sparrows of St. Paul's mirrors God's solicitude for the most humble of his creatures (Luke 12:6; Luke 12:7; Matthew 10: 29-31), of course, and is also suggestive of St. Francis of Assisi's famously close relationship to these birds, but because the simultaneous chiming of the City's clocks resounds like a salvo of cannon, and the sparrows take fright at such an ominous and war-like explosion, the Irish associations of the sparrow, and more specifically the Siege of Drogheda, perhaps, are evoked once again. Finally, given that St. Paul's and the Houses of Parliament epitomized, for Woolf, the entrenched patriarchal power of Church and State, when we read at the beginning of the "1891" chapter of *The Years* that sparrows and starlings "whitened the heads of the sleek statues holding rods or rolls of paper in Parliament Square" (*TY* 79), it would be unwise to assume these birds are defecating at random. Could it be, indeed, that they are targeting the statue of Oliver Cromwell in particular? Situated just off Parliament Square and unveiled much to the outrage of Irish Nationalist MPs in 1899, Cromwell is not depicted holding "rods or rolls of paper," but far more controversially, with his zealous campaign in Ireland in mind, a sword and a Bible.

Overall, it is important to appreciate that the novel's Irish theme—beginning with Delia's idealistic commitment to "the Cause" (*TY* 101); finding its pathetic fulfilment in the spuriousness of "her *imitation* Irish flattery" (*TY* 326; italics added), her "*assuming* the manner of a harum-scarum Irish hostess" (*TY* 329; italics added), and "her *rather exaggerated* Irish sing-song" (*TY* 361; italics added), before reaching its grotesque apotheosis in Patrick's blinkered view that the Irish would "be glad to join the Empire again" (*TY* 362)—is only partly conveyed through the story of Delia's capitulation to the entrenched values of her upbringing and her husband's Establishment mindset. Delia's fantasy of a romantic entanglement with Parnell is travestied in her long marriage to a scion of the Protestant Ascendancy, whose sympathies are clearly Unionist and whose family "has served its king and country for three hundred years" (*TY* 362)—almost certainly having planted its roots, that is, on land seized from Catholics by Cromwell and his army during his forcible Settlement of Ireland in the mid-seventeenth century. But the Irish theme also encompasses, among other things, the "Irishmen of birds" and the Apsley House graffito. This is not to claim, of course, that every sparrow in *The Years* is an avian Irishman; what Charlotte M. Yonge called these "poor despised creatures" are also associated with the masses, the excluded and the immured Pargiter women of Abercorn Terrace in the novel. But some of its sparrows have a distinctly Hibernian ring to them, it seems reasonable to suggest, once we adjust our ears to their clamor.

One of the first steps of Mao Zedong's Great Leap Forward (1958-1962) was to order the extermination of what he deemed the four great pests of China: rats, flies, mosquitoes and sparrows. "Everyone come and fight sparrows" proclaimed one propaganda poster featuring a boy with a catapult and his admiring sister looking skyward for targets. Mao's campaign led to ecological disaster as the near elimination of China's sparrows meant that crop-eating insects, especially locusts, flourished ("Four Pests Campaign"), but for students of Woolf, Mao's grave underestimation of the humble sparrow reminds us, yet again, that when we fail to attend to her texts with sufficient diligence, precision and imagination, it is more than likely that, one way or another, those texts will escape us. Accordingly, the main point of this essay is not necessarily to be found in its interpretative speculations (claims which must always be debatable, if not controversial), but in its reaffirmation of the rich potentiality of Woolf's fiction and the ongoing need for her readers to approach all her writings with ever more open minds. We must be un-noddingly alert not just to Woolf's elevated preoccupations, but her everyday events; not just to her grand and imposing structures, like St. Paul's, but to the ordinary things that move about outside them, such as London's maligned and plumeless sparrows.

Works Cited

Abbott, Reginald. "Birds Don't Sing in Greek: Virginia Woolf and 'The Plumage Bill'." *Animals and Women: Feminist Theoretical Explorations*. Eds. Carol J. Adams and Josephine Donovan. Durham NC and London: Duke UP, 1995. 263-289. Print.

Alt, Christina. *Virginia Woolf and the Study of Nature*. Cambridge: Cambridge UP, 2010. Print.

Blyth, Ian. "Do Not Feed the Birds: *Night and Day* and the Defence of the Realm Act." *Contradictory Woolf: Selected Papers from the Twenty-First Annual Conference on Virginia Woolf*. Eds. Derek Ryan and Stella Bolaki. Clemson, SC: Clemson U Digital P, 2012: 278-84. Print.

Clark, J. F. McDiarmid. "Eleanor Ormerod (1828-1901) as an Economic Entomologist: 'Pioneer of Purity Even More than of Paris Green'." *British Journal for the History of Science* 25.87 (December 1992): 431-452. Print.

Clark, John F. M. "The Irishmen of Birds." *History Today*. 50.10 (October 2000): 16-18. Print.

"Four Pests Campaign" http://en.wikipedia.org/wiki/Four_Pests_Campaign

Gifford, Don with Robert J. Seidman. *"Ulysses" Annotated: Notes for James Joyce's "Ulysses."* Berkeley, Los Angeles and London: U of California P, 1988. Print.

Goldman, Jane. *The Feminist Aesthetics of Virginia Woolf: Modernism, Post-Impressionism and the Politics of the Visual*. Cambridge: Cambridge UP, 1998. Print.

Gurney, J. H., Colonel C. Russell and Elliott Coues. *The House Sparrow*. London: William Wesley, 1885. Print.

"The House Sparrow." *History of British Birds: The Figures Engraved on Wood by T. Bewick. Vol. I. Containing the History and Description of Land Birds*. Newcastle: Beilby and Bewick, 1797: 154-157. Print.

Joyce, James. *Ulysses*. Eds. Hans Walter Gabler with Wolfhard Steppe and Claus Melchior. New York: Vintage, 1986. Print.

Morris, F. O. *The Sparrow Shooter*. London: S.W. Partridge, 1886. Print.

Pankhurst, E. Sylvia. *The Suffragette: The History of the Women's Militant Suffrage Movement, 1905-1910*. London: Gay and Handcock, 1911. Print.

Scott, Bonnie Kime. *In the Hollow of the Wave: Virginia Woolf and Modernist Uses of Nature*. Charlottesville and London: U of Virginia P, 2012. Print.

Stallworthy, Jon. *Between the Lines: Yeats's Poetry in the Making*. Oxford: Clarendon Press, 1965. Print.

Tegetmeier, W. B. "Appendix." *The House Sparrow (The Avian Rat) in Relation to Agriculture and Gardening, with Practical Suggestions for Lessening its Numbers*. London: Vinton, 1899: 73-90. Print.

Wallace, Robert, ed. *Eleanor Ormerod, LL.D. Economic Entomologist: Autobiography and Correspondence*. London: John Murray, 1904. Print.

"Westminster Gazette." http://en.wikipedia.org/wiki/Westminster_Gazette

Woolf, Virginia. *The Essays of Virginia Woolf*. Eds. Andrew McNeillie and Stuart N. Clarke. 6 vols. London: Hogarth Press, 1986-2011. Print.

———. *The Letters of Virginia Woolf*. Eds. Nigel Nicolson and Joanne Trautmann. 6 vols. London: Hogarth Press, 1975-1980. Print.

———. *Mrs Dalloway*. Ed. David Bradshaw. Oxford: Oxford UP, 2000. Print.

———. *Night and Day*. Ed. Suzanne Raitt. Oxford: Oxford UP, 1999. Print.

———. *Orlando: A Biography*. Ed. Brenda Lyons. London: Penguin, 2000. Print.

———. *A Passionate Apprentice*. Ed. Mitchell A. Leaska. London: Pimlico, 2004. Print.

———. *The Waves*. Ed. Michael Herbert and Susan Sellers with research by Ian Blyth. Cambridge: Cambridge UP, 2011. Print.

———. *The Years*. Ed. Anna Snaith. Cambridge: Cambridge UP, 2012. Print.

Woolf, Virginia, Vanessa Bell and Thoby Stephen. *Hyde Park Gate News: The Stephen Family Newspaper*. Ed. Gill Lowe. London: Hesperus, 2005. Print.

Yonge, Charlotte M. *An Old Woman's Outlook in a Hampshire Village*. London and New York: Macmillan, 1892. Print.

VIRGINIA WOOLF

Three Guineas

Narrow Gates and Restricted Paths: The Critical Pedagogy of Virginia Woolf
Rod C. Taylor

> No man who worships education has got the best out of education.
> Without a gentle contempt for education no man's education is complete.
> —G. K. Chesterton

> Education is an admirable thing, but it is well to remember from time to time that nothing that is worth knowing can be taught.
> —Oscar Wilde

The 1963 Harvest edition cover to *Three Guineas* speaks powerfully to the conflict expressed in the pages found beyond it, even though Woolf had no hand in choosing it (see illustration). The photograph on the cover features three women traveling on bicycles toward a university entrance, each wearing a black, formal university gown and black shoes, with hair neatly pinned up. Trees, full and green, border the road on which the women ride, and the bright, yellow sky casts a warm glow over their surroundings.[1] When viewing the image, one's attention is drawn away from the women, located in the lower third of the cover, and toward the towering institution, which fills most of the frame. The only face offered to readers is that of the university, toward which all three women ride on a path that provides ample room for each to maneuver.

Two aspects negatively shadow this otherwise pleasant image. The first is a narrow gateway that appears at the base of the tower in the center, one that will ultimately restrict the path on which the women ride, forcing them to adjust into a tighter group or even to abandon their collective travel and go it alone. Beyond the gate the university awaits them, with its internal structures and high walls made of carved stone. Even as the image gestures to women advancing in the world, progressing toward their degrees, it also invokes Woolf's fear that in taking this road women will be forced to mold themselves into narrowly defined educated subjects. The pathway to the university allows for more mobility than its gateway and what lies beyond, for once inside the women will be surrounded by long-standing, rigid boundaries. Viewed from Woolf's perspective, then, the gateway represents the constricting channels early twentieth-century women were forced to negotiate in order to gain their formal education. Imposing structures and borders of the college

---

[1] The image, a photograph taken by Chris Ware, shows three Girton College students entering the campus on their bikes. Interestingly, the presence of human subjects is a marked modification from the original cover, designed by Woolf's sister, Vanessa, which featured a simple drawn image of three paper guineas, a pen, and an inkwell against a dark background.

correspond to the reductive and limiting environments that were inevitably a part of England's male-governed university institutions. Additionally, the writing of a fluid hand floats over the image, the words indecipherable. Perhaps this overlaid script represents the multiple letters Woolf drafts within this work, letters that cast a dark shadow over the sunny prestige typically associated with a university education. Read this way, the picture of these "outsiders" on their way to becoming "insiders" invites but also threatens, an appropriate effect for reading an author who remained, for most of her life, ambivalent toward an education she never received.[2]

Woolf's ambivalence results from a view of education that mirrors my reading of this cover photograph. From the outside, education represents promise and potential, but the path toward it forces its participants into longstanding and harmful ruts, restricting the ways in which they can realize their potential and benefit from their learning. In *Three Guineas*, Woolf demonstrates that upward mobility, which higher education promises, is not so easily attained, nor are the intellectual independence and social equality that supposedly come with it. In her failure to embrace women's inclusion enthusiastically, Woolf might seem overly harsh, especially given the newly-won rights of women in the early twentieth century. But a closer look at the underlying reasons for her suspicion of higher education aids in comprehending her constant vacillation between supporting and undermining formal learning in Britain.

In just a few pages, Woolf sums up much of her educational philosophy by offering radical changes regarding the purpose and structures of higher education (42-44).[3] Her specific ideas connect her to Frankfurt School writers, whose theories would later be adopted by Paulo Freire and Henry Giroux to propose what is now called "critical pedagogy."[4] Woolf's critique of traditional education and her pro-

---

[2] While Woolf's autodidacticism is well established among critics and biographers, in "'Tilting at Universities': Woolf at King's College London," Kenyon Jones and Snaith draw attention to a certain level of familiarity with formal education—via the women's college at King's College London—that Woolf appears to downplay in her writings on the subject of education. As they point out, perhaps the reason for this omission was the high importance she placed on self-learning over formal experiences in the classroom.

[3] Apart from the cover image discussed above, all references to *Three Guineas* in this essay come from the Harcourt 2006 annotated edition.

[4] For the purposes of this essay, the main tenets of "Critical Pedagogy" are largely derived from two key texts: Paulo Freire's *Pedagogy of the Oppressed* (1970) and Giroux's *Theory and Resistance in Education: A Pedagogy for the Opposition* (1983). In *Empowering Education* (1992), Ira Shor defines critical pedagogy as the "[h]abits of thought, reading, writing, and speaking which go beneath surface meaning, first impressions, dominant myths, official pronouncements, traditional clichés, received wisdom, and mere opinions, to understand the deep meaning, root causes, social context, ideology, and personal consequences of any action, event, object, process, organization, experience, text, subject matter, policy, mass media, or discourse" (129).

posed alternative education call for a pedagogical philosophy that works to create subjects dedicated to critical inquiry and devoted to addressing social injustices of all kinds. In doing so she shares with Freire and other critical pedagogues a philosophy of education that consistently calls for a reevaluation of any given education model. With this essay, I join Melba Cuddy-Keane in a desire to "take Woolf outside the borders that would limit her sphere to Bloomsbury, or to high modernism, or to feminism, and to locate both the person and her ideas in a different context—one that involves public debates about books, reading, and education. . ." (8). Although Cuddy-Keane's treatment of education centers specifically on reading practices in the early twentieth century and Woolf's personal interest and efforts in matters of literacy, our tasks are similar by virtue of seeing Woolf's pedagogy as ultimately non-gendered. Throughout, I argue that Woolf demonstrates that she is more than an innovative artist and pioneering feminist. Her evaluation of higher education and the influence of that assessment ultimately make her an early "Transformative Intellectual," a term, coined by Giroux, used to describe those educators able to critique and transform inequities in social structures.

A quick academic search on critical pedagogy easily confirms that, for the most part, the fight is over. Interest in debating this controversial pedagogy's validity seemed to peak somewhere around the turn of the millennium and has steadily waned ever since. From the beginning, critical pedagogy caused controversy among academics, often resulting in a substantial divide between those who staunchly opposed it and those who insisted upon the necessity of its implementation.[5] Almost two decades of intense argument—via books, journals, and blogs—did little to resolve such differences, and perhaps that explains one of the reasons interest has dropped so dramatically. Proponents could never seem to agree on how, when, where, and why critical pedagogy should be implemented, and it did not take long for both sides to become entrenched along clearly defined battle lines. As a result, readers might easily challenge the value of revisiting the issue now, especially—as this essay's title suggests—through a literary lens. But there are at least two reasons why we should.

One of those reasons lies in the educational philosophy that Woolf espouses in *Three Guineas*. At its core, Woolf's pedagogy anticipates Freire's in that both systems inquire into knowledge and how the production of knowledge is constituted, but Woolf's orientation toward knowledge is that of ambivalence toward new

---

[5] For an iconic example of resistance, see Maxine Hairston's controversial 1992 CCC's essay, "Ideology, Diversity, and Teaching Writing," or her more pointed *Chronicle of Higher Education* essay from the previous year, "Required Writing Courses Should Not Focus on Politically Social Issues." Gregory Jay and Gerald Graff's "A Critique of Critical Pedagogy," in *Higher Education Under Fire: Politics, Economics, and the Crisis of the Humanities* (1995) provides another pointed example. On the other side of the issue, we have the works of key critical pedagogy proponents like Shor, McLaren, and Giroux.

understanding—even that which resists oppressive systems—rather than political absolutism on one side or another. In other words, for her, ambivalence represents true progress, whereas common interpretations of Freire's approach emphasize new, resistant knowledge (and action based on that knowledge) as primary evidence of satisfactory progress.[6] As such, I argue that Woolf's pedagogy provides a way to move us beyond a teleological approach to critical pedagogy and thus the simple good/bad binary that often results from a highly politicized application of Freire's system of thought.

Current educational challenges provide another reason for revisiting critical pedagogy through a new lens. The current problems facing institutes of higher education go beyond the trifecta of race, class, and gender, and as such are not easily assigned left and right political affiliations. Pressure on universities to adopt corporate models of efficiency, the legitimacy of online learning, a growing lack of tenure-track positions, overreliance on assessment, the integrity of for-profit colleges—to name just a few—all pose challenges that an inquiry-based approach could help solve, but not if we hold that only new knowledge is the ultimate goal.[7] Woolf provides us with a critical approach to pedagogy that privileges individual experience, skepticism, and reflection in the learning process over the simple acquisition of new knowledge. To be sure, the ambivalence Woolf encourages toward one's education does indeed generate new knowledge, but it also encourages a healthy skepticism toward that new knowledge, one that keeps imagination (and humility) alive in the student. New content is not the goal of Woolf's process; new conclusions are not the end game here but rather the product of it.

A brief introduction to *Three Guineas* kicks off my exploration of Woolf's argument regarding the role perspective plays in solving educational problems and provides some better understanding as to her own evaluation of personal experience and its relationship to pedagogical purpose. My reading of *Three Guineas* then serves to organize her thoughts on teaching into a more distinct pedagogical system. Such organization aids in one's ability to abstract her thoughts on teaching and learning from this particular work and find broader application. After offering

---

[6] Here I refer to those approaches (i.e., of theorists like McLaren, Shor, and Giroux) that place great emphasis on students coming to practical and absolute conclusions that aid in their practical ability to resist their oppressors. This approach typically opens critical pedagogy up to the challenge that it does not create genuinely critical agents but rather its practitioners simply replace one set of political values with another.

[7] Kurt Spellmeyer's "Saving the Social Imagination: The Function of the Humanities in the Present Time" (2012), David Youngberg's "Why Online Education Won't Replace College—Yet" (2012), John Boe's "Don't Call Me Professor!" (2011), and Anne Borrego's "Trading Ivy for an Office Park" (2002) provide just a small sample of the current conversations surrounding such topics.

a reading of *Three Guineas* that works to extend this famously feminist author's pedagogy beyond feminism, I re-connect Woolf to Freire's thoughts, establishing the manner in which her critical pedagogy provides a way for us to complicate and reinvigorate our own approach to this system of thought. Ultimately, this essay provides one example of how modernist works preoccupied with teachers, classrooms, universities, and other pedagogical spaces, objects, and theories—like Woolf's *A Room of One's Own* and *Three Guineas*—provide a productive lens through which literary critics and pedagogues can reevaluate their approach to the contemporary classrooms in which such literature is taught.

War and Education

In both *A Room of One's Own* and *Three Guineas* Woolf reveals her suspicion that formal education operates as a subtle vehicle for ideological induction into a male-centered, warring society, and yet at the same time she also demonstrates her distrust regarding the motives of emerging forms of higher education in Britain. For Woolf, this ambivalence is key to a healthy pedagogy that works against mindless indoctrination of all kinds. Ultimately, her ambivalence toward formal education emerges not simply as a corresponding attribute of a critical pedagogy that predates Freire's, but rather as an intellectual activity essential to operating productively within established educational systems that, purposefully or not, work to advance the dominant ideologies of the governments and cultures to which they belong.

In literary realms, *Three Guineas* is not often analyzed as an educational treatise.[8] As Mark Hussey points out, *Three Guineas* ultimately "established Woolf as a significant voice in the cause of pacifism" (285), and much criticism

---

[8] Melba Cuddy-Keane's *Virginia Woolf, the Intellectual, and the Public Sphere* (2003) provides one of a few examples of literary criticism pointedly concerned with Woolf's pedagogy in *Three Guineas*. In this work, Cuddy-Keane seeks to combat a view of Woolf as an elitist, arguing that she was in many ways a pedagogical intellectual, concerned with public literacy. Nicholas Midgley's "Virginia Woolf and the University" argues that Woolf's views on education, especially in *Three Guineas*, function as a type of education in and of itself. Additionally, Robin Hayes' dissertation *Virginia Woolf's Treatise on Education:* Three Guineas (2003), as well as my own, *Modernism and the Wreck of Education: Lawrence, Woolf, and the Democratization of Education* (2007), provide yet another example of a literary focus on the pedagogical message in *Three Guineas*. One is more likely, however, to find *Three Guineas* being discussed as an educational text in works specifically dedicated to matters of pedagogy, especially those concerned with women and education. *Women in Higher Education: Empowering Change* (2002) by Joann DiGeorgio-Lutz, "Bearing Witness to Differends: Virginia Woolf and Postmodern Composition Pedagogies" by Lisa Hill, and "Virginia Woolf: Postmodern Writing Instructor" by Bradley R. Bowers provide a few examples.

supports this assertion.[9] For Woolf, however, pacifism and pedagogy are intimately linked. In matters closely connected to learning, early twentieth-century and contemporary critics alike have focused on the form of this work, its epistolary framing, and the use of endnotes—all aspects that undergird Woolf's attempt to re-educate the mis-educated. Jane Marcus argues that the style of this work, along with its content, connects it to "the literature of the oppressed" (*Languages* 79), an idea seconded by Lynn Kramer's assertion that the included endnotes "represent, in textual format, the way women's voices, especially feminist voices, have been fragmented and marginalized" (100).[10] Due to her unapologetic anger and controversial assertions in this work, Woolf endured a host of negative reviews that highlight early resistance to the goals and methods of that re-education: from Graham Greene's assessment that her arguments were "a little provincial, even a little shrill" (*The Spectator* 1111) to Vita Sackville-West's comment that despite its "lovely prose," *Three Guineas* was filled with "misleading arguments" (*L6* 412). In "Caterpillars of the Commonwealth Unite" (1938), Q.D. Leavis argues that this work demonstrates Woolf's inability to identify with those outside her social and economic class. Woolf anticipated such a response, telling her sister that once the book was published, "I shan't . . . have a friend left" (*L6* 218). Both in form and content, *Three Guineas* proved to be an obstacle for readers. Pointing to the ways in which Woolf's aesthetics enact her philosophies, Victoria Middleton argues that *Three Guineas* "works not by transcending but unsettling our ideological assumptions about culture and power" (407). One of the systems of power she unsettles is that of education.

While *A Room of One's Own* contains an evaluation of formal education that subtly critiques the epistemological framework beneath it, *Three Guineas* more explicitly challenges various ideologies perpetuated by current modes of education. One of the ideologies it contests is patriotism, a notion that an educated man defines differently than his uneducated sister. As evidence of this difference, Woolf cites the Lord Chief Justice of England's explanation regarding the kind of patriotism that leads young men to go to war: "For those who have been trained in English schools and universities, and who have done the work of their lives in England, there are few loves stronger than the love we have for our country" (12). Barred from formal learning, an educated man's sister has held a "position in the home of freedom" different from that of her brothers, however, and thus her interpretation of

---

[9] Jane Marcus refers to *Three Guineas* as "the bible of a new generation of pacifists" (*Art and Anger* xiv), "a manifesto," and "peace propaganda" (*TG* xlix-l), and Sandra Gilbert and Susan Gubar see this work as "the postwar era's great text of pacifist feminism" (*Sexchanges* 306).
[10] For a treatment of the epistolary form, see Anne Herrmann's "'Intimate, Irreticent and Indiscreet in the Extreme': Epistolary Essays by Virginia Woolf and Christa Wolf" (1986).

patriotism presumably differs as well. So, while *Three Guineas* is clearly a pacifist text, Woolf's attention to education allows one to concentrate on the progressive and innovative pedagogical theories contained within it.[11] In fact, Woolf's reflections on the three guineas ultimately revolve around the purpose, methods, history, and influence of higher education in Britain.

In this work, Woolf raises numerous questions regarding the purpose and benefit of formal learning, and in seeking to answer them she exposes higher education's flaws, its hypocrisy, and, at times, its inability to produce "good people" (those who would oppose war and promote peace). The playful and mischievous tone found throughout *A Room of One's Own* is notably absent in *Three Guineas*, for here she vehemently expresses her disgust with higher education's role in creating mindless, obedient, patriotic, war-loving citizens unable or unwilling to question those in authority. Her evaluation of British education, which involves lampooning highly regarded universities, government organizations, and even the established Church, demonstrates her view that academic training functions as one of the most common means by which men and women are inducted into a male-centered, and thus, according to Woolf, violent society.

Dissatisfied with merely criticizing education, alongside her critique of higher education's purposes and methods Woolf includes a proposal for an alternative pedagogy. Her proposed pedagogy is characterized by calls for self-reflexivity, a reassessment of the teacher/student relationship, a reevaluation of curriculum needs, and a learning environment that discourages ideological conformity and promotes critical thinking. Her presentation of this pedagogy privileges philosophy over bureaucracy. According to Patricia Laurence, Woolf's response to fascism in *Three Guineas* centers on "a social and philosophical analysis that allows for more subtlety and casts itself into a future when changed relations between the sexes will lead to changes in human relations in general" (127). Woolf's goal seeks first to encourage a change of mind that would consequently result in long-lasting changes in policies, governments, and social institutions that currently encourage fascism. The same pattern emerges in her pedagogy, which also functions philosophically first. The necessary corresponding structures and methods of this pedagogy would ultimately be determined by the alternative motivations at work within it, so Woolf focuses her attention on the prerequisite to successful transformation, one that starts from within and works its way out.

[11] Although my argument on Woolf's pedagogy will concern the first chapter of *Three Guineas*, I will be drawing on comments made throughout the whole work, although not always chronologically. As critics note, Woolf often repeats herself in this work, yet in many cases her repetitions contain subtle nuances that elucidate the ideas being revisited. Because of this tendency, I will move between various points in this work, attempting to piece together in a more orderly fashion her criticisms and proposed solutions to the problems of higher education.

A Gulf So Deeply Cut

The structure of *Three Guineas* is perhaps best summarized by the three requisitions found within its pages. Woolf frames the entire work as a response to a barrister who has solicited her support for anti-war efforts. After addressing two other financial requests, one from a local women's college and one from a society dedicated to helping women enter into various professions, Woolf finally turns her full attention toward the barrister's initial requests. He has asked that she sign a manifesto pledging "to protect culture and intellectual liberty" and also to join a society "whose aim is to preserve peace" (102). Woolf ultimately rejects the offer to join his association, opting instead to participate in one she labels "The Outsider's Society," an organization that consists of "educated men's daughters working in their own class . . . and by their own methods for liberty, equality and peace" (125). Her rejection likely comes as no surprise to readers, for by this point she has incorporated drafts of other letters in her response to the barrister that reveal her skepticism of the benefits of joining schools, professions, and societies governed by men. She divides the work into three chapters, each one devoted to addressing the three different requisitions.[12] In examining this work with attention to matters of pedagogy, one notices that the first chapter specifically foregrounds education, and the two that follow, despite their shift in focus, offer clear connections between formal learning and media, religion, and war.

Before addressing the concerns introduced by the barrister or her other correspondents, however, Woolf highlights the role education plays in shaping individual perspectives by presenting it as the most obvious cause of the chasm that exists between the barrister and herself. Although both come from what is "convenient to call the educated class," only the barrister received formal training, having begun his education at "one of the great public schools and finished it at the university" (6). In the course of addressing the "gulf so deeply cut" between them, so vast that she "wonders whether it is any use to try and speak across it" (6), Woolf reflects on the numerous sacrifices women have made for men's education and questions the productivity of men and women jointly attempting to evaluate such a longstanding tradition as war. This reflection, in turn, causes her to ponder the significance of "informal" education and to evaluate the meaning of patriotism and its connection to formal learning. Woolf invites the barrister (and thus her readers) to follow her

---

[12] As Jane Marcus points out, the format of this work led to it enjoying far fewer readers than *A Room of One's Own*. "It is difficult to read," she argues, "because the role of the reader in overhearing the narrator's responses is uncomfortable. We are eavesdroppers twisting our necks to hear what she says, and we are never sure we aren't being addressed as well, as part of the problem" (*TG* xlv-xlvi).

train of thought as she works to answer his initial question: "How in your opinion are we to prevent war?" (5).

Woolf wastes no time in pointing to the difficulty of arriving at simple answers to complicated questions, modeling the very self-reflection she encourages throughout both texts. Asked to provide her opinion on how to prevent war (a request that implies a certain amount of respect for her position and ideas), Woolf begins her response with a seemingly self-deprecating comment. "A whole page could be filled with excuses and apologies; declarations of unfitness, incompetence, lack of knowledge, and experience: and they would be true," she writes, "[b]ut even when they were said there would still remain some difficulties so fundamental that it may well prove impossible for you to understand or for us to explain" (5). Woolf understands that her position in society as a woman, an "uneducated" citizen (one inexperienced in war and politics) will surely lead to a skeptical reception of any answer she might supply. Still, her first concern is not this obstacle, but rather the likelihood that she and the barrister will misunderstand each other. Despite that risk, she must attempt to answer the question, "even if it is doomed to failure" (5), so she takes on the barrister's request and its accompanying obstacles in a way that is almost predictable at this point in her career: she creates a character.

In drawing "a sketch" of the barrister, Woolf first points to that which she and the barrister have in common, information that later only serves to emphasize the role their disparate educational experiences have played in creating the gulf that exists between them. She draws attention to the fact that they both come from "the educated class," "speak with the same accent," observe similar dining etiquette, and depend upon servants for their care. Both are able to discuss politics and religion "without much difficulty," as well as other issues such as "war and peace" and "barbarism and civilization" (6). More important, however, she and the barrister both earn their own livings, he through his job and she through her writings. For readers familiar with Woolf, the importance she places on the power of earning one's own living is no surprise, as *A Room of One's Own* makes clear.

And yet at the end of this extensive list of common characteristics, her tone dramatically shifts with a single and powerful word: "But." The significance of this three-letter word should not be underestimated, especially in Woolf's writings. With it she begins *A Room of One's Own*, where it marks the beginning of a resistance to her audience's expectations, as it also does in *Three Guineas*. In both instances, the word "but" registers Woolf's misgivings regarding common assumptions in her culture, and, perhaps more significantly, this conjunction contains within it the seed of her resistance. With this small word she begins her counterarguments, subverting the "truths" about men, women, and war in which many around her believe. Given the barrister's similarities to Woolf, he most likely expects a certain amount of sympathy and camaraderie from her, but she is not so easily co-opted. With the word "but," and three dots that "mark a precipice" between her and the barrister, she informs him that there exists "a gulf so deeply cut between us that for three years and more I have been sitting on my side of it wondering whether it is any use to try to speak across it" (6). Interestingly, Woolf has afforded herself the same amount of time allowed for one to complete a college degree, perhaps gesturing to an unpaid-for degree on the subject. Armed with her own "degree," and after pointing to all their similarities, Woolf highlights that which they don't have in common—their education.

The effects of "Arthur's Education Fund" provide Woolf with one way of explaining the differing perspectives between women and men and why education plays such a large role in shaping these differing perspectives.[13] Because of "Arthur's Education Fund," men like the barrister have been able to enjoy the benefits of formal learning, although Woolf is quick to mention that the education of those benefiting from this "voracious receptacle" was not merely bound up in "book-learning" (6). In their youth, men like the barrister experienced friendships with other educated men, whose talk "broadened [their] outlook[s] and enriched [their] mind[s]." "In the holidays you traveled," she tells him, "[you] acquired a taste for art; a knowledge of foreign politics, and then, before you could earn your own living, your father made you an allowance upon which it was possible for you to live while you learnt the profession which now entitles you to add the letters K.C. to your name" (7).[14] While such positive events occur in the lives of these young men, the daughters of educated men pay, with their lack of education and experience, into an account that does little to fund anything for them. "The result," Woolf concludes, "is that though we look at the same things, we see them differently." The reality of Arthur's Education Fund "magically" turns the landscape of "noble courts and quadrangles of Oxford and Cambridge" into "petticoats with holes in them, cold legs of mutton, and the boat train starting for abroad while the guard slams the door in their faces" (8). Here Woolf juxtaposes educated, privileged men with uneducated, underprivileged women. Shabby "petticoats" mark the alternative perspective as distinctively feminine, while cold mutton points to the lack of excess and slammed doors to lack of access. The education of men has perpetuated illogical and unethical gender hierarchies, yet these same inequities have also ironically contributed to a healthier and more balanced psychology in women.

[13] She takes this term from William Thackeray's nineteenth-century novel *Pendennis* (1848-50), from which she also borrowed the term "Oxbridge," used in *A Room of One's Own*.
[14] "King's Counsel," a mark of distinction awarded to outstanding members of the British bar. (*OED*) Woolf's reference to the award can be seen as indicating the prestigious positions that the barrister occupies and the power of influence that he possesses.

The informal ways in which her female predecessors learned provide Woolf with the basis for proposing a learning process that benefits from a politics of positionality between what she calls a "paid-for" and "unpaid-for" education. Paid-for education refers to the formal training and academic knowledge made available via money and opportunity, a form of education that in Woolf's day was becoming increasingly more available to women.[15] "Unpaid-for" education is "that understanding of human beings and their motives which, if the word is rid of its scientific associations, might be called psychology" (9). Because of their long history of "choosing the human being with whom to live life successfully," Woolf thinks that women have some skill in this arena (9). For her, women of the nineteenth century benefited from the unpaid-for education that resulted from their oppression, and the sum of the lessons learned must not be abandoned, even as twentieth-century women continue to strive for the paid-for education that has eluded them for so long.

Ultimately, the differences between the sexes result in different viewpoints, making it difficult to try and find answers together. "Complete understanding could only be achieved by blood transfusion and memory transfusion—a miracle still beyond the reach of science," she claims (9). In such a way, Woolf again emphasizes the power of perspective. It is "an indisputable fact," Woolf informs the barrister, that women, who "are made up of body, brain and spirit, influenced by memory and tradition must still differ in some essential respects from 'you,' whose body, brain and spirit have been so differently trained and are so differently influenced by memory and tradition." "Though we see the same world, we see it through different eyes," she writes (22). Despite their advance in the professional realm, women's viewpoints remain relegated to a place far beneath men's. Acknowledging the extent to which, for women, the doors of law, business, religion, and politics are "at best ajar," Woolf encourages a look in another direction, "in a direction natural to educated men's daughters, in the direction of education itself." "The part that education plays in human life is so important ... so considerable," she argues, "that to shirk any attempt to see how we can influence the young through education against war would be craven" (28-30). To that end, she turns to theorizing how women might influence the educational institutions and pedagogy of the future while exposing the flaws inherent in the systems and methods that currently exist.

Freire, Giroux, Woolf, and the Practice of Freedom

---

[15] According to Woolf's records, the yearly income of Oxford University in 1933 was £435,656 and £212,000 at Cambridge in 1930. These numbers provide just a small example of "the immense sum of money that has been spent on education in the last 500 years" (31). In today's economy, the larger of the two amounts would be equivalent to at least £23,882,661 (or $38,087,698), according to the Bank of England's CPI calculator.

In the first chapter of *Three Guineas*, Virginia Woolf drafts a letter to the honorary treasurer of a local women's college who has requested a donation for the school's rebuilding. In her response, which indecision has kept her from producing in a timely fashion, Woolf wonders whether or not it is worthwhile to support the reconstruction of existing educational institutions. "Shall I send it or shan't I?" she asks herself. "If I send it, what shall I ask them to do with it? Shall I ask them to rebuild the college on the old lines? Or shall I ask them to rebuild it, but differently? Or shall I ask them to buy rags and petrol and Bryant & May's matches and burn the college to the ground?" (42). Woolf's speculations on the various conditions attached to her donation foreground her ambivalence toward formal education. For Woolf, there appear to be only three possible responses to this request. With her money, she can support existing goals and methods of education, fund futile attempts at developing new ones, or subsidize the ultimate destruction of the buildings themselves—key symbols of Britain's ostensibly enlightened culture. To Woolf's mind, reconstructing the college on the "old lines" will not do, yet rebuilding it on new ones seems difficult, especially given the male-centeredness of education in Britain and the impossibility of implementing many radical but necessary changes. Should she perhaps burn the college to the ground, she wonders. Since higher education cannot help produce "good people," the guinea might be best used to purchase materials that will aid in its ruin.[16]

Woolf does finally commit to sending the first guinea to the women's college, with no strings attached, grudgingly admitting that in order to gain financial independence women must "follow the old road to the old end . . ." (46). Before arriving at this decision, however, she first proposes an alternative pedagogy, one that seeks to redefine the goals, methods, and environments commonly associated with higher education. The fact that within moments of introducing a new pedagogy she discards it does not lessen its significance, for her hesitation is rooted in recognizing that the present "reality" makes the acceptance and adoption of her educational ideas highly unlikely (45). The pedagogy she envisions is not impossible, just improbable in her time, a fact confirmed by the emergence and widespread acceptance of a similar one several decades later. Critical pedagogy, both in its past and present forms, owes much to modernism, but not just to the members of the Frankfurt school. By encouraging a pedagogy that centers on critical thinking,

---

[16] In Woolf's "A Society" (1921), the "society for asking questions" seeks to determine whether "Oxbridge professors help to produce good people and good books," which are considered "the objects of life" (122). This debate as to whether or not education can produce "good" people is hardly new. Plato's *Meno* and *Protagoras* both reveal the difficulty of answering the question, "Can virtue be taught?" In the latter work, Protagoras contends that virtue can be taught didactically, while Socrates asserts that such a quality is inevitably a part of a person's nature, just as knowledge is, and therefore it can only be drawn out through instruction—not imparted by it.

personal reflection, and political activism, Woolf anticipated the direction educational philosophy would travel in post-World War II Europe and North America.[17]

For those critics who have bought into the stereotype of Woolf as elitist, it might be an odd conjunction to think of her alongside such a radical figure in educational history as Paulo Freire, a man specifically dedicated to the lower class. Yet, Woolf often objected to the charge that she was elitist. Hermione Lee points out that on several occasions Woolf argued against accusations, made by individuals such as Ben Nicolson and Desmond McCarthy, that she could not relate to the working class. Furthermore, she claimed that her own educational background gave her the right to use the pronoun "we" when speaking to the Workers' Educational Association in 1940 on the topic of education (Lee 742). In fact, in this lecture, entitled "The Leaning Tower," she claims that education is elitist, unconcerned with the needs of the masses, and she ultimately calls for a classless society (179). Still, she lived most of her life away from the lower classes, and often her comments on education are grounded in a middle-class context. How curious, then, that she and Freire share certain pedagogies, although hers remains more gloomily inflected because she didn't share his hope that such changes could flourish in the social world in which she lived.

Richard Shaull's foreword to Paulo Freire's *Pedagogy of the Oppressed* gives us our first glimpse of the way in which Woolf's views on learning anticipate critical pedagogy. "There is no such thing as a *neutral* educational process," Shaull claims, for "[e]ducation either functions as an instrument which is used to facilitate the integration of the younger generation into the logic of the present system and bring about conformity to it, *or* it becomes 'the practice of freedom,' the means by which men and women deal critically and creatively with reality and discover how to participate in the transformation of their world" (34). The application of Shaull's comments to Woolf's requires little parsing. Having already rejected an educational system that has, since its inception, sought to indoctrinate its members "into the logic" of an existing hegemony, Woolf encourages a "practice of freedom" strikingly similar to that later proffered by Freire.

Firmly rooted in the dialectical social criticism characteristic of the Frankfurt school theorists, critical pedagogy was popularized by Freire with the publication of *Pedagogy of the Oppressed*. In it, he presents his now famous rejection of "banking education" and the traditional teacher-student dichotomy. Convinced that both conventions contribute to oppression, Freire offers a pedagogy he believes will aid in liberating the oppressed from their oppressors. This pedagogy, writes Freire,

---

[17] In America, John Dewey and George Counts more formally promoted this progressive approach to education through Dewey's *Democracy and Education: an Introduction to the Philosophy of Education* (1916) and Counts's *Dare the School Build a New Social Order* (1932).

"must be forged *with* not *for* the oppressed . . . [and] makes oppression and its causes objects of reflection by the oppressed" (33). From this reflection, he insists, will come the impetus for the oppressed to engage in their own liberation. This pedagogy, he claims will "be made and remade" many times as its practitioners learn and respond to their changing realities.

Freire outlines two stages in the development of a pedagogy of the oppressed, both of which correspond to the progression suggested decades earlier by Woolf's treatment on the topic of education in *Three Guineas*. In the first, the "world of oppression" is revealed to the oppressed. Confronted with the reality of their subjugation, the oppressed commit themselves to the transformation of their world. In the second stage, during which the transformation has succeeded, this form of pedagogy "ceases to belong to the oppressed and becomes a pedagogy of all men in the process of permanent liberation" (40). In its initial stage, a change in perception is the goal, and in the second the impact of this change in perception results in an "expulsion of the myths created and developed in the old order, which like specters haunt the new structure emerging from the revolutionary transformation" (40).

While Woolf most likely had no such structured plan in mind when she formed her pedagogy, she was nonetheless involved in attempting to bring about the first stage Freire describes and hoped that the second might one day, in the far distant future, become a reality. In drawing attention to the history of prejudice that resulted in the lack of professional and educational opportunities available to women of her era, she seeks to open the eyes of women around her to their oppression and to encourage activism that might lead to a transformation of their world. Some of the difficulty with that task lies in the fact that part of the oppression women experienced came in the form of the "freedom" to participate in educational structures designed and implemented by men.[18] Her hope for the qualities of the second stage is more easily found in *A Room of One's Own* than in *Three Guineas*. It appears that the ten years that transpired between these two texts worked to discourage much of the optimism she possessed in 1928. Still, the fact that she offers such a pedagogy suggests that she held onto some hope that a transformation might yet occur that would usher in a new educated subject, one who embraced inquiry and dialogue rather than recoiling from it.

Key to such a dialogue for Woolf was the acknowledgement of no unlimited or unbiased perspective from which to enter into any given inquiry. Early in *Three Guineas*, speaking to the barrister, Woolf questions the existence of an "absolute point of view" (13), and her answer, or lack thereof, is central to understanding her pedagogy and the new educated subject she envisions. Confronted with the reality that she and the barrister cannot understand each other because of the numerous

---

[18] In 1920, women students were allowed to become full members at Oxford but Cambridge did not follow suit until 1948.

differences between them, she considers whether it would be better for her letter "to be torn across and thrown into the waste-paper basket" (13). In looking to Woolf for an answer to his question, the barrister has failed to acknowledge the different circumstances, sociological and biological, that influence their perspectives, differences that determine the way in which each approaches the question and the answer to it. The more information she gathers in her search, the more evasive the answer to the question becomes, along with the possibility of reaching "a moral judgment which we must all, whatever our differences, accept." "Indeed," she writes, "the more lives we read, the more speeches we listen to, the more opinions we consult, the greater the confusion becomes and the less possible it seems . . . to make any suggestion that will help you to prevent war" (13). The importance of this admission lies in the implications that no neutral perspective exists by which she, the barrister, or anyone else can claim absolute objectivity. Her invitation to the barrister for them to examine together the pictures supplied by the Spanish government of dead bodies speaks to her frustration with the lack of neutral perspectives.[19]

Indeed, later in *Three Guineas*, these same pictures from the war are the catalyst for her educational proposal. In light of the questions surrounding the purpose of formal education and the pictures of dead bodies and ruined houses, Woolf feels she must first revisit some very basic questions regarding the kind of education her money will support. She tells the treasurer that as a result of these pictures and the questions they raise, she should consider carefully the aims of her college, as well as the educational subject it seeks to produce. For these reasons, Woolf tells the treasurer, "I will only send you a guinea with which to rebuild your college if you can satisfy me that you will use it to produce the kind of society, the kind of people that will help to prevent war" (33). But since she has no such assurance and can get no immediate response to her questions, Woolf offers her own answers by way of recommending a university designed to produce a new educated subject.

In a very short space, Woolf's proposal to the treasurer captures many of the concerns subtly presented in *A Room of One's Own* and haphazardly spread across all three chapters of *Three Guineas*; her entire formal proposition spans no more than a few pages (42-44). Compare this to her contemporary D. H. Lawrence's "Education of the People," in which he reinvents public education from the ground up, taking more than seventy pages to do so.[20] Despite its brevity, however, Woolf's

---

[19] Interestingly, readers don't see these pictures, which were never included. Julia Duffy and Lloyd David note the irony of Woolf discussing photographs she doesn't include while failing to even mention those she does, a fact they feel perhaps contributed to the omission in subsequent editions of the five photographs Woolf did include in the first edition. (129).
[20] Despite his personal experience in the classroom as a teacher from 1908-1911, Lawrence's doomed essay would be rejected by a number of publishers and would only be brought to light in his posthumous papers. Despite the essay's inherent shortcomings when it comes to solving the problems of education, he and Woolf shared many of the same criticisms.

proposal is filled with many provocative and complicated ideas on education, many that demonstrate more ambitious goals than just equity. As Lucio Ruotolo argues, Woolf felt that "modern education needs something more than equal opportunity," and as such she advocates for a system that can shake off old, static, and what Ruotolo refers to as "unregenerative ideas" (286). Unlike many past educational theorists, Woolf does not go into great detail regarding age, selections of students, administrative structures, and the like. Instead, she offers radical revisions of five key categories involved in a university education: the foundations on which it is constructed, teacher/student relationships, the kind of teachers to be hired, the pedagogical aims of its curriculum, and the physical and psychological environment created by its participants. Such changes, however, must be cast in a new mold; the old will not work.

    The role that imagination must play in liberation from that old mold, however, ultimately complicates Woolf's vision of a new pedagogy for women. Within the first few pages of Freire's iconic work, he explains how the liberation of the oppressed, first and foremost, depends upon a formal and strategic break from the structures of the oppressors. Too many times, he argues, the oppressed revolt and win only to fall into the same traps of their former oppressors. In the initial struggle for their freedom, "the oppressed, instead of striving for liberation, tend themselves to become oppressors, or 'sub-oppressors'" (29-30). "The Oppressed must be their own example in the struggle for their redemption," Freire claims. Models from among the oppressors will not work (39). For Woolf, though, the necessity of a model is more problematic because women of the early twentieth century had few, if any, educational examples of their own to mimic. Even Emily Davies, who founded Girton, the Cambridge women's college, in 1870, insisted that its female students be taught and prepared in the same manner as their male counterparts in British universities (Hussey 102). As such, female education—even when run by women—often failed to provide a non-oppressive model. The old and rich colleges of men, Woolf contends, have led to "neither a respect for liberty nor a particular hatred of war," and so the new college must take advantage of its youth and poverty and found itself on the advantages of both conditions. "[I]t must be an experimental college, an adventurous college," she states, one "built on lines of its own" (43). "Experimental" and "adventurous" here mark the need for an imaginative task on the part of her audience. Her suspicion of women categorically subscribing to the standards and methods of existing universities speaks to Woolf's fear of a similar outcome. She insists that women must not become like men in this regard, but in order for that trap to be avoided a new foundation must be embraced, one that has little in common with that found supporting universities like Oxford and Cambridge, or even those of colleges like Girton and Newnham.

    Woolf's description of the physical construction of this new kind of university works as a powerful metaphor for a unique quality that must be a part of this new form of education: the willingness to change repeatedly. After introducing the need for *new* construction instead of reconstruction, Woolf explains that this new, "adventurous college" must be built "not of carved stone and stained glass, but of some cheap, easily combustible material which does not hoard dust and perpetrate traditions" (43). While this reference to carved stone and stained glass points to the expensive trimmings associated with higher education, it also gestures toward the hard, immutable, inanimate environments of Cambridge and Oxford. In this description, the traditional university gathers dust, revealing its archaic status and lifeless state of existence. Here education works to perpetuate traditions and crush attempts at change. Woolf envisions a university built out of combustible material, which is not only cheap, but also easily ignited if necessary.[21]

For Woolf, the ease with which one can destroy an existing institution does not signify a weakness but a strength; it is a mark of its flexibility—and flexibility in education is key for Woolf. Unlike various proponents of critical pedagogy over the years, Woolf does not simply seek to overturn an oppressive pedagogy and install its opposite, or at least not permanently. To that end, her educational philosophy demands a state that encourages constant renewal. One finds it easier to wipe the slate clean when there is little thought given to the materials wasted in the process or to the construction costs associated with replacing the one destroyed. Likewise, the task of tearing down and setting ablaze the old structures appears simply a matter of having the will to do so (and locating a match, of course). All the stone and stained glass in Oxford and Cambridge, both in the buildings and in the minds of their leaders, make the prospect of their demolition unthinkable, and so Woolf knows it is useless to try and rebuild. As such, she posits the building of this new center for higher learning and in doing so outlines what type of traditional internal structures should not be constructed in its creation.

Woolf promotes an orientation toward knowledge as inevitably mutable—always necessarily changing—by calling for a ban on museums and libraries that house old books filled with unchanging facts. Instead of shelves filled with "chained books and first editions under glass cases," she requests that "the pictures and books be new and always changing" (43). Woolf anticipates formal theories of constructivism, that is, the philosophy that knowledge is a product of our active involvement in gathering and interpreting information gained through observation, experience, and reflection.[22] In critical pedagogy, knowledge is treated as largely

---

[21] This reference to flammable materials is significant, especially given Woolf's repeated references in this work and in private letters to wanting to burn down the old schools.
[22] Theories on constructivism have impacted a wide-variety of scholarly fields, such as literature, philosophy, psychology, sociology, education, and mathematics. Interestingly, even in mathematics the language used to articulate the epistemological shift works when looking at

socially constructed, not as immutable and fixed somewhere outside us, waiting to be found. As Christopher Robbins, a former student and now colleague of Giroux points out, critical pedagogy "has the consequence of subjecting all knowledge and their modes of production to public engagement and contestation" (xxi). As mentioned above, Woolf seeks to do that in *Three Guineas*, and in proposing a new educational institution works to ensure that such reflection and change is not only encouraged but also required. In her directions regarding decorations ("Let it be decorated afresh by each generation with their own hands cheaply," she says), we can see her insistence that future modifications to all new conclusions reached in one's education are essential to creating a virtuous educated subject (43). She wants no dust gathering on the materials or the ideas on which this school is built.

In addition to structural impositions, Woolf demands that instruction at this university transcend that of the traditional institutions in England. "[W]hat should be taught in this new college?" she asks. This question reflects more of an attempt to condemn the subtle "truths" taught in Oxford and Cambridge than a desire to see a specific curriculum overhaul. The new college must not teach "the arts of dominating other people; not the arts of ruling, of killing, of acquiring land and capital." What it should teach, she argues, are "the arts of human intercourse; the art of understanding other people's lives and minds, and the little arts of talk, of dress, of cookery that are allied with them" (43). In this brief statement, Woolf expresses a central philosophy of her pedagogy: dialogue is necessary for true learning to occur. She enacts this view though *A Room of One's Own*, but couched as it is here in *Three Guineas*—that is, as a formal pedagogy—her insistence on the necessity of dialogue in learning can be treated in a more specifically educational context.[23] Woolf understands that the absence of dialogue in education further enables learning to function as an "exercise of domination" (Freire 65), and her proposal here works to condemn a pedagogy that Freire would later famously refer to as "banking education."

In banking education, students are viewed as empty vessels waiting to be filled with the superior knowledge of the teacher, a notion Woolf rejects in theory and practice. Traditional education views teaching as "an act of depositing, in which the students are the depositories and the teacher is the depositor." The teacher,

Woolf's treatment of education. For example, "constructive mathematics," Douglas Bridges explains, "is distinguished from its traditional counterpart, classical mathematics, by the strict interpretation of the phrase 'there exists' as 'we can construct'" (par. 1). Woolf might argue that information found in the books located on the shelves of the British Museum often present their "knowledge" as if it "there exists," rather than as knowledge that one is able to construct through a subjective treatment of evidence.

[23] Woolf's appreciation for dialectical exchange and for investing in "the art of understanding other people's lives and minds" is also central to her aesthetic choices, which she explains in "Mr. Bennett and Mrs. Brown" and models in her novels from *Jacob's Room* forward.

often through lectures, provides the information, and students "receive, memorize, and repeat" (Freire 58). In his description of this oppressive methodology, Freire offers an extensive, but surely not exhaustive, list of practices and attitudes associated with those who embrace this pedagogy, many of which Woolf addressed in *Three Guineas* and in *A Room*.[24] More interesting than their common objections, however, are their common solutions, for in Woolf's new university we see her desire to encourage what Freire later will refer to as "problem-posing education."

Woolf's approach to problem-posing education, even years before Freire describes it, offers a unique perspective on how educators can model their own pedagogy rather than just preach it. Problem-posing education manifests itself in four distinct ways, all of which coincide with Woolf's pre-World War II pedagogical practices and goals. Banking education, Freire argues, operates by "mythicizing reality," whereas problem-posing education works to demythologize it (71). Much of Woolf's use of biography and history in *Three Guineas* operates in a similar way, revealing how certain "mythicized" truths about the world are closely connected to concrete situations and people, and are often rooted in prejudice and ignorance. There is no mystery, in her mind, behind the assumption that women are less intelligent than men. A simple gloss of history demonstrates that limited education and opportunity have given women little chance to discover or demonstrate their abilities, and men, enjoying their position of power, are hardly motivated to alter a system that has served them so well. The transparency of Woolf's thought process also serves this goal. And although one might argue that this transparent presentation of her methodology is merely a clever rhetorical strategy, I would suggest that in allowing the barrister (and thus her readers) insight into how she gathers and interprets information that so powerfully informs her deductions she allows her readers to come to their own conclusions more easily. In short, she presents her thoughts

---

[24] Here I provide the list in full. In reading it, one can easily see how similar Freire's pedagogical concerns are to those of Woolf.
- the teacher teaches and the students are taught;
- the teacher knows everything and the students know nothing;
- the teacher thinks and the students are thought about;
- the teacher talks and the students listen—meekly;
- the teacher disciplines and the students are disciplined;
- the teacher chooses and enforces his choice, and the students comply;
- the teacher acts and the students have the illusion of acting through the action of the teacher;
- the teacher chooses the program content, and the students (who are not consulted) adapt to it;
- the teacher confuses the authority of knowledge with his own professional authority, which he sets in opposition to the freedom of the students;
- the teacher is the Subject of the learning process, while the pupils are mere objects (Freire 59).

here as a problem that needs solving, and as such, models a method that avoids indoctrinating her readers and demystifies her status as one "who simply knows."

In fact, Woolf's entire letter to the barrister can be viewed as a problem-posing education in this regard, and connects to the second quality of this kind of pedagogy: dialogue. From the beginning, she presents the problem and then a series of dialogues between her and other letter writers in an attempt to "dialogue" with her correspondents. By encouraging dialogue, Woolf works to engage her readers in the critical thinking process, and her demand for the positive role of dialogue in the school she imagines further reflects her aversion to banking concepts of education.[25] In this new university, an appreciation for dialogue would ensure that all would teach and all would learn. What we get in Woolf's work that we don't get as much in Freire is the form following the content closely. The experience that Woolf offers her readers gives them a chance to test out the benefits of her pedagogy, which in turn puts them in direct dialogue with the author.

Creativity and reflection form the third and fourth qualities of problem-posing education and are manifested in Woolf's argument that "[t]he aim of the new college ... should be not to segregate and specialize, but to combine" (43). Whereas banking education "inhibits creativity" (Freire 71), Woolf's model thrives on it. Part of this creativity can be found in the presentational style common to problem-based pedagogy, but creativity is also necessary in one's reflective practices. Freire argues that a pedagogy of oppression maintains that humans are abstract, isolated, and independent, "unattached to the world," but "education as a practice of freedom" works to teach just the opposite. True reflection, for Woolf and Freire, seems to hinge on being willing to "explore the ways in which mind and body can be made to cooperate" and to "discover what new combinations make good wholes in human life" (*TG* 43). Creativity is also essential to this form of pedagogy, as both teachers and students are required to adapt themselves to each other and to their specific circumstances.

Woolf demonstrates her understanding that revolutionary pedagogy is not enough, however, by following her comments with suggestions regarding the kind of teachers that must be hired to ensure the success of this program. Her imagined university would be run by teachers "drawn from the good livers as well as from the good thinkers." These are individuals who first and foremost love to learn. There should be no difficulty in attracting them, she declares, for these artists, mu-

---

[25] Years earlier, and on the other side of the Atlantic, John Dewey expressed his own frustration with the lack of dialogue in educational practices in the United States. "Why is it, in spite of the fact that teaching by pouring in, learning by a passive absorption, are universally condemned, that they are still so entrenched in practice? That education is not an affair of 'telling' and being told, but an active and constructive process, is a principle almost as generally violated in practice as conceded in theory" (5).

sicians, and writers who would teach here would do so because they would learn. "What could be of greater help to a writer," Woolf asks, "than to discuss the art of writing with people who were thinking not of examinations or degrees or of what honour or profit they could make literature give them but of the art itself?" (44). Compare such a teacher with the kind Woolf has described previously in *Three Guineas*. This teacher would not thrive on ornamentation or encourage students to do so, but rather would flourish in an environment of cooperative learning. In *Three Guineas*, Woolf continues to champion the benefits of students and teachers acting as critical co-investigators.

Her celebration of the creative individual and a sincere commitment to intellectual and artistic freedom for students significantly informs Woolf's criticism of education, but her proposed solutions are, for the most part, first and foremost philosophical. Woolf's proposal, even as it relates to Freire's theories, has its critics. As an education major in the early nineties, I often found myself at odds with certain aspects of critical pedagogy being taught by professors in my education classes, specifically its apparent attempt to "de-center" the authority of the classroom. At other times, I found this philosophy of teaching guilty of romanticizing students' experiences or personal views. Such tendencies have been recognized and addressed by educational theorists for and against critical pedagogy. For example, Giroux argues that "some versions of critical pedagogy reduce its liberatory possibilities by focusing almost exclusively on issues of dialogue, process, and exchange." In these cases, teaching is "reduced to getting students to merely express or assess their own experiences." Furthermore, Giroux criticizes those teachers who engage in a "flight from authority," which results in a pedagogy that, at its best, is merely facilitation (49). But this is critical theory at its worst, says Giroux.

While Woolf's pedagogy is undoubtedly concerned with issues of "dialogue, process, and exchange," her ultimate purpose for proposing a new university enables educators to avoid the type of pedagogy alluded to above. At its best, "critical pedagogy is developed as a cultural practice that enables teachers and others to view education as a political, social, and cultural enterprise" (Giroux 50). Ideally, Giroux argues, it "calls into question forms of subordination that create inequities among different groups *as they live out their lives*" (50, emphasis mine). Woolf's ambitions go even further, though, beyond the classroom and even beyond her nation. In re-educating the educated and offering a new education for those not yet educated, she seeks to reduce the animosity brought about by difference, competition, greed, and jealousy. In short, she wants a genuinely democratic education, one that celebrates inquiry and creativity, one that longs for change and increased understanding, one that isn't afraid to tear down the old and build the new. And all of these desires are framed in a letter that has at its heart a desire to stop war.

When Giroux offers a detailed description of critical pedagogy at its best, he might well have been describing the very one Woolf promotes both in *A Room of One's Own* and *Three Guineas*, although I would argue Woolf is a bit more skeptical of what constitutes a "good citizen." According to Giroux, such a pedagogy

> rejects classroom relations that relegate difference as an object of condemnation and oppression, and it refuses to subordinate the purpose of schooling to narrowly defined economic and instrumental considerations. This is a notion of critical pedagogy that equates learning with the creation of critical rather than merely good citizens. This is a pedagogy that links schooling to the imperatives of democracy, views teachers as engaged and transformative intellectuals, and makes the notion of democratic difference central to the organization of curriculum and the development of classroom practice. (50)

At its core, Woolf's views on learning are connected to a sincere commitment to ethics and peace, and she does indeed desire an education that would produce good people. At the same time, however, she understands that definitions of "good" change, and her calls for a university that will "hoard no dust" gestures to the critical reflection that must continue beyond the moment of its conception. She mistrusts any single definition of "good." In 1938, a "good citizen" would have been a patriot, a team player, a follower. To avoid the same kind of trap, Woolf pushes her readers and thus her fellow citizens to forge ahead skeptically and carefully onto new educational paths, but forge they must.

In the halls of Oxford and Cambridge and in her society, Woolf sees a pedagogy that oppresses, and, daring to imagine one that might work to usurp it, she offers the groundwork for a place where "society was free; not parcelled out into the miserable distinctions of rich and poor, of clever and stupid; but where all the different degrees and kinds of mind, body and soul merit co-operated" (44).[26] But, in the middle of envisioning a new college where degrees don't matter and lectures are obsolete and vanity and displays of competition and jealousy are notably absent, Woolf hesitates, and seemingly gives up and gives in, ending her proposal just as she began *A Room of One's Own*: *in medias res*. Her fictional response to the honorary treasurer breaks off, "not from lack of things to say," but rather because Woolf imagines the reader of the letter recalling that "students of Newnham and Girton, since they could not put B.A. after their name, were at a disadvantage in obtaining appointments" (44). As such, how could a college forced to work so hard at obtaining appointments for its students begin to dream of deviating from long-standing pedagogical forms and procedures? "Fire off your rhetoric, but we

---

[26] As Morag Shiach points out, "Woolf finds that in both Oxford and Cambridge the values of competition, acquisition, and militarism dominate both research and teaching" (xxiii).

have to face realities," Woolf imagines the treasurer saying to her, and so Woolf suspends her plans for a new kind of university and faces the "reality on which [the treasurer's] eyes were fixed" (45).

Woolf's abandonment of her proposal, however, does not weaken the power of the ideas espoused within it. Ultimately, she knows how unwelcomed her pedagogy would be by those who have the power to change the educational landscape of her time, and she resigns herself to this fact: she might "dream [her] dreams," but women such as the honorary treasurer must deal with the pressure of delivering an education that will get students jobs. It would seem that the only realistic option is for the college to rebuild itself on the old lines, to produce practical results, award degrees, participate in egocentric ceremonies, and accumulate wealth that they would then refuse to share. In other words, the only option seems for women to become like men.[27] That reality, Woolf tells the barrister, means that in the future "that college, too, must ask the same question that you, Sir, are asking now: 'How in your opinion are we to prevent war?'" (45).

Still, even as Woolf sends a guinea to the treasurer, she dreams of the daughters of educated men dancing around the fires of a burning school, while their mothers look down upon them and cry "Let it blaze! Let it blaze! For we have done with this education" (46). A mere three years later, with war still weighing heavily on her mind, she would end her life by walking into a river. She would never see the lasting effects of her thoughts on higher education, how her theories on learning are beginning to be realized in various universities and secondary institutions in and outside of England, how more and more difference is being embraced and celebrated in education, or how women are now teaching men. It would seem that we have advanced far down the path she envisioned.[28] And yet, as I am finishing this essay, I see in the news that ten more have been killed in Afghanistan, and I find myself wondering, "How can we prevent war?" Inasmuch as war seems inevitably to result from the desire of one party to oppress another, the question leads me back to the critical pedagogy espoused by Virginia Woolf and Paulo Freire.

I find Woolf's question as difficult now as I imagine Woolf did then. In *Three Guineas*, she demonstrates that there are tragic consequences for not thinking,

---

[27] One of the rejected titles for *Three Guineas* was "*Men Are Like That*" (*D4* 77). Such a title nods to Woolf placing the cause of war squarely on the shoulders of men, and, since education plays such an important role in shaping the psychology and perspectives of men, she suggests that if women drive in the same old ruts, so to speak, they will unavoidably end up in the same town.

[28] Indeed, in Michèle Barrett's introduction to the 1993 Penguin Classics version of *Three Guineas*, she writes that the book "has now found its time." Whereas its original audience was "by and large uncomprehending and hostile," contemporary audiences see its "equation between masculinism and war" a worthy "topic of heated political debate rather than a cranky eccentricity" (ix).

acting, and teaching critically. In the same year of the publication of her book, Hitler was hailed *Time Magazine*'s "Man of the Year," and within nine months of this accolade he had invaded Poland. With Europe on the brink of another major war, it seems as if the time was just not right for Woolf's ideas on education to take root, but such environmental impediments to a revolutionary pedagogy would finally succumb to the passion of those dedicated to critical reflection as the atrocities of the war pushed philosophers and artists to reexamine the potential progress of the human race. Respected psychologists and educators joined in the reevaluation of the impact of education on the modern subject, and soon a pedagogy that Woolf abandoned in frustration began to gain traction in various forms. Although critical pedagogy still remains marginalized in many educational environments (in practice more than in theory), discussions surrounding its perceived mission continue to result in occasional public reactions from educators and public intellectuals. Its power, however, lies not in its mere inclusion in dialogues on education but rather in our reflection on the role that critical thinking plays in the democratic classroom and how that role must continue to evolve as we do. For that, dialogue is essential, as is our putting such theories to the test in our classrooms.

"Critical inquiry and exchange are supported by a pedagogy that levels the playing field," James Slevin argues, "not just by bringing academic norms and expectations into the open, but through classroom practices explicit in their interrogations and critiques of those norms" (53). Woolf understood that and, along with proposing a new approach to learning, she sought to model it within her work. Using Woolf's theories as a lens through which we re-examine the tenets of critical pedagogy allows us to see ambivalence not as a side-effect of a critical orientation toward knowledge but rather as the goal. It also challenges educators to move beyond teaching about the need for critical thinking, encouraging us also to model it in our very delivery—to make the form match the content of our message. But perhaps most importantly, it keeps the conversation surrounding critical thinking—what it means, what it looks like, and why we need to consider its role in our classrooms—alive. In the end, there will always be those who question whether educational spaces provide the best places to explore social problems or to attempt to answer questions like "How can we prevent war?" And perhaps, at best, education can only provide part of the answers to such longstanding cultural challenges that have put us on a seemingly circular path; nevertheless, I find Woolf's critical pedagogy a useful place to begin imagining a different journey, for us and for our students.

Works Cited

Barrett, Michèle. Introduction. *A Room of One's Own/Three Guineas*. By Virginia Woolf. 1938. London: Penguin Books, 1993. ix-liii. Print.
Boe, John. "Don't Call Me Professor!" *Pedagogy* 11.1 (2011): 33-42. Print.
Borrego, Anne Marie. "Trading Ivy For An Office Park." *Chronicle of Higher Education* 48.24 (2002): A10-A12. Print.
Bowers, Bradley. "Virginia Woolf: Postmodern Writing Instructor." *Resources in Education*, April (1994): 377-499. Print.
Bridges, Douglas. "Constructive Mathematics." *The Stanford Encyclopedia of Philosophy* (Winter 2004 Edition). Ed. Edward N. Zalta. 5 February 2007. Web.
Counts, George S. *Dare the School Build a New Social Order?* New York: The John Day Company, 1932. Print.
Cuddy-Keane, Melba. *Virginia Woolf, the Intellectual, and the Public Sphere*. New York: Cambridge UP, 2003. Print.
Dewey, John. *Democracy and Education: An Introduction to the Philosophy of Education*. New York: Macmillan, 1916. Print.
DiGeorgio-Lutz, Joann. *Women in Higher Education: Empowering Change*. Westport: Praeger, 2002. Print.
Duffy, Julia and Lloyd Davis. "Demythologizing Facts and Photographs in *Three Guineas*." *Photo-textualities: Reading Photographs and Literature*. Ed. Marsha Bryant. Newark: U of Delaware P, 1996. 128-140. Print.
Freire, Paul. *Pedagogy of the Oppressed*. New York: Continuum, 2000. Print.
———. *Politics and Education*. Los Angeles: UCLA Latin American Center Publications, 1998. Print.
Gilbert, Sandra M. and Susan Gubar. *Sexchanges*. New Haven, Yale UP, 1988-1994. Print.
Giroux, Henry. *On Critical Pedagogy*. New York: Continuum, 2011. Print.
———. *Theory and Resistance in Education: Towards a Pedagogy for the Opposition*. Westport: Bergin & Garvey, 2001. Print.
Greene, Graham. "From the Mantelpiece." *The Spectator* 17 (1938): 1110-12. Print.
Hairston, Maxine. "Diversity, Ideology, and Teaching Writing." *College Composition And Communication* 43.2 (1992): 179-193. Print.
———. "Required Writing Courses Should Not Focus On Politically Social Issues."*Chronicle of Higher Education* 37.19 (1991): B1-B3. Print.
Hayes, Robin Donna. *Virginia Woolf's Treatise On Education*: Three Guineas. Dissertation Abstracts International, Section A: The Humanities and Social Sciences 63.8 (2003): 2831. Print.
Herrmann, Anne. "'Intimate, Irreticent and Indiscreet in the Extreme': Epistolary Essays by Virginia Woolf and Christa Wolf." *New German Critique: An*

Interdisciplinary Journal of German Studies 38 (1986): 161-80. Print.

Hill, Lisa. "Bearing Witness to Differends: Virginia Woolf and Postmodern Composition Pedagogies." *The 49th Annual Meeting of the Conference on College Composition and Communication.* Chicago, 1998. Print.

Hussey, Mark. *Virginia Woolf A-Z.* New York: Oxford UP, 1995. Print.

Jay, Gregory and Gerald Graff. "A Critique of Critical Pedagogy." *Higher Education Under Fire: Politics, Economics, and the Crisis of the Humanities.* Eds. Michael Bérubé and Cory Nelson. New York: Routledge, 1995. 201-213. Print.

Kenyon Jones, Christine, and Anna Snaith. "'Tilting At Universities': Woolf At King's College London." *Woolf Studies Annual* 16 (2010): 1-44.

Kramer, Lynn. "One Retrospective Lupine View: A Terrified Student's View of Virginia Woolf's *Three Guineas*." *Virginia Woolf: Themes and Variations.* Eds. Vara Neverow-Turk and Mark Hussey. New York: Pace UP, 1993. 97-102. Print.

Laurence, Patricia. "A Writing Couple: Shared Ideology in Virginia Woolf's *Three Guineas* and Leonard Woolf's *Quack, Quack!*" *Women in the Milieu of Leonard and Virginia Woolf: Peace, Politics, and Education.* Eds. Wayne K. Chapman and Janet M. Manson. New York: Pace UP, 1998. 125-143. Print.

Lawrence, D. H. "Education of the People." *Phoenix: The Posthumous Papers of D. H. Lawrence.* New York: The Viking Press, 1936. 587-668. Print.

Leavis, Q. D. "Caterpillars of the Commonwealth Unite!" *Scrutiny* 7 (1938): 203 14.

Lee, Hermione. *Virginia Woolf.* New York: Random House, 1996. Print.

Marcus, Jane. *Art and Anger: Reading like a Woman.* Columbus: Ohio State UP, 1988. Print.

———. Introduction. *Three Guineas.* By Virginia Woolf. 1938. Ed. Jane Marcus. Orlando: Harcourt, 2006. xxxv-lxxii. Print.

———. *Virginia Woolf and the Languages of Patriarchy.* Bloomington, IN: Indiana UP, 1987. Print.

McLaren, Peter, and Joe L. Kincheloe. *Critical Pedagogy : Where Are We Now?.* New York: Peter Lang, 2007. Print.

Middleton, Victoria. "*Three Guineas*: Subversion and Survival in the Professions." *Twentieth Century Literature* 8 (1982): 405-17. Print.

Midgley, Nicholas. "Virginia Woolf and the University." *Woolf Studies Annual* 2 (1996): 147-159. Print.

Plato. *Protagoras and Meno.* Trans. Adam Beresford. New York: Penguin, 2005. Print.

Robbins, Christopher. Introduction. *The Giroux Reader.* Ed. Christopher Robbins. Boulder: Paradigm Publishers, 2006. vii-xxvii. Print.

Ruotolo, Lucio P. "'The Lord Must Have His House': Virginia Woolf's Romantic Anarchism." *Virginia Woolf: Themes and Variations*. New York: Pace UP, 1993. 277-287. Print.

Shaull, Richard. Foreword. *Pedagogy of the Oppressed*. By Paulo Freire. 1970. New York: Continuum, 2000. 39-34. Print.

Shiach, Morag. Introduction. *A Room of One's Own and Three Guineas*. By Virginia Woolf. 1928, 1938. Oxford: Oxford UP, 2008. xii-xxviii. Print.

Shor, Ira. *Empowering Education: Critical Teaching for Social Change*. Chicago: U of Chicago P, 1992. Print.

Slevin, James. "Keeping the University Occupied and Out of Trouble." *ADE Bulletin* 130 (2003): 50-54. Print.

Spellmeyer, Kurt. "Saving the Social Imagination: The Function of the Humanities at the Present Time." *College English* 74.6 (2012): 567-587. Print.

Taylor, Rod C. *Modernism and the Wreck of Education: Lawrence, Woolf, and the Democratization of Learning*. Diss. Indiana University, 2007. Print.

Thackeray, William. *The History of Pendennis: His Fortunes and Misfortunes, His Friends and His Greatest Enemy*. Oxford: Oxford UP, 1999. Print.

Woolf, Virginia. *The Diary of Virginia Woolf*. Eds. Anne Olivier Bell and Andrew McNeillie. 5 vols. London: Hogarth Press, 1977-84. Print.

———. *Jacob's Room*. New York: Harcourt, Brace and Company, 1922. Print.

———. "The Leaning Tower." *Collected Essays*, Vol. 2. New York: Harcourt, Brace, and World. 1967. 162-181. Print.

———. *The Letters of Virginia Woolf*. Eds. Nigel Nicolson and Joanne Trautman. 6 vols. New York: Harcourt Brace Jovanovich, 1975-1980. Print.

———. "Mr. Bennett and Mrs. Brown" (1924). *The Essays of Virginia Woolf*. Vol. 3. Ed. Andrew McNeillie. San Diego: Harcourt Brace Jovanovich, 1988. Print.

———. *A Room of One's Own*. Orlando: Harcourt, 1997. Print.

———. "A Society." *The Complete Shorter Fiction of Virginia Woolf*. Ed. Susan Dick. New York: Harcourt Brace, 1985. 124-136. Print.

———. *Three Guineas*. 1938. Orlando: Harcourt, 1963. Print.

———. *Three Guineas*. 1938. Annotated and with an introduction by Jane Marcus. Orlando: Harcourt, 2006. Print.

Youngberg, David. "Why Online Education Won't Replace College—Yet." *Chronicle of Higher Education* 53.14 (2012). Web. 13 August 2012.

Guide to Library Special Collections

This guide updates the information in volume 19 according to information received by January 2014.

Name of Collection: The Beinecke Rare Book and Manuscript Library

Contact: Kevin Repp, Curator of Modern Books and Manuscripts
Patricia Willis, Curator of American Literature

Address: Yale University Library
P.O. Box 208240
New Haven, CT 06520-8240

URL: www.beinecke.library.yale.edu

Hours: Mon.–Thu. 8:30 AM–8 PM
Fri. 8:30 AM–5 PM

Access Requirements: Registration required at first visit.

Holdings Relevant To Woolf: General Collection includes autograph manuscript of "Notes on Oliver Goldsmith." Comments on Edward Gibbon, William Beckford Collection. Letters from Virginia Woolf in the Bryher Papers, the Louise Morgan and Otto Theis Papers, and the Rebecca West Papers. Related material: 41 letters from Vita Sackville-West to Violet Trefusis; files relating to Robert Manson Myers's *From Beowulf to Virginia Woolf* in the Edmond Pauker Papers.

Yale Collection of American Literature includes typewritten manuscripts of "The Art of Walter Sickert," "Augustine Birrell," "Aurora Leigh," "How Should One Read a Book?" "Letter to a Young Poet," "The Novels of Turgenev," "Street Haunting." Dial/Scofield Thayer Papers: manuscripts of "The Lives of the Obscure," "Miss Ormerod," and "Mrs. Dalloway in Bond Street." Letters from Virginia Woolf in the William Rose

Benet Papers, the Benet Family Correspondence, Henry Seidel Canby Papers, the Seward Collins Papers, the Dial/Scofield Thayer Papers, and the Yale Review archive. Material relating to translations of Woolf in the Thornton Wilder papers. Related material: Clive Bell, "Virginia Woolf" (Dial/Scofield Thayer Papers); 43 letters from Leonard Woolf to Helen McAfee (*Yale Review*); 11 letters from Leonard Woolf to Gertrude Stein.

Name of Collection: The Henry W. and Albert A. Berg Collection of English and American Literature

Contact: Isaac Gewirtz, Curator

Address: New York Public Library, Room 320
Fifth Avenue & 42nd Street
New York, NY 10018

Telephone: 212-930-0802
Fax: 212-930-0079
Email: isaacgewirtz@nypl.org

Hours: Tue.–Wed. 11 AM–7 PM
Thu.–Sat. 10 AM–6 PM
Closed Sun., Mon. and legal holidays

Access Requirements: After acquiring Library card in room 315, check outerwear and all containers (briefcases, computer cases, handbags, folders, etc.) in Ground Floor cloakroom, and proceed to the Berg Collection. Traceable and photo identification required. Undergraduates working on honors theses need letter from faculty advisor. No books may be brought to the reading tables, including notebooks.

Restrictions: Virginia Woolf's bound MSS are now made available on microfilm and CD. URL for Berg finding

GUIDE TO LIBRARY SPECIAL COLLECTIONS 85

aid: http://www.nypl.org/research/manuscripts/berg/brgwoolf.xml. N.B. All the Berg's Woolf MSS are on microfilm and 90 percent of them on CD published by Research Publications and available at many research libraries.

Holdings Relevant To Woolf: Manuscripts/typescripts of all of the novels except *Orlando*, including: *Between the Acts, Flush, Jacob's Room, Mrs. Dalloway* (notes and fragments), *Night and Day, To the Lighthouse, The Voyage Out, The Waves, The Years*; 12 notebooks of articles, essays, fiction and reviews, 1924–1940; 36 volumes of diaries; 26 volumes of reading notes; correspondence with Vanessa Bell, Ethel Smyth, Vita Sackville-West and others. Su Hua Ling Chen's Bloomsbury correspondence.

Recent Acquisitions: Proof copy of *A Room of One's Own* (July 1929); ALS Vanessa Bell to Vita Sackville-West, April 29, 1941 [in Marler, *Selected Letters* 478-80]; Frank Dean, *Strike While the Iron's Hot: Frank Dean's Life as a Blacksmith and Farrier in Rodmell*, ed. Susan Rowland (S. Rowland, 1994) [includes map, accounts of search for VW's body and of her funeral]; Vita Sackville-West, *Marian Stranways*, autograph manuscript, [1913].

Name of Collection: The British Library Manuscript Collections

Contact: Manuscripts Enquiries

Address: 96 Euston Road
London NW1 2DB
England

Telephone: 0207-412-7513
Fax: 0207-412-7745
Email: mss@bl.uk

Hours: Mon. 10 AM–5 PM; Tue.–Sat.: 9:30 AM–5 PM

Access Requirements: British Library Reader Pass (signed I.D. required and usually proof of postgraduate academic status, or other demonstrable need to use the collections—see www.bl.uk). In addition, access to most literary autograph material only available with letter of recommendation.

Restrictions: Paper Copies, Microfilms, and Photography of selected items available upon receipt of written authorization for photo duplication from the copyright holder.

Holdings Relevant to Woolf: Diaries 1930–1931 (microfilm); *Mrs. Dalloway* and other writings (1923–1925) three volumes; letter from Leonard Woolf to H. G. Wells (1941); two letters from Virginia Woolf and three letters from Leonard Woolf to John Lehmann (1941); letter written on behalf of Leonard Woolf to S. S. Koteliansky (1946); notebook in Italian kept by Virginia Woolf; notebook of Virginia Stephen (1906–1909); A sketch of the past revised ts (1940); letters from Virginia Woolf in the correspondence files of Lytton and James Strachey; letter from Virginia Woolf to Mildred Massingberd; letter from Virginia Woolf to Harriet Shaw Weaver (1918); letters from Virginia Woolf to S. S. Koteliansky (1923–1927); letter from Virginia Woolf to Frances Cornford (1929); letter from Virginia Woolf to Ernest Rhys (1930); correspondence of Virginia Woolf in the Society of Authors archive (1934–1937); letter and postcard from Virginia Woolf to Bernard Shaw (1940); three letters (suicide notes) from Virginia Woolf (1941); two letters from Virginia Woolf and three from Leonard Woolf to John Lehmann (1941). "Hyde Park Gate News" 1891–1892, 1895 (add. MSS 70725, 70726). Letters of Virginia and Leonard Woolf to Lady Aberconway, 1927–1941. Letter from Virginia Woolf

GUIDE TO LIBRARY SPECIAL COLLECTIONS 87

to Frances Cornford. Letters from Virginia Woolf to Macmillan Co. 1903, 1908. Collection of RPs ("reserved photocopies" – copies of manuscripts exported, some subject to restrictions).

Name of Collection: Harry Ransom Humanities Research Center

Contact: Research Librarian

Address: The University of Texas at Austin
P.O. Box 7219
Austin, TX 78713-7219

Telephone: 512-471-9119
Fax: 512-471-2899
Email: reference@hrc.utexas.edu

Hours: Mon.–Fri. 9 AM–5 PM
Sat. 9 AM–12 NOON
Closed holidays; intersession Saturdays; one week each in late May and late August.

Access Requirements: Completed manuscript reader's application; current photo identification.

Holdings Relevant To Woolf: The manuscript collection includes the typed manuscript with autograph revisions of *Kew Gardens*, and the typed manuscript and autograph revisions of "Thoughts on Peace in an Air Raid." The Center holds 571 of Woolf's letters, including correspondence to Elizabeth Bowen, Lady Ottoline Morrell, Mary Hutchinson, William Plomer, Hugh Walpole and others. Further mss. relating to Virginia Woolf include letters to her from T. S. Eliot and reviews of her work. A substantial collection of the first British and American editions of Woolf's published works, as well as 130 volumes from Leonard and Virginia Woolf's library and a collection of books published by the Hogarth Press, is also housed.

An art collection holds a landscape painting of Virginia's garden and a series of Cockney cartoons in a sketch book, signed "V.W." The center also has extensive holdings of materials related to Leonard Woolf, Ottoline Morrell, Mary Hutchinson, Lytton Strachey, Dora Carrington, E. M. Forster, Clive Bell, Roger Fry, Vanessa Bell, Bertrand Russell, Elizabeth Bowen, William Plomer, Stephen Spender and Hugh Walpole.

Name of Collection: King's College Archive Centre

Contact: Patricia McGuire, Archivist

Address: King's College
Cambridge CB2 1ST

Telephone: 01223-331444
Fax: 01223-331891
Email: archivist@kings.cam.ac.uk

Hours: Mon.–Thu. 9:30 AM–12:30 PM and 1:30 PM–5:15 PM. *Closed during public holidays and the College's annual periods of closure.*

Access Requirements: Proof of ID, letter of introduction, appointment in advance.

Holdings Relevant To Woolf: Woolf MSS and letters: Minute book, written up by Clive Bell, of the meetings of a play-reading society, with cast lists and comments on performances by CB. Dec. 1907–Jan. 1909, Oct. 1914–Feb. 1915. Players included variously Clive and Vanessa Bell, Roger and Margery Fry, Duncan Grant, Walter Lamb, Molly MacCarthy, Adrian and Virginia Stephen, Saxon Sydney-Turner. *Freshwa-*

ter, A Comedy—photocopy of editorial typescript prepared from the MSS at Sussex University and Monk's House; photocopy of covering letter from the publisher to "Robert Silvers," Jan. 29, 1976. Papers relating to the Virginia Woolf Centenary Conference held at Fitzwilliam College, Cambridge, Sept. 20-22, 1982. TS with corrections of "Nurse Lugton's Curtain." Typed transcript of R. Fry's memoir of his schooldays. Correspondence with Clive Bell, Julian Bell, Vanessa Bell, Richard Braithwaite, Rupert Brooke, Mrs. Brooke, Katharine Cox, Julian Fry, Roger Fry, John Davy Hayward, J. M. Keynes, Lydia Keynes, Rosamond Lehmann, Charles Mauron, Raymond Mortimer, Frances and Ralph Partridge, G. H. W. Rylands, J. T. Sheppard, W. J. H. Sprott, Thoby Stephen, Madge Vaughan. Woolf-related archival collections held: Charleston Papers; Rupert Brooke Papers; E. M. Forster Papers; Roger Fry Papers; J. M. Keynes Papers; Frances Partridge Papers; George Humphrey Wolferstan ('Dadie') Rylands Papers; J. T. Sheppard Papers; W. J. H. Sprott Papers. Various works of art by Vanessa Bell, Duncan Grant, and Roger Fry, held in various locations around King's College. Access via Second Bursar's secretary.

Name of Collection: The Lilly Library

Contact: Joel Silver, Director
Cherry Williams, Curator of Manuscripts

Address: The Lilly Library, Indiana University
1200 East Seventh Street
Bloomington, IN 47405-5500

Telephone: 812-855-2452
Fax: 812-855-3143
Email: liblilly@indiana.edu, silverj@indiana.edu
chedwill@indiana.edu

Hours:	Mon.–Fri. 9 AM–6 PM; Sat. 9 AM–1 PM; *Closed Sundays and Major Holidays*
Access Requirements:	Valid photo-identification; brief registration procedure.
Restrictions:	Closed stacks; material use confined to reading room; wheelchair-accessible reading room and exhibitions (but no wheelchair-accessible restroom).
Holdings Relevant To Woolf:	Corrected page proofs for the American edition of *Mrs. Dalloway*; letters to Woolf from Desmond and Mary (Molly) MacCarthy; 77 letters (published in Letters) from Woolf to correspondents including Donald Clifford Brace, Robert Gathorne-Hardy, Barbara (Strachey) Halpern, Richard Arthur Warren Hughes, Desmond MacCarthy and Molly MacCarthy; "Preliminary Scheme for the formation of a Partnership between Mr Leonard Sidney Woolf and Mr John Lehmann to take over The Hogarth Press" (includes contract signed by Lehmann, Leonard Woolf, and Virginia Woolf and receipt for Lehmann's payment to Virginia Woolf to purchase Virginia Woolf's share in the Hogarth Press); photographs of Virginia Woolf, Leonard Woolf, Lytton Strachey, Strachey family, Roger Fry, and Vanessa Bell (Hannah Whitall Smith mss.); (Richard) Kennedy mss. (four hand-colored lithographs of Virginia Woolf: artist's proofs for RK's portfolio, VIRGINIA WOOLF: "AS I KNEW HER"; Sackville-West, V. mss. (10,529 items: includes the correspondence of Vita Sackville-West, and Harold Nicolson); MacCarthy mss. (ca. 10,000 items: papers of Desmond and Molly MacCarthy); correspondence between LW and Mary Gaither regarding publication of *A Checklist of the Hogarth Press* (1976, repr. 1986); Todd Avery, *Close and Affectionate Friends: Desmond and Molly MacCarthy and the Bloomsbury Group*

GUIDE TO LIBRARY SPECIAL COLLECTIONS

(The Lilly Library/Indiana University Libraries, 1999).

Name of Collection: Literature & Rare Books, Special Collections, University of Maryland, College Park, Libraries

Contact: Lauren Brown,
Manager Special Collections

Address: University of Maryland Libraries
College Park, MD 20742

Telephone: 310-405-9212
Fax: 301-314-2709
Email: askhornbake@umd.edu

Hours: Dates and hours of operation subject to change. Contact Lauren Brown before planning a research visit.

Access Requirements: Photo ID.

Holdings Relevant To Woolf: Papers of Hope Mirrlees contain five autograph letters and postcards (1919–1928) from Virginia Woolf to Mirrlees. Also in the collection are 113 letters from T. S. Eliot to Mirrlees, and three letters from Lady Ottoline Morrell to Mirrlees. A finding aid is available at http://hdl.handle.net/1903.1/1536.

Name of Collection: Monks House Papers/Leonard Woolf Papers/Charleston Papers/Nicolson Papers

Contact: University of Sussex
Special Collections

Address:	The Keep Woollards Way Brighton & Hove BN1 9PB
Telephone:	01273-482349
Email:	library.specialcoll@sussex.ac.uk
URL:	www.thekeep.info
Access Requirements:	By appointment. Identification to be presented on arrival. Registration and material requests can be made through our website.
Restrictions:	Photocopying strictly controlled.
Holdings Relevant To Woolf:	The University of Sussex holds two large archives relating to Leonard and Virginia Woolf: The Monks House Papers, primarily correspondence and MSS of Virginia Woolf, including the three scrapbooks relating to *Three Guineas*, and Virginia Woolf's engagement diaries from 1930 to her death in 1941; and The Leonard Woolf Papers, primarily correspondence and other papers of Leonard Woolf. (Monks House Papers are available on microfilm in many research libraries.) The Charleston Papers consist in the main of letters written to or by Clive and Vanessa Bell and Duncan Grant which had accumulated in their home; the library houses Quentin Bell's photocopied set; letters from Roger Fry, Maynard Keynes, Lytton Strachey, Virginia Woolf, Vita Sackville-West, E. M. Forster, T. S. Eliot, Frances Partridge and others. The Maria Jackson letters comprise some 900 letters from Maria Jackson to Julia and Leslie Stephen. The Nicolson Papers complement these three Sussex archives relating to the Bloomsbury Group, and consist of Nigel Nicolson's correspondence relating to his editorial work as principal editor of the six-volume *Letters of Virginia Woolf*, published between 1975 and 1980.

GUIDE TO LIBRARY SPECIAL COLLECTIONS 93

The Bell Papers. A. O. Bell's correspondence relating to her editorial work on Virginia Woolf's diaries, a parallel collection to the Nicolson Papers. Collection level description may be accessed at www.archiveshub.ac.uk

Name of Collection: The Morgan Library & Museum

Contact: Reading Room

Address: 225 Madison Ave.
New York, NY 10016

Telephone: 212-590-0315
Email: readingroom@themorgan.org
URL: www.themorgan.org

Access Requirements: Admission to the Reading Room is by application and by appointment. See http//www.themorgan.org/research/reading.asp for application form.

Holdings Relevant To Woolf: Virginia Woolf. Autograph manuscript notebook, 1931 Sept. 24. 1 item (52 p.) ; 265 x 208 mm. Contains drafts of "A Letter to a Young Poet," a brief letter to the press entitled "The Villa Jones" [ff. 3–5] and a monologue by a working-class woman [ff. 44–46]. MA 3333. Purchased on the Fellows Fund with the special assistance of Anne S. Dayton, Enid A. Haupt, Mrs. James H. Ripley, Mr. and Mrs. August H. Schilling, and John S. Thacher, 1979.

Virginia Woolf. Autograph letters signed (2) and typed letter signed, dated London [etc.], to E. McKnight Kauffer, 1931 Apr. 4–23, and undated. 3 items (4 p.). Concerning a drawing of her and a bibliography of her works. MA 1679. Purchased in 1959.

Vanessa Bell. 84 autograph letters, 3 typed letters, 7 postcards, and 3 telegrams. Most, but not all, are written by Vanessa Bell to John Maynard Keynes. Concerning Duncan Grant, Roger Fry, Clive Bell, the Bell children, Leonard and Virginia Woolf, Lytton Strachey, John Maynard and Lydia Lopokova Keynes, David Garnett, Ottoline Morrell, and others. MA 3448. Items in this collection are described in 97 individual records (MA 3448.1-97). Purchased on the Fellows Fund, special gift of the Gramercy Park Foundation (Mrs. Michael Tucker), 1980.

Name of Collection: University of Reading Special Collections

Contact: Special Collections Service

Address: Special Collections Service
University of Reading
Redlands Road
Reading RG1 5EX

Telephone: 0118-378-8660
Fax: 0118-378-5632
Email: specialcollections@reading.ac.uk
URL: www.reading.ac.uk/special-collections

Access Requirements: Prior appointment suggested to consult material. Permission required to consult or copy material in the Hogarth Press, Jonathan Cape, and Chatto & Windus collections from Random House:
Random House Group Archive & Library
1 Cole Street
Crown Park
Rushden
Northants. NN10 6RZ

Holdings Relevant To Woolf: Hogarth Press (MS 2750): editorial and production correspondence relating to publications of the Press including Woolf's own titles. Production ledgers 1920s–1950s. Correspondence between Leonard Woolf and Stanley Unwin about progress with his collected edition of the works of Freud. Order books – e.g. lists of booksellers, book clubs and how many books they have ordered for a particular title. Newscuttings—press clippings of advertisements for Hogarth Press books including Virginia Woolf publications.

Chatto & Windus (CW): small number of letters 1915–1925; 1929–1931.Various letters and notes by Leonard Woolf; outgoing letters to Leonard Woolf: 22 November 1927 (CW A/119); outgoing letters to Virginia Woolf: 29 January 1936 (CW A/172), 22 December 1931 (CW A/135), 31 December 1931 (CW A/135), 15 December 1920 (CW A/100), 20 December 1920 (CW A/100).

George Bell & Sons (MS 1640): 5 letters from Leonard Woolf 1930–1966.

Routledge (RKP): Reader's report by Leonard Woolf on George Padmore's "Britannia rules the blacks" (1935); "How Britain rules Africa." 1 letter from Leonard Woolf (June 1941) from Miscellaneous publishing correspondence 1941-1942 Wi-Wy RKP 174/15. Draft introduction by Leonard Woolf to *Letters on India* by Mulk Raj (1942) and 1 letter to Leonard Woolf from Mulk Raj Anand 1942-1943 RKP 178/3. Correspondence concerning the publication of *The War for Peace* by Leonard Woolf, 1939-1940 RKP 160/5. 1 letter from Virginia Woolf declining an invitation from Routledge to write a biography of Margaret Bondfield, 25 May 1940 RKP 160/5.

Megroz (MS 1979/68): 2 letters from Leonard Woolf, 1926.

Allen & Unwin (MS 3282): Correspondence with

Leonard Woolf c.1914-1918 (re. his book *International Government*), 1923-1924; 1939-1940; 1943; 1946; 1950-1951; 1953; 1965 (concerning ill-founded rumors about the Hogarth Press); 1967 (concerning a reprint of *Empire and Commerce in Africa*).

Jonathan Cape (MS 2446): All correspondence from file JC A43. Correspondence between Jonathan Cape and Virginia Woolf and Cape and A. C. Gissing concerning Virginia Woolf's introduction to George Gissing's *Ionian Sea* to which A. C. Gissing objects. 1 postcard (1935), 1 letter (1933), 2 letters (1932) from Virginia Woolf. 1 letter (1932) from Virginia Woolf declining to write an introduction to Jane Austen's Northanger Abbey. 4 letters (1931) from Virginia Woolf declining to write an introduction to one of Miss Thackeray's books.

Letters from Vanessa Bell: 1 letter from Bell CW 152/2; 1 letter from Bell CW 171/10; 2 letters from Bell CW 578/1; 1 letter from Bell CW 59/9; 1 letter from Bell (1936) CW 61/10. Artwork by Vanessa Bell for various Virginia Woolf titles.

Artwork by Angelica Garnett, Philippa Bramson and others for various books in the Chatto & Windus archive.

Name of Collection: Frances Hooper Collection of Virginia Woolf Books and Manuscripts Elizabeth Power Richardson Bloomsbury Iconography Collection.

Contact: Karen V. Kukil
Associate Curator of Special Collections

Address: Mortimer Rare Book Room

GUIDE TO LIBRARY SPECIAL COLLECTIONS 97

William Allan Neilson Library
Smith College
7 Neilson Drive
Northampton, MA 01063

Telephone: 413-585-2908
Fax: 413-585-2904
Email: kkukil@smith.edu
URL: www.smith.edu/libraries/libs/rarebook

Hours: Mon.–Fri. 9 AM–5 PM

Access Requirements: Appointment to be made with the Curator.

Holdings Relevant To Woolf: The Hooper Collection emphasizes Woolf as an essayist but also includes many Hogarth Press first editions, limited editions of Woolf's works, and translations. The collection includes page proofs of *Orlando*, *To the Lighthouse*, and *The Common Reader*, corrected by Woolf for the first American editions, a proof copy of *The Waves* that Woolf inscribed to Hugh Walpole, and the proof copies of *The Years* and of *Flush*. The Collection also has one of the deluxe editions of *Orlando* that was printed on green paper. Other items include twenty-two pages of reading notes from 1926, three pages of notes on D. H. Lawrence's *Sons and Lovers*, thirty-three pages of notes for Roger Fry, a six-page ms. "As to criticism," a five-page ms. of "The Searchlight," and a fourteen-page ms. of "The Patron and The Crocus." The Hooper Collection also owns 140 letters between Woolf and Lytton Strachey as well as other correspondence, including a 13 February [1921] letter to Katherine Mansfield and ten letters to Mela and Robert Spira.

The Richardson Collection is a working collection of books and materials used by Richardson in preparing her *Bloomsbury Iconography*. It includes Leslie Stephen's photograph album, ninety-eight original exhibition catalogs dating back to 1929, clippings and photocopies of such items as reviews of early Woolf works, and Bloomsbury material from British *Vogue* of the 1920s. The Collection also has three preliminary pencil drawings by Vanessa Bell for *Flush*.

The Mortimer Rare Book Room also owns Woolf's 1916 Italian ms. notebook and her corrected typescripts of "Reviewing" and "The Searchlight." In addition, there is a 1923 photograph of Woolf at Garsington. Original cover designs for Hogarth Press publications include *The Common Reader*, *On Being Ill*, and Duncan Grant. The Mortimer Rare Book Room also has a Sylvia Plath collection that includes eight of Woolf's books from Plath's library, several of which are underlined and annotated, as well as Plath's notes from her undergraduate English 211 class at Smith (1951–1952) in which she studied *To the Lighthouse*. The collection also includes Woolf's 26 February 1939 letter to Vita Sackville-West, a 1931 bronze bust of Virginia Woolf by Stephen Tomlin, a 1923 Hogarth Press edition of T. S. Eliot's *The Waste Land*, a 1919 Hogarth Press edition of *Paris* by Hope Mirrlees and first editions of Vita Sackville-West and Katherine Mansfield publications. Additional Bloomsbury items include *Original Woodcuts* (Omega Workshops, 1918), Vanessa Bell's original woodcut for the cover of *Monday or Tuesday* (1921), and exhibition catalogs for *Manet and the Post-Impressionists* (Grafton Galleries, 1911), Friday Club Members (Mansard Gallery, 1921) Paintings and Drawings by Vanessa Bell (Independent Gallery, 1922). Additional photographs include the Mary L. S. Bennett (née Fisher) Family Photographs. Online exhibitions are available on the Mortimer Rare Book Room's website.

Name of Collection: Woolf/Hogarth Press/Bloomsbury

GUIDE TO LIBRARY SPECIAL COLLECTIONS 99

Contact: Lisa J. Sherlock

Address: Victoria University Library
71 Queens Park Crescent E.
Toronto M5S 1K7
Ontario Canada

Email: victoria.library@utoronto.ca
URL: library.vicu.utoronto.ca/special/bloomsbury.htm

Hours: Mon.–Fri. 9 AM–5 PM

Access Requirements: Prior notification; identification.

Restrictions: Limited photocopying.

Holdings Relevant To Woolf: This collection, the most comprehensive of its kind with nearly 5,000 items, contains all the work of Virginia and Leonard Woolf in various editions, issues, variants and translations; all the books hand-printed by Leonard and Virginia Woolf at the Hogarth Press, including many variant issues and bindings, association copies and page proofs; a nearly comprehensive collection of Hogarth Press machine printed books to 1946 (the year Leonard Woolf and the Press joined Chatto & Windus) including presentation copies, signed limited editions, page proofs, variants as well as substantial amounts of ephemera, such as the *Catalogue of Publications to 1939* with annotations by Leonard Woolf. The collection is also very strong in Bloomsbury Art and Artists, especially the decorative arts, including important examples of Omega Workshops publications and exhibition catalogues. Materials include the catalogue of the second post-impressionist exhibition, 1912; catalogues relating to Vanessa Bell and Duncan Grant exhibitions; bronze medal of Virginia Woolf by Marta Firlet; oil on canvas portrait of Amaryllis Garnett by Vanessa

Bell (c.1958); Portrait sketch of Leonard Woolf by Vanessa Bell; Duncan Grant and Vanessa Bell designed Clarice Cliff dinner plates; original Vanessa Bell and Duncan Grant sketches and designs for dust jackets, novels, and other special projects; bronze busts of Lytton Strachey and Virginia Woolf by Stephen Tomlin (1901–1937); as well as the Marcel Gimond bust of Vanessa Bell and the Tomlin bust of Henrietta Bingham. Original correspondence and mss. material includes that by Vanessa Bell; Leonard Woolf; Ritchie family re: Anne Thackeray Ritchie/Stephen family; Duncan Grant; Quentin Bell; S. P. Rosenbaum mss. Letters from E. M. Forster, Bertrand Russell, James Strachey, Raymond Mortimer, David Garnett, Nigel Nicolson and others in the Bloomsbury Circle; as well as biographers, scholars and bibliographers such as Joanne Trautmann, Carolyn Heilbrun, J. Howard Woolmer, Leon Edel, Leila Luedeking, P. N. Furbank, Noel Annan and others. Large Ephemera Collection includes items revealing Virginia Woolf's effect on popular culture.

Name of Collection: Library of Leonard and Virginia Woolf (Washington S U)

Contact: Trevor James Bond
Head, Manuscripts, Archives, and Special Collections

Address: Washington State University Libraries
Pullman, WA 99164-5610

Email: tjbond@wsu.edu
URL: www.wsulibs.wsu.edu/holland/masc/masc.htm

Hours: Mon.–Fri. 8:30 AM–4:30 PM

Access Requirements: Letter stating nature of research preferred; student

GUIDE TO LIBRARY SPECIAL COLLECTIONS 101

or other identification.

Restrictions: Materials must be used in the MASC area under supervision. Photocopying or photographing is permitted only when it will not harm the materials and is permitted by copyright.

Holdings Relevant To Woolf: WSU has the Woolfs' basic working library including many works which belonged to Woolf's father, Sir Leslie Stephen, and other family members. Over 800 titles came from their Sussex home, Monks House, including some works bought at auction soon after Leonard Woolf died in 1969. Later additions include: 1,875 titles from his house in Victoria Square, London; 400 titles from his nephew Cecil Woolf; and over 60 titles from Quentin and Anne Olivier Bell. WSU has been actively collecting: all works in all editions by Virginia Woolf; all titles by Leonard Woolf; dust jackets; works published by the Woolfs at the Hogarth Press through 1946; books by their friends and associates, especially those by Bloomsbury authors and about Bloomsbury artists; relevant correspondence and original works of art. Original artwork by Vanessa Bell; scattered letters by Vanessa Bell, E. M. Forster, Roger Fry, Leslie Stephen, Lytton Strachey, and Leonard Woolf. Original artwork by Richard Kennedy for illustrations in his book *A Boy at the Hogarth Press*; scattered letters by Roger Fry, Leslie Stephen, Ethel Smyth, and Leonard Woolf. Virginia Woolf's initialed copy of *Cornishiana*; Leonard Woolf's annotated copy of *An Anatomy of Poetry* by A. Williams-Ellis; Leslie Stephen's copy of *Lapsus Calami and Other Verses*, inscribed by James Kenneth Stephen. Several letters from Virginia Woolf, including two written in 1939 to Ronald Heffer, and a letter to Edward McKnight Kauffer. New in the Hogarth Press Collection are a copy of E. M. Forster's *Anonymity, an Enquiry*, bound in cream paper boards, and what Woolmer calls the third label state of Forster's *The Story of the Siren*. The Library of Leonard and Virginia Woolf is once again shelved separately so that scholars visiting Pullman may see the collection apart from the other rare book collections.

Name of Collection: Yale Center for British Art

Contact: Elisabeth Fairman,
Senior Curator of Rare Books and Manuscripts

Address: 1080 Chapel Street
P.O. Box 208280
New Haven, CT 06520-8280

Telephone: 203-432-2814
Fax: 203-432-9613
E-mail: elisabeth.fairman@yale.edu

Hours: Tue.-Fri. 10 AM-4:30 PM

Access Requirements: Permission needed in order to reproduce.

Holdings Relevant To Woolf: Rare Books & Mss Department: 94 letters from Vanessa Bell and Duncan Grant to Sir Kenneth Clark; Prints & Drawings Department: 4 drawings by Vanessa Bell; 4 drawings by Duncan Grant; 6 drawings by Wyndham Lewis; 1 drawing by Frederick Etchells; Paintings Department: 1 painting by Vanessa Bell, 4 paintings by Duncan Grant (including portrait of Vanessa Bell); 3 paintings by Roger Fry. 6 letters from Lytton Strachey (to Clive Bell, Siegfried Sassoon, et al.).

Reviews

Virginia Woolf's Essayism. Randi Saloman (Edinburgh: Edinburgh UP, 2012) vii +184pp.

Randi Saloman has written an exciting book. *Virginia Woolf's Essayism* urges readers to think differently about essays and the essay genre, portrays Woolf as actively experimenting throughout her career to combine the advantages of the essay and the novel in a new form, and provides fresh and provocative readings of several of Woolf's least-studied novels. Virginia Woolf emerges from this study not as a writer who wrote essays on the side, but as a writer with a lifelong essay project, one that sought to reconcile the ultimately irreconcilable novel and essay genres.

In her introduction, Saloman briefly surveys other approaches to Woolf's essays and to essayism in general, stakes out her interest in what the essay contributes to the modern novel, makes her case for Woolf's centrality to that contribution, and sets up the framework for her study. She "consider[s] the essay as a format that Woolf used to solve artistic problems," a place where Woolf examined both the writing process and herself as a writer (8). Saloman organizes her intricate and suggestive study in concentric circles, beginning with a look at one essay, "Street Haunting," and one novel, *Mrs. Dalloway*, as a way to introduce the tension between essayistic freedom and novelistic authority she will examine repeatedly, with fascinating variations, throughout her book. She then moves outward to Woolf's *Common Readers*, and next, out again to Woolf's two longest essays, *A Room of One's Own* and *Three Guineas*. These first three chapters establish what Woolf loves about the essay genre—"the essay's implicit desire to spark discussion, putting the exchange between itself and its readers at the forefront of its concerns" (49) and her belief that readers, "[u]nited by the work and by an appreciation for the act of reading . . . contribute to the work and to the ongoing process of its reading" (69). They also show what she achieves with it—a "democratic aesthetic [that] allows her to think aloud about the possible meanings of her subject, and to side with process and reflection" in *A Room of One's Own* (84-85) and a sustained model of "protecting individual thought" against group thinking even when such intellectual work "yield[s] little beyond frustration at [its] own inefficacy" and no "predetermined resolution" in *Three Guineas* (94, 104). Saloman next looks at how Woolf experiments with and uses essayistic techniques from *The Voyage Out* through *To the Lighthouse*. In her last chapter, Saloman focuses on Woolf's herculean efforts to create a hybrid essay/novel form in *The Pargiters* and then *The Years*.

Saloman reads Woolf's career as a conscious, consistent, and courageous struggle to meld the essay and novel genres together, arguing that Woolf used many essayistic techniques to revolutionize the modern novel. As a result, everything in Woolf's canon looks different. Seen through Saloman's lens, the essays look even more speculative and open; *The Voyage Out* and *Night and Day* look more experimental; the great novels of mid-career look less radical; and *The Years* looks more successful. In a steadily cumulative way, Saloman builds her argument and, in the process, revises everything we thought we knew about Woolf, genre, and Woolf's use of genre, an amazing critical feat. Plus, her book both challenges and gives pleasure.

Woolf's struggle with genre stems from her desire to have a relationship with the reader in the novel that is more like the relationship she enjoys with the reader in her essays, a relationship she creates and sustains through her essayistic voice. As Saloman notes, "So much of Woolf's essay-writing is concerned not merely with what the essayist desires to get across, but with how to shrink the space between reader and writer, how to ensure or make likely that readers will understand what the writer wishes them to, without taking away the free will or playfulness of those readers" (52). So, for Saloman, *Jacob's Room* marks a shift in Woolf's novel canon because that is when Woolf gives up her essayistic voice and increases her use of essayistic techniques:

> Woolf comes into her own stylistically not by moving from a conventional approach to an experimental one, but by reframing her experiments, moving away from her attempts to adopt an essayistic voice to a more authoritative narration, balanced by increased formal experimentation and a willingness to break the conventional structure of the novel. (126)

In Woolf's earlier novels, she allowed her characters to "live out their essayistic tendencies" and thus created "a more genuine or truthful portrait of their struggles to reconcile understanding and action," but the result was "decidedly forced and slow-moving" (132). In Woolf's later novels, characters "confine their essayism to their internal reflections" (132). Woolf's gain in narrative control, however, means that "the reader loses the sense of identification and genuine affinity that the earlier books offer" (133). In Saloman's argument, then, the essay allows the author to grant the reader all sorts of dialogic freedom—to participate in the creation of the art, to ramble, to hold contradictory views, to debate with the author, to play. But the novel requires the author to maintain authority, create distance between writer and reader, and curtail the reader's ability to enter into dialogue. Although Saloman certainly understands that essayists control and craft their work just as much as novelists do, she argues that choice of genre controls the range of voices that narrators of either genre can use.

Robert Atwan claims the essay has, since the Renaissance, "continuously permeated and shaped what we normally think of as imaginative literature" (6). He traces a long tradition of novelists who regularly included essays within their fictions to take "a recognizable essayistic stance in relation to fictive material" or "[explore] the limits of imaginative literature" (7, 9). Saloman, by contrast, focuses on how modernists used the "essayistic mode of the nineteenth century . . . to produce the 'high modern novel' itself" (2). She frames her examination of Woolf's essayism around Woolf's awareness that "the modernist novel's use of essayistic techniques concealed an inescapable and fatal contradiction" (2). Entering a conversation in which many critics argue for the permeability of genre in Woolf, Saloman argues instead that although Woolf did more to bring together the essayistic and the novelistic than any other modernist, she could not ultimately blend the two most important components of the two genres into something new. The authorial relationship with the reader in the novel depends on narrative authority no matter how seemingly abdicated, whereas the authorial relationship with the reader in the essay depends on the reader's seeming freedom no matter how constructed. Narrative authority and essayistic freedom are thus incompatible, and in her struggles to combine them, Woolf's experiments reveal a line that cannot be crossed or blurred. If Woolf could have given up her "authoritative novelist's position," then perhaps she could have produced the essay-novel she envisioned with such excitement late in 1932 (165). Yet, paradoxically, if narrative authority is crucial to the novel as a genre, which Saloman argues it is, then such an essay-novel would not really have been the hybrid Woolf sought. Writers can use fictional techniques in the essay and essayistic techniques in the novel, but a true blending of the two genres, in which the writer both allows the reader and characters to ramble *and* governs readers' and characters' reactions, Saloman indicates, is impossible. Thus, Woolf's supposed "failure" in *The Years* actually acknowledges the power of genre to determine what an author can do.

Routinely insightful and tightly argued, Saloman's study sometimes confuses the reader trying to keep distinctions between essayism, essayistic techniques, and essayistic voice straight. Sometimes the argument leaves too much left unsaid. The overall arc of the argument is clear, and Saloman's brilliant readings support that argument, but at times, the reader wants more clarification, explanation, or supporting evidence. On the one hand, Saloman seems to be trying to refresh academic prose, to write a more subtle criticism. On the other hand, and this is pure speculation on my part, Saloman seems constrained by external forces— time? academic conventions? length restrictions?—that make her compress her argument. Each short section within a chapter is understandable, but how the sections fit together, particularly in the last chapter, is not always clear. Moves from section to section sometimes seems abrupt, and transitions between chapters are marked more by purpose statements than claims. Circumstances may have forced Saloman to condense. Or perhaps her elliptical style was her attempt to combine essayism and the academic essay. If so, her book about the uneasy tension between the essay and novel genres also highlights an uneasy tension between the essay and literary criticism.

Nevertheless, Saloman's book is quite lively and well-written, so I am responsible for not connecting the dots better, and upon rereading, the book's pieces did seem to fit together more snugly. Even so, the book feels cut to *below* the bone, meaning that basic information sometimes goes missing. For example, Saloman uses and argues with Rachel Stephens's article about *The Pargiters* on pages 140-41 (which is where Stephens is in the index), but then Stephens, presumably Rachel again, shows up on page 157 with no warning or introduction or citation or place in the index. Surely an earlier paragraph or reference was cut and the resulting gap not patched over. The book ended abruptly, too, with my turning the last page expecting more.

That literal reading experience captures my overall reaction to *Virginia Woolf's Essayism*. I thoroughly enjoyed it, but wanted more: a chapter on *Orlando*, *The Waves*, and *Between the Acts*, narratives that also seem to work with essays or essayism, yet differently from the novels included here; a conclusion that pulled everything together; conclusions *to* chapters; more evidence and argument; more circling back to the beginning of the book; more conversation about Woolf's essays; more discussion of essayism; more of the pleasure of Randi Saloman's company. I wanted the book to have a more leisurely feel to it. I wanted Saloman to feel free to digress, to elaborate, to follow her observations where they took her, like Woolf does in "Street Haunting," and to unpack her argument more thoroughly. I suspected she could have said (and probably did say) much, much more, and I wished she'd had the chance to do so.

What my speculations and desires make plain, though, is just how much this book achieves, how impressive and stimulating both its form and content are. Managing to successfully incorporate *some* essayism into her criticism, Saloman invites the reader's questions. Do Woolf's descriptions of Elizabeth's, Rezia's, and Miss Kilman's movements around the city provide a hint of "Street Haunting" in *Mrs. Dalloway* that are not totally subordinate to Clarissa's or Septimus's narratives? Does Eleanor's question at the end of *The Years*, along with her decision to walk home through the empty streets and the narrator's nonfictional description, carry any trace of essayistic freedom?

Saloman's exhilarating approach in this book widens and deepens our thinking about genre and its place in modernism, and her focus on genre, form, and mode is anything but exclusively formalist; indeed, it complicates and enriches feminist and cultural studies. Most admirable, though, is that in every sentence she writes, Saloman portrays Woolf as a writer with agency, a writer who knew what she was doing and what the stakes were. That Woolf eventually came up against genre barriers she could not cross illustrates just how far she went. Most important, Saloman brings a sense of possibility to Woolf studies. She has blazed the way, so perhaps the "more" I wanted from her is actually up to us.

—Beth Rigel Daugherty, *Otterbein University*

Work Cited

Atwan, Robert. "Essayism." *The Iowa Review* 25.2 (Spring-Summer 1995): 6-14. JSTOR. Web. 21 Jan. 2013.

Woolf & the City: Selected Papers of the Nineteenth Annual Conference on Virginia Woolf. Ed. Elizabeth F. Evans and Sarah Cornish (Clemson U Digital P, 2010) xiv + 249 pp.

The conference program (included as an appendix to *Woolf & the City*) indicates the sheer breadth and variety of work that was on display at the Nineteenth Annual Conference on Virginia Woolf held at Fordham University's Lincoln Center campus in New York in June 2009. The essays selected for inclusion in this collection address topics from tortoises to the Tube in discussions of Woolf's engagement with urban spaces in her writing. The results are occasionally mixed, but as a whole the collection justifies the editors' claim in their introduction that this subject "still has unplumbed depths," and there is much to relish in the diverse range of interpretations and research evident throughout (viii).

The book is divided into eight different sections: "Keynotes" (which includes one keynote paper by Tamar Katz and abstracts for two more by Anna Snaith and Jessica Berman due to be published elsewhere at the time the collection was put together); "Navigating London"; "Spatial Perceptions and the Cityscape"; "Regarding Others"; "The Literary Public Sphere"; "Border Crossings and Liminal Landscapes"; "Teaching Woolf, Woolf Teaching"; and "Inspired by Woolf: A Conversation" (a transcription of a round-table discussion that brought together three women of different generations and careers on whom

Woolf's writing has had a significant influence). Across the collection as a whole, a wide range of Woolf's body of work is discussed, with particular emphasis on major novels such as *Mrs. Dalloway*, *Jacob's Room*, and *The Years*, as well as more critically neglected texts such as *Flush*. It is especially gratifying to see so much scholarship on Woolf's essays (though there is certainly scope for further consideration of her short stories).

The cluster of essays on "Navigating London" offers some of the clearest insight into Woolf's London in the collection. Two essays on transport systems discuss in detail the impact of the ways in which people traversed the city on Woolf's writing—Eleanor McNees's "Public Transport in Woolf's City Novels: The London Omnibus" and Alexandra Harris's "Virginia Woolf Underground"— while Kathryn Simpson's essay on "Street Haunting" provides a compelling discussion of commodity culture, the woman artist, and the gift economy. This section as a whole traces movement around London, but elsewhere in the collection there are attempts to consider Woolf's move beyond urban spaces. Vara Neverow considers the ways in which *Jacob's Room* distinguishes between urban and pastoral spaces in depicting transgressive sexuality, and Rishona Zimring considers Woolf's writing about her 1938 trip to Scotland as evidence of "the expression of an urbanized, disenchanted, but not-yet-globalized and media-saturated modernity where the terms 'center' and 'periphery' are still relevant" (165). Later in the collection, in "An Archive in the City: 'True Pictures' and Animated News Films of Suffragettes in the Holograph of Virginia Woolf's 'The Movies' in the Berg Collection," Leslie Kathleen Hankins offers interesting insight into Woolf's engagement with one aspect of this "media-saturated modernity" that did have a telling impact on her: the cinema (165).

The emergence of a *globalized* information age in the years since Woolf's death provides the impetus for Paula Maggio's "Virginia Woolf in the Cyber City: Connecting in the Virtual Public Sphere," which considers the potential for "a democratic and inclusive approach to the author" and the significance of her work in a digital age for the common (or otherwise) reader (215). Woolf's common reader recurs across several of the essays in the collection, including Melissa Sullivan's lively discussion of Woolf's challenge to social and cultural hierarchies in "The Bestseller and the City: *Flush*, *The Barretts of Wimpole Street* and Cultural Hierarchies" and Cheryl Hindrichs's useful essay on the role played by *Orlando* in teaching courses on critical theory, "'Find Our Own Way For Ourselves': *Orlando* as an Uncommon Reader in the Critical Theory Classroom." Further scope for employing Woolf's writing as a pedagogical tool is explored in Sevinc Kurt's "Recreating Woolf's Public and Private Spaces in Architectural Design Education," an account of a fascinating project in which students created spatial interpretations of extracts from Woolf's novels.

The collection comes to a close with a transcript of a round-table discussion with Kris Lundberg (artistic director of Shakespeare's Sister Theater Company), Susan Sellers (scholar and novelist), and Ruth Gruber (journalist and author—at a remarkably young age—of an early thesis on Woolf in the 1930s). Much is made in this discussion of Gruber's correspondence with Woolf and their meeting in 1935, providing a direct link between the present moment and a woman who died 70 years ago. This symbolic erasure of the years that separate Woolf from the present time is a tendency enacted throughout many of the most memorable essays that make up this collection, which draw implicit links between Woolf's reactions to the conditions of modernity and our own. Nowhere is this more apparent than in Mark Hussey's provocative piece, "Woolf and the Falling Man," in which he considers Woolf's discussion of the spectator's ethical response to images of trauma and relates it to contemporary responses to the 9/11 attacks.

Ultimately, *Woolf & the City* suggests that the diversity and scope of Woolf scholarship continues to respond to on-going developments in critical methodologies, theory, and contemporary events. Many of the essays offer thought-provoking and insightful commentary on Woolf's writing and open up the possibility for future scholars to respond to questions posed by the work included here. That said, there are limitations to the collection as a cohesive whole. As a gathering of conference proceedings, at times the overarching theme of "Woolf and the city" does not come through as strongly as it might, and there is some discrepancy in the quality of the essays, in particular in structural terms, as some still read as conference papers that would have benefitted from further editing and elaboration for publication. What's more, the book is somewhat difficult to negotiate, hampered by the lack of an index (a shortcoming that will be corrected when a digital version is archived online). At its best, though, *Woolf & the City* raises sufficient questions and offers enough insight that the editors' hopes that "readers will not only find much of interest in these essays but will be inspired" to pursue future work on the topic stands a good chance of being realized (xii).

—Jenny McDonnell, *IADT, Dun Laoghaire*

The Years. Virginia Woolf. Ed. Anna Snaith. The Cambridge Edition of the Works of Virginia Woolf (Cambridge: Cambridge UP, 2012) xi + 870pp.

The Years is arguably the most allusive and the most elusive of Woolf's ten novels. Its fifty-year time span alone—1880 to the Present Day of the early 1930s—demanded an unusual degree of compression, especially at the stage of final revision late in 1936 when Woolf cut "two enormous chunks" from the galley proofs. Throughout her diaries and letters from the first conception on January 20, 1931 ("an entire new book … about the sexual life of women" [*D*4 6]) to her reaction to Stephen Spender's evaluation of the novel on April 30, 1937 ("But I'm very glad you saw that the tend of the book, its slope to one quarter of the compass and not another, was different from the tend in my other books" [*L*6 122]) Woolf alternately soared and sank through the writing process though the agony of revision brought her dangerously close to despair. In tackling this nearly 400-page novel for the scholarly Cambridge edition, Anna Snaith has provided readers with an impressively authoritative and comprehensive tome in which the 411 pages of explanatory notes, textual apparatus and textual notes exceed the length of the actual novel. Snaith justifies this extensive editorial apparatus in her introduction when she argues that the novel forces us to "read metonymically" from detail to "larger social structure" (lv). It becomes the editor's job then to unpack the slightest of allusions and to provide the multiple textual variants among the versions of the novel from holograph through galley and page proofs. As Snaith aptly remarks, "Beneath the most fleeting of references lie layers of contextual meaning" (lxiii). In keeping with the general editors' dictum—"to engage the reader in a process of informed exploration and interpretation that continues beyond the edition" (xviii), this edition of *The Years* opens up avenues of exploration from suggestions about the various sources of family names to historical accounts of political and legal issues pertinent to each of the eleven chronological sections. The textual apparatus allows us to compare the significant differences between the eight holograph notebooks and the galley and page proofs in order to observe Woolf's arduous process of revision and especially to see the persistent attempts at compaction as Woolf fought against conflicting temptations of expansion—"It should include satire, comedy, poetry, narrative, & what form is to hold them all together?" *(D*4 152) and contraction—"Oh Lord how am I ever going to pull all that into shape! What a tremendous struggle it'll be!" (*D*4 172). It is to Snaith's credit that she is able in both the textual apparatus and the textual notes to demonstrate this accordion-like push and pull of such a "baggy monster" (Henry James, Preface to *The Tragic Muse* 1907).

The General Preface by Jane Goldman and Susan Sellers that precedes each novel in *The Cambridge Edition of the Works of Virginia Woolf* stipulates both the method and structure individual editors are to follow: "textual process" should take precedence over "interpretative conclusions" (xv). The editor's introduction is to chart three principal aspects of the novel: its composition history, its publication history and its early critical reception until Woolf's death in 1941. In the case of this penultimate novel, and the last published in Woolf's lifetime, Snaith extends this account forty years to Grace Radin's 1981 study of the novel's evolution from holograph to galley and page proofs, including the "two enormous chunks" extant in the galleys but cut late in 1936. Though Snaith closely follows the overall goal of the Cambridge editions to make the complex history of the novel as transparent and accessible as possible for both common reader and textual scholar, she proffers some insightful interpretative comments in her introduction. Like Radin before her, she views *The Years* as "a haunted text" (xlix) because of the large amount of material omitted throughout the four-year writing process. Though Radin identified a "reverberative structure" (Radin xxii) that allowed Woolf to suggest details finally expunged from the published novel, she wondered if the galley proofs and parts of the holograph perhaps contained "another unwritten novel" (Radin xviii). With more complete access to all of the extant materials from subsequent textual critics' studies of page proofs to Jeri Johnson's 1998 annotated Penguin edition to cultural historians' identification of particular London sites and newspaper accounts, Snaith synthesizes her sources to argue for a dual method of reading the novel synchronically and diachronically. Such a reading, she asserts, allows us to map Woolf's "urban geography" over a fifty-year span via the spatial and temporal movements and thoughts of the characters. We both see and hear the progress from Victorian to Edwardian to Georgian London through the novel's attention to the material environment, a process that anchors the text to its earlier novel-essay form. As Snaith rightly insists, Woolf's "decision to cut the essays was not a rejection of the project's basis in non-fiction, but affirmation of its centrality to the project…" (lxiii).

The Cambridge edition includes two chronologies—the first of Woolf's Life and Work and the second, more usefully, of the Composition of *The Years*. The latter allows us to date quite precisely Woolf's writing progress through allusions to the novel and its shifting titles in the diaries and letters. And in recording both Woolf's reading and her published essays during the period of the novel's composition, this chronology adds a kind of shorthand context. It also charts the stages of revision—of deletion and insertion—through the dating of the chapter heads as late as mid-December 1936.

Perhaps the most useful aspects of the Cambridge edition are the 143 pages of Explanatory Notes and the 219 pages of Textual Apparatus. The Explanatory

Notes range widely from the first one on the book's final title, suggesting that Woolf may have drawn it from Thomas Hardy's poem "During Wind and Rain" with its line, "Ah, no; the years, the years; / Down their carved names the raindrop ploughs" (393), to one on Morris wall-papers and another on the possible origin of the character Nicholas's name. In the Present Day section, notes about new inventions—traffic lights, the wireless, electric lights—jostle with references to politics, specifically to symbols of fascism in Britain (Mosley's British Union of Fascists and the Woolfs' friend Harold Nicolson's involvement with Mosley's New Party), and to Irish Home Rule and the establishment of the Irish Free State in 1922. These notes not only provide essential context for the novel, they also help to round out the characters and in some cases to make them more contradictory.

The extensive Textual Apparatus, marked, like the Explanatory Notes and the Textual Notes, at the bottom of the pages of the novel proper, compare the copy text—B1, the first British edition of 1937—with three sets of galley proofs (BG, BGR1, BGR2), two sets of page proofs (BP1, BP2), the first American edition (A1) and the Uniform Edition of *The Years* (BU) published in 1940. Apart from a set of uncorrected page proofs housed at Smith College in Northampton, Massachusetts, the galley and page proofs in the Textual Apparatus, along with the 8 holograph notebooks, are in the Berg Collection at the New York Public Library. Only two typescripts from the 1910 section are housed in the Monks House Papers at the University of Sussex. Particularly significant are the large cuts at the galley proof stage like Peggy's extensive interior monologue at the final party of the Present Day section where she feels separate, excluded from the exuberance. A representative of the new professional woman in a field (medicine) only recently opened to women, Peggy draws the debate on women's status that underlies the entire novel into the present. Omission of the bulk of her dissatisfied musings, like the late deletion of the 1914 and 1921 sections (largely from Eleanor's point of view), undermines the original intent—"a sequel to a Room of One's Own—about the sexual life of women: to be called Professions for Women perhaps" (*D4* 6). The Textual Apparatus salvages the earlier material and encourages us to read in the two ways Woolf suggested in her 1926 essay "How Should One Read a Book?": first as accomplices, and later as critics or "after readers" (*E4* 390, 396) for whom "[h]olding this complete shape in mind it now becomes necessary to arrive at some opinion of the book's merits…" (*E4* 397).

Likewise, the Textual Notes lead us back to the holograph notebooks and to Mitchell Leaska's 1978 edition of the first two notebooks, *The Pargiters*, as well as Mark Hussey's *Major Authors on CD-Rom: Virginia Woolf*. In general, the notes demonstrate Woolf's greater reliance on editorializing and her reference to specific historical events. In particular, the two most outspoken female characters, Sara (Elvira in the holograph), and Rose, receive more attention and explanation throughout the holograph, leading Snaith to observe, "Generally, the manuscript includes more details about women's relationship to patriotism" (792). Snaith also remarks on Woolf's excisions and word changes in the manuscript and incorporates some of these via strike-through lines in the notes. The final fifty-page appendix comprises the two sections from 1914 (originally dated by Radin as 1917) and 1921 excised at the galley proof stage in 1936. Though these have been known since Charles Hoffmann's 1969 *PMLA* essay, "Virginia Woolf's Manuscript Revisions of *The Years*," and Grace Radin's first transcription of the galley proofs in her 1977 article, "'Two enormous chunks': Episodes Excluded during the Final Revisions of *The Years*," in the *Bulletin of the New York Public Library*, Snaith's edition would not be complete without reprinting them. Like the Textual Apparatus, these two sections considerably amplify our understanding of the novel. Specifically, the 1914 section set just one month into the Great War in the third week of September, captures a moving picture of class attitudes toward the war from three points of view before shifting to Eleanor's ambivalent response as she rides an omnibus home from a West End play. The second "chunk" is the novel's only foray into the 1920s; set in 1921 it gives us a glimpse of the recently widowed Kitty Lasswade at Richmond Park with her old admirer Edward Pargiter. This section too, however, ends with Eleanor alone in an unusually somber mood regarding the people on a nighttime London street as having "the faces of beasts…in a jungle" (855). The ending to the 1921 section would have better prepared the reader for Peggy's cynicism in The Present Day and for a link sufficiently repressed in the published novel between Eleanor, representative of the old, and Peggy, of the new, female generation.

As Snaith notes in her introduction, eventually readers will be able to examine *The Years* in digital version and instantly click through to the textual variants in the holograph, galley and page proofs to achieve a simultaneity the material text with all its textual apparatus and explanatory notes still precludes. Yet, that such a material text now exists, allowing readers to approach a simultaneous (or synchronic/diachronic reading) demands a large dose of gratitude to Snaith and the Cambridge edition's general editors. Like George Eliot's *Middlemarch*, a nineteenth-century precursor of *The Years* in its sweeping story of a culture caught on the cusp of the Victorian period, *The Years* captures a culture caught in a similar transitional period. The latter novel runs in a narrower channel, its tributaries more subterranean and invisible, but with this new edition, we have acquired both a broader and a deeper view of a twentieth-century author on a par with her predecessor.

—Eleanor McNees, *University of Denver*

Work Cited

Radin, Grace. *Virginia Woolf's* The Years: *The Evolution of a Novel*. Knoxville, TN: U of Tennessee P, 1981.

Social Dance and the Modernist Imagination in Interwar Britain. Rishona Zimring (Farnham, UK: Ashgate, 2013) 229 pp.

Rishona Zimring presents the period between the two world wars as a series of tense duets between recuperation and paralysis, nostalgia and experimentation, obsessions with the symptomatic individual and with the health of the community. Social dance, Zimring argues, epitomizes the contradictions of the period, serving as "both symptom and cure for a war-ravaged, cosmopolitan modernity" (10). The interwar period saw a surge of dancing in couples and groups as waltzes, polkas, and quadrilles competed with new dance practices like swinging, fox-trotting, and romping. Zimring's study is refreshing in its close attention to these nontheatrical and participatory dances rather than the solos of modern dance and the experiments of the Ballets Russes that have dominated scholarship on dance and modernism. Canonical modernists like Virginia Woolf, D. H. Lawrence, and T. S. Eliot look different when social dance is at the center of analysis, and lesser known figures gain in significance; Zimring examines Katherine Mansfield, the Bloomsbury associates Gwen Raverat and Frances Partridge, folk-revivalist Cecil Sharp, and dancer-choreographer Margaret Morris. While literature, particularly fiction, is the focus of the book, Zimring includes film, portraiture, poetry, design, and choreographic analysis in her important contribution to interdisciplinary studies of modernism.

The prologue, "Social Dance, Musical Entertainments, and the Question of Sociability," documents the historical transformation of social dancing in the early twentieth century. Zimring describes the Cave of the Golden Calf, Margaret Morris's Chelsea Club, Lady Ottoline Morrell's artistic salon, and the huge new dance clubs. In these diverse venues, social dance was not simply a sign of avant-garde decline; the regenerative possibilities of social dance as a form of leisure coexisted with its potential to encourage frenetic denial. Zimring examines two representative interwar texts that focus on musical entertainments: Virginia Woolf's short story "The String Quartet" (1921) and the film *Piccadilly* (1929), with a screenplay by Woolf's rival Arnold Bennett. Both suggest that the pastime of listening to music in groups can be sources of solace and of escapism, introducing one of the most fascinating themes of the book: Modernist writers and artists appreciated the ways that social dancing promoted communal bonds, but they worried that social groups, especially groups moving in choreographed formations, resembled armies and even fascist parades.

Chapter One, "Couples and Flirts: Dance After War in Lawrence and Mansfield," opens with a reading of Mark Gertler's 1916 painting *Merry-Go-Round* as an iconic anti-war image and warning of the dangerous power of social dancing to turn leisure into a force for mindless conformity. D. H. Lawrence described "the violent mechanized rotation and complete involution" of Gertler's soldier-figures as the same group violence that led to war (58). His antidote was the heterosexual couple, and he repeatedly represented the destruction of social groups and the triumph of the couple through images of dance. In a masterful reading of Lawrence's *Women in Love* (1920), Zimring demonstrates that the challenging novel is structured as a "triptych of dance scenes that both consolidate and exhibit the power of couples" (73). As a counterpoint to Lawrence's promotion of the heterosexual dyad and a "rebuttal" of his story "The White Stocking" (1914), Zimring turns to Katherine Mansfield's story "Her First Ball" (1921) (78). For Mansfield's young Leila, the joy of dancing with multiple partners allows her to temporarily escape the normative trajectory toward marriage and motherhood. Zimring argues that Mansfield's fiction presents dancing in social groups as an opportunity for women to explore "open-ended flirtation that actively *resists* the channeling of erotic energies into formal courtship, romance and domesticity" (80). Yet Mansfield, like other women artists whom Zimring discusses, ambivalently represents social dance in her fiction; women can experience only a circumscribed emancipation as they temporarily dissolve into the group dance but remain contained within the conventions of the ball.

Readers of *Woolf Studies Annual* will find much of interest in Chapter Two, "How Bloomsbury Danced," which offers a rich analysis of the complex dance cultures Bloomsbury inhabited and focuses on how gender and sexuality influence representations of dancing. The chapter discusses four women: the famous sisters Vanessa Bell and Virginia Woolf, the diarist and Bloomsbury chronicler Frances Partridge, and Gwen Raverat, designer for the ballet *Job* presented by the Camargo Society in 1931. Zimring's analysis reveals that women's art and responses to dance challenge the received notion that Bloomsbury unequivocally embraced the Ballets Russes with which it shared a transgressive sexual and erotic terrain. Vanessa Bell's colorful 1927 portrait of the Ballets Russes dancer Lydia Lopokova contrasts with the staid portrait by Roger Fry (1922); Bell depicts Lopokova kneeling onstage in a strapless white-lace costume while the Bloomsbury economist John Maynard Keynes holds a bouquet backstage. Whereas Fry confines the dancer in a Madonna-like pose and long dress designed by Duncan Grant, Bell appears to celebrate her makeup and bodily display but fixes her in a man's gaze and conventional gender roles. Further complicating any clear interpretation of Bell's representation of dance is another portrait she painted of Lopokova sitting in the same dress designed by Grant. Zimring mentions but does not analyze this second portrait. If the meanings of the dueling Lopokova portraits for Zimring's study are unclear, this is partly because of Bell's ambivalence and that of Bloomsbury more generally.

One of the great strengths of Zimring's study is her attention to women artists' contradictory responses to social dance. She suggests that Bell and Woolf's ambivalence might stem from their distaste for the balls they were forced to attend with their family. In her letters, Woolf variously claims that social dance enforces conformity and that she would trade her "profound Greek to dance really well" (109). In her fiction, Woolf uses dancing "to stage struggles over individual and group identities" and depicts "dance as a scene of attempted yet unsuccessful solidification of British identity and coherence" (114). Zimring demonstrates that dance features at important moments in nearly all of Woolf's major novels and offers fresh readings of her interwar fiction. From Fanny Elmer to Jinny to Lily Briscoe, Woolf's characters figure as dancers at conspicuous moments in the narrative. Lily Briscoe at her easel "attain[s] a dancing rhythmical movement" yet "the formidable ancient enemy… suddenly laid hands on her" like a dangerous dance partner (*TTL* 158). Woolf focuses on the "precariousness or fragility" of the communal feelings that social dancing encourages (111). Zimring's most remarkable example is from *Mrs. Dalloway*'s party, where Clarissa had "meant to have dancing" (*MD* 177). In a fascinating journal entry from June 1920, Woolf details her sister's account of a young man who fell from a roof during a dance party and how his fellow dancers merely looked for other parties: "to come to a dance among strangers & die—to come dressed in evening clothes, & then for it all to be over, instantly, so senselessly" (*D2* 50-51). Zimring provocatively reads this "*death involving social dancing* as a source for *Mrs. Dalloway*'s poetics of mourning" (118). For Woolf, the potential pleasures of dancing that might have been at Clarissa's party coexist with the danger of falling into a dance of death.

With her analysis of the ballet *Job* and the work of the Bloomsbury-affiliated Camargo Society at the end of Chapter Two, Zimring convincingly expands the scope of social dance to include the culturally reparative work of staged dance. Chapter Three, "Dancing in Place: Folk, Mass, and Visions of Community," extends this concern by examining the English Folk Song and Dance Society and Mass Observation, a project to create an ethnography of everyday life in Britain using a team of observers and writers. Both organizations regarded participatory social dancing as a practice that instilled "authentic Britishness," although the English Folk Song and Dance Society celebrated rural agrarian dancing and Mass

Observation championed urban life and nightclubs (133). Folk revivalism is a crucial context for T. S. Eliot's "East Coker" (1940), the second poem in *Four Quartets* (1943). Zimring argues in Chapter Four, "'Feet Rising and Falling': Dance, Meter, and Modernity in Eliot's 'East Coker,'" that Eliot deplored folk revivalism and forms of therapeutic dance as misguided desires to recover what he called a "dead ritual" without its attendant faith (175). Reading against interpretations of the poem's redemption and hopefulness, Zimring analyzes the scene of peasants dancing in "East Coker" as a "haunting, hallucinatory" *danse macabre* with a frantic, disorienting rhythm (194).

Social Dance and the Modernist Imagination in Interwar Britain offers a rich description of the dance cultures of the modernist period and the contradictory literary impulses they provoked, particularly celebrations of community and warnings about the destruction of the individual. While dance is increasingly being included in interdisciplinary studies of modernism, social dance has been overlooked. Zimring's research fills an important gap, showing that the inclusion of social dance requires a revision of the usual narratives about how dance performance inspired and responded to experiments in the other arts. Zimring offers a refreshing account of interwar modernism's ambivalent view of dance as a practice that seemed to mobilize communities toward cultural recuperation but might also mobilize them toward conformity, consumerism, and worst of all, the militarism that led to the deadly war.

—Carrie J. Preston, *Boston University*

Virginia Woolf in Context. Bryony Randall and Jane Goldman, eds. (Cambridge and New York: Cambridge UP, 2012) xi + 502 pp.

In the late 1990s Cambridge University Press began issuing the *Cambridge Companion* series of guides to literary periods, movements, and individual authors. The *Cambridge Companion to Virginia Woolf*, first published in 2000, was a particularly successful volume in the series, with twelve article-length essays on large aspects of Woolf's work by some of the most eminent Woolf critics. Addressed to students and common readers, the *Cambridge Companion* was a cross between a reference work and a collection of critical articles providing intelligent, often provocative contexts for Woolf's writing.

If a Companion provides contexts, what does an In Context volume do? *Virginia Woolf in Context*, part of a new major authors series from Cambridge called *Literature in Context*, covers some of the same ground as the previous Cambridge volume and features some of the same writers. But there are key differences in format, which make the new collection more of a grab bag than the previous one. The essays are shorter, around eight pages apiece, and there are 37 of them. Perhaps inevitably, they differ in quality and usefulness. More intriguingly, however, they display different understandings of what "context" means.

In putting together this collection following Cambridge's general guidelines, the editors, Bryony Randall and Jane Goldman, had to wrestle with this question. The answer initially might seem easy. A context is information that helps us interpret a literary text. But this definition is unhelpfully broad: what writing about a literary text is *not* a context? In the range of topics, from Michael Whitworth's "Historicizing Woolf: Context Studies" (which opens the book by suggesting, against the assumptions of many other entries, that "context" means historical circumstance), to Darya Protopopova's "Woolf and Russian Literature," to Carole Bourne-Taylor's "Woolf's Mediterranean Experience," to Ruth Hoberman's "Woolf and Commodities," to Clare Colebrook's "Woolf and 'Theory,'" to Margaret Homans's "Woolf and the Victorians," to Linden Peach's "Woolf and Eugenics," to Pam Morris's "Woolf and Realism," to Ian Blyth's "Woolf, Letter Writing and Diary Keeping," we encounter context as critical practice, literary influence, biographical background, reference, approach, analogue, and genre. "Context," thus construed, is elastic enough to comprehend various kinds of topic, if not quite every topic that could be described after the words "Woolf and."

There is also a certain amount of apparent overlap. To an extent, the editors have separated two kinds of context by dividing the essays into a short section on "Theory and Critical Reception" and a much longer section called "Historical and Cultural Context." Often the relation between an essay in the first section to one or more essays in the second section is one of overview to more specific instance. For instance, Anne Fernald's "Woolf and Intertextuality" briefly sets up one aspect of the relation we see in "Woolf and Russian Literature" or "Woolf and the Victorians." But the relations between an essay like Lisa L. Coleman's "Woolf and Feminist Theory: Woolf's Feminism Comes in Waves" and Judith Allen's "Feminist Politics: 'Repetition' and 'Burning" in *Three Guineas* (Making It New)" are more difficult to discern; they certainly do not amount to a difference between theory and practice. Both essays are theoretical, and both attempt the kind of play of critical language that characterized *écriture féminine* in the 1980s, although neither explicitly reflects on this context. In still another case, Patricia Morgne Cramer's "Woolf and Theories of Sexuality" in the first section, and Madelyn Detloff's "Woolf and Lesbian Culture: Queering Woolf Queering" in the second, gain in richness and complexity when read together. Detloff reads Woolf's lesbian productions and desires with recent queer theory while Cramer suggests that the extended sense of "queer" in current theorizations is so capacious and directed toward formal innovation (in this respect queer theory resembles *écriture féminine*) that it loses its sexual specificity. Again, the two treatments are equally theoretical, but the relation between them might most productively be viewed as a debate.

These pairings bring out what to me is one of the most interesting aspects of *Virginia Woolf in Context*: the variety of essay genres that different critics have chosen. Although this collection is more a research tool than an assembly of new critical articles, not all the contributors have written an introduction to a topic, describing and citing primary and secondary materials and tendencies in criticism over a period of time. Having said that, I'll note that many of the essays do provide exactly this kind of guidance, which students and scholars pursuing their own projects will probably find most useful. Among the most comprehensive and helpful of the essays clearly aimed at aiding others' research are Bonnie Kime Scott's "Regionalism, Nature, and the Environment," Bryony Randall's "Woolf and Modernist Studies," Sanja Bahun's "Woolf and Psychoanalytic Theory," Jane Lilienfeld's "Woolf, War and Peace," Emma Sutton's "Music," Maggie Humm's "Science and Technology," Anna Snaith's "Race, Empire, and Ireland," and the essays by Fernald, Protopopova, Homans, and Blyth that I mentioned earlier. These critics are dealing with subjects that they have already explored in depth, but they are generous in their synopses and evaluations of other critics' writings, even those with which they disagree.

A second genre of essay selects a few examples and allows them to stand synecdochically for the larger topic. Mark Hussey, who has already written several articles about the reception history of Woolf's writing, chooses in "Woolf: After Lives" to focus on a forgotten but (by that token) representative critic, Ray Monk. Using Monk's antagonistic judgments as impetus to elucidate what Woolf was *not* doing, Hussey finds evidence of both genre and gender policing in the attacks on and trivializations of her writing. David Bradshaw's "Woolf's London, London's Woolf" continues this critic's fascinating project of mapping the London of various novels and exploring how precise geographical and topical references build important subtexts. And Jessica Berman in "Woolf and the Private Sphere" constructs out of references in the novels and essays a narrative in which Woolf herself moves away from privacy into the public sphere.

Another genre of essay differs from this last in obliquely or overtly using an example as if it were the sole or true manifestation of the larger subject. In "Woolf and Contemporary Philosophy," Derek Ryan uses one strand of contemporary philosophy, a philosophy of science that draws on Heisenberg's and Bohr's differing interpretations of quantum phenomena, as an analogue to what he calls "intra-action" in Woolf's novels. In "Woolf and 'Theory,'" Claire Colebrook dismisses poststructuralism—and incidentally, all the Woolf criticism that arose from Derridean, Lacanian, Kristevan, and Foucauldian thought—to describe how she taught *A Room of One's Own* as part of a theoretical tradition presided over by Deleuze and Guattari's *Anti-Oedipus*. And Perry Meisel presents the scaffolding of a major critical article in "Woolf and Freud: The Kleinian Turn," which tries to make a case, in too little space, for Melanie Klein's influence on *To the Lighthouse*.

Still another genre of essay considers a topic as manifested in one book or the relations between two books. Heidi Stella uses the historical fact of European anti-Semitism as a point of entry into *Jacob's Room* (not a self-evident conjunction: Stella's middle term is the proposition that Leonard Woolf was one model for Jacob). Vassiliki Kolocotroni explores Woolf's ambivalence toward Greek language and culture in her rendering of the unintelligible song that the children sing at the end of *The Years*. And Elena Gualtieri's "Woolf, Economics, and Class Politics: Learning to Count" charts a growing awareness of the complexities of class in the transition from *A Room of One's Own* to *Three Guineas*.

Finally, one essay exemplifies an old genre that is nearly extinct in academic publishing. Drew Patrick Shannon's "Woolf and Publishing: Why the Hogarth Press Matters" is a personal appreciation, celebrating small presses, book collecting, and most of all the joys of the printed book. Unlike the other essays in the collection it is addressed to common readers and also about common readers. It provides information but also, consciously, pleasure, and reminds us that in her own Common Reader pieces, reviews, and long essays like "Phases of Fiction" and "Reading," Woolf herself wrote in the mode of appreciation.

Some of these essay genres seem better suited to brief exposition than others. Perhaps paradoxically, the essay providing an overview of the general topic while summarizing and evaluating criticism appears most often successful, although my discussion above notes plenty of exceptions. Readers consulting *Virginia Woolf in Context* for information on particular subjects will likely be less concerned about whether a particular entry seems incomplete or whether a field of inquiry is oddly framed. But the collection also invites more casual readers to dip into it, following fancy rather than a plan. Most of the articles are very readable, and many will provide little jolts of recognition or insight, sending us back to Woolf's novels and essays with a stronger sense of their complexities.

—Molly Hite, *Cornell University*

Julian Bell: From Bloomsbury to the Spanish Civil War. Peter Stansky and William Abrahams (Stanford: Stanford UP, 2012) xi + 314 pp.

The "search for Julian Bell" has preoccupied Peter Stansky for half a century, dating to his undergraduate years (xi). Over four decades after he and William Abrahams published their landmark study, *Journey to the Frontier: Two Roads to the Spanish Civil War* (1966), Stansky has returned to the topic. In between, the eminent historian and literary scholar has given us a remarkable range of studies of the British left and its interwar fate, including *On or About December 1910: Early Bloomsbury and Its Intimate World* (1996), which is known to many Woolf scholars. *Journey to the Frontier* treated Bell and John Cornford, emblematic figures of the 1930s who died in Spain. Now, Stansky (who credits Abrahams, deceased in 1998, as co-author of the present work) has issued *Julian Bell: From Bloomsbury to the Spanish Civil War*, and one immediately sees in it that he has returned to Bell because of the availability of new materials and archives—not the least among them Woolf's letters and diaries, and Quentin Bell's biography of her—since the first book's publication. Furthermore, Stansky now writes in a socio-cultural climate that permits disclosing facts about homosexual relationships among Bloomsbury members and families that could not be printed safely in 1966, before the decriminalization of homosexuality in Britain. The same holds true for accounts of interwar and post-World War II Communists, and even of Bell's romantic affairs. The result is a revision and expansion of *Journey to the Frontier* that is deeply personal in two ways: it is focused both on Bell's private life and on Stansky's own relationship to his subject and the world of Bloomsbury's second generation that he first probed long ago.

Bell, son of Vanessa and beloved nephew of Virginia, who felt her sister's "children were like my own," proved to be a paradoxical "violent pacifist," as Patricia Laurence has called him in a recent title (280). Conscious of the weight of intellectual history that he bore, Bell began his poem "Autobiography" with "I stay myself—the product made / By several hundred English years, / [...] Of high Victorian intellects, / Leslie, Fitzjames" (*Essays* 228). Torn between the ideals of the Bloomsbury climate and the energies of political activism in the 1930s, Bell edited a collection of memoirs by conscientious objectors to the Great War in 1935, and then, only two years later, decided to take up arms in Spain before acceding to his mother's wishes and serving as a noncombatant ambulance driver. Woolf, who was profoundly saddened by his death in July 1937, wrote the brief, understudied "Memoir of Julian Bell" that Quentin published in part as "Reminiscences of Julian" (only later was the full text published by S. P. Rosenbaum). Woolf notes here that "I have never known anyone of my generation to have that feeling about a war" as Bell did about the Spanish Civil War, which in part made him such a vital imagined interlocutor for her in *Three Guineas* ("Memoir" 28). Woolf concludes that he necessarily "had to be killed in Spain— an odd comment upon his education & our teaching"—a reflection of the doubts she had about Bloomsbury and about art's relation to politics in the 1930s (*D5* 126). We can understand Bell better in the present moment, Stansky suggests, by recognizing that he saw and experienced the contradictions and hypocrisies of his own era in ways that many of his elders and peers could not.

Chapter one of *Julian Bell*, "A Bloomsbury Childhood," is barely revised from Stansky and Abrahams's 1966 study, save some quotations from Vanessa's letters and incidental details about relationships among members. In chapter two, "A Young Apostle," one finds a more granular archival reconstruction of Bell's formation as an aspiring poet among the societies and literary magazines of Cambridge. Drawing on the expanded Charleston Papers at King's College, Cambridge; on letters among Bell and his family and colleagues; and on the history of near-forgotten reviews including *The Venture and Experiment*, Stansky situates Bell as a provocative literary figure of uneven talent. He also treats his affair with Anthony Blunt, a fellow Apostle who later became infamous once he was outed as a Soviet spy and stripped of his knighthood. Similarly, more details on Bell's affair with Helen Soutar, who was called simply "A" in *Journey to the Frontier*, are brought to light. Chapter three, "Searching," addresses Bell's intellectual development in the early 1930s, in which his "poetic, academic, literary-critical, philosophic, political, and romantic existence" seemed to be thriving (130). New material includes excerpts of the long discussions with his mother about marrying Soutar, details of his affair with Lettice Ramsey ("B" in *Journey to the Frontier*), and more evidence for why Bell remained a pacifist leftist, refusing to join a party even when nearly all of his literary generation had become "Communists, or almost Communists," as he wrote. In contrast to Cornford, Bell considered communism "very largely a literary phenomenon—an attempt of a second 'post-war generation' to escape from the Waste Land," one that "provides the activity, the sense of common effort, and something of the hysteria of war" (158).

In 1935, Bell left England to teach in China, where a war between Communists and Nationalists, carried out while under partial Japanese occupation, attracted his Byronic strain, offering him what he called a "genteel form of suicide" (182). In chapter four, "China," Stansky provides more details of Bell's affair with "K" (from *Journey to the Frontier*), since identified as Ling Shu-hua, wife of the dean at Wuhan University, where Bell was teaching. (For her part, Ling Shu-hua, a well-known writer and painter in China, would be published by the Hogarth Press in 1953.) Unable to extricate himself from another awkward position, Bell found that Spain called to him, a new romantic plunge and an escape from affairs and over-intellectualizing. He was driven to Spain by his "beliefs, and my ancestors and environment," even as Vanessa tried desperately to convince him not to go: "You object to cutting down trees—isn't war that, a million times worse?" (237, 231). But perhaps his most cutting comments came in his disagreements with Woolf: "It's too late too," he wrote, "for democracy and reason and persuasion and writing to the *New Statesman* and Virginia signing letters saying it's all a pity. The only real choices are to submit or to fight. ... There's only one thing to be done with Fascists, and that's kill them" (235). His full-throated rejection of Bloomsbury pacifism was complete when he wrote in an essay that "Non-resistance to war means non-resistance to fascism and a resignation to the disappearance of most, if not all, that we value" (249).

Thus, in the final chapter, "Spain," Bell's dramatic interpersonal tension with elder Bloomsbury comes through most fully. Woolf finds him, during his brief stay in England between China and Spain, to be "vigorous, controlled, as I guess embittered, ... changed: taut, tense, on the defense: yet affectionate: but no longer spontaneous" (262). She could never comprehend "what made him feel it necessary, knowing as he did how it must torture Nessa, to go?" (264). Even so, Woolf's objection was "waver[ing]": "I'm sometimes angry with him; yet feel it was fine, as all very strong feelings are fine; yet they are also wrong somehow: one must control feeling with reason" (264). In this chapter, one can see Bloomsbury's ingrained rebelliousness turning on its own ideals in the person of Bell. Accounts from other artist-figures who drove ambulances in Spain, such as Richard Rees, fill out Stansky's portrait of Bell's death, and Vanessa's writings on him make for painful but necessary reading. Woolf scholars will appreciate the challenge that Bell issues to her thought—one that he now issues more robustly, thanks to Stansky's revisions.

Those who know *Journey to the Frontier*, however, might miss the juxtaposition of Bell and Cornford, and might wish for a different sort of revision from Stansky: about three-quarters of *Julian Bell* reproduces the Bell sections of the former study. But when Stansky revises and expands, he does so archivally and personally, with an introspective historian's eye. This makes for some captivating passages not only about Bell's private life and his intellectual journeys, but also about Stansky and Abraham's research for their first book in the 1960s: what surviving Bell family members could not tell them, or what was known by "those in the know" and shared only in code (xi). Woolf scholars and those interested in Bloomsbury more generally will wish that Stansky's study incorporated some of the wealth of publications on this topic that have issued forth in the past four decades. He cites a few publications that have appeared since 1966, but they are editions of letters or revised biographies of relevant figures— hardly any critical resources, literary or otherwise. (Laurence's *Lily Briscoe's*

Chinese Eyes: Bloomsbury, Modernism, and China [2003], for instance, receives only a passing mention.) For those who wish to revisit Bell's life and its telling by Stansky, *Julian Bell* will prove refreshing, shedding further light on a figure whose aunt's star continues to outshine his, but whose life and death affected her final years in indelible ways.

—Gayle Rogers, *University of Pittsburgh*

Works Cited

Bell, Julian. *Essays, Poems and Letters*. Ed. Quentin Bell. London: Hogarth Press, 1938. Print.

Woolf, Virginia. "Memoir of Julian Bell." *The Platform of Time: Memoirs of Family and Friends*. Ed. S. P. Rosenbaum. London: Hesperus Press, 2007. Print.

The Labors of Modernism: Domesticity, Servants, and Authorship in Modernist Fiction. Mary Wilson (Burlington: Ashgate, 2013) x + 176pp.

The Vanessa Bell painting (*Interior with a Housemaid*, 1939) that ornaments the cover of Mary Wilson's lively and instructive book shows, in the upper half of the canvas and to the left, a cluttered desk, reasonably well lit; next to it an open door, better lit, dividing the painting in half; and in shadow, to the right, an aproned housemaid, standing and cleaning with a mop. In the bottom half of the painting, its vertical legs and slats thrusting upward into the painting's center, is the chair that goes with the desk. Draped over the chair is an article of clothing, perhaps a coat or shawl. Its form and color echo the shadowy housemaid, though like the desk and door it is much brighter, as if the inanimate object were intended to reveal how much more interesting the housemaid might look if she were ever to emerge from the shadows. All in all, the cover is an astonishingly apt crystallization of Wilson's argument. According to Wilson, modernist fiction continues the long literary tradition that represses and marginalizes the lives of all working people while at the same time it also finds formal means of hinting that these lives are not marginal after all: for example, by suggesting that there exists a rich if mysterious relationship between the servant's labors with the mop (a visual rhyme with the chair) and the mistress's writing at the desk. Thus in *Mrs.*

Dalloway, Wilson argues, "Lucy's housekeeping work, preparing for the party, enables Clarissa to engage in the creative labor of buying the flowers" (42).

Beyond the fact that their work frees their mistresses to do other, more creative things, what does it mean to say that these servants are not, after all, marginal? The declared assumption behind these four chapters, covering Virginia Woolf, Gertrude Stein, Nella Larsen, and Jean Rhys, is that servants were "necessary laborers in the creation of modernist domesticity and the conditions of production of modernist fiction" (3). Necessary? Well, yes, but in what sense exactly? When Woolf visited the Docks, she proposed to the readers of *Good Housekeeping*, how ironically it's impossible to say, that the system of world trade displayed in London's ships, cranes, and warehouses depended on their habits of consumption—that they were necessary to it, hence possessed the power to change it. Are prosperous consumers (Woolf makes it clear she is addressing women with some purchasing power) "necessary" to the capitalist system in the same sense of the word that would apply to domestic servants? If they are, then necessity does not signify, as it might seem to, labor, or suffering, or exploitation. Marx observed in *Capital* that for all the harshness of their lives, domestic servants weren't necessary to the system at all. What drives the system is the profit motive; servants are a way of disposing of your profits, not making any. Employing them is no more necessary to capitalism than, say, building bonfires of pound notes in your backyard and inviting the neighbors in to watch. To see this is to see that the sort of necessity Wilson has in mind has less to do with labor than with gender: "a domesticity supported by servants actually helps to make possible both [the] critique of domesticity and the ideal of middle-class women's fiction" (3). In other words, she asks how women's writing was inflected by the fact that it depended on servants who were also women and who did the labor that would otherwise have filled the writers' days and thus prevented them from writing. Is their shared gender strong enough to override the overwhelming difference in class, even if (as she suggests) its force is too weak to oblige servants' lives to be represented fully and directly?

The answer is interestingly unclear. That Woolf's conscience was troubled by the fact that Sophie Farrell and Nellie Boxall devoted their entire lives to her family's welfare is well documented in Alison Light's *Mrs. Woolf and the Servants: An Intimate History of Domestic Life in Bloomsbury* (2008). As Light shows, Woolf's emotions on the subject were extensive, powerful, and complicated. She was immensely exasperated both at her servants and at herself for accepting what she perceived as their tyrannical irrationality. In this she was largely a creature of her class and time. Wilson cites Victoria Rosner's comment that to offer as evidence of momentous social change "the character of one's cook," as Woolf famously does in "Mr. Bennett and Mrs. Brown," is to assume that one is speaking to women whose meals are prepared by cooks and that cooks themselves will not be raptly listening in the audience (33). This is not quite the assumption one would take away from Woolf's picture of a new democratic age in which the cook emerges from her dark basement to borrow the newspaper. On the other hand, there was something unbearable to Woolf in the idea that Sophie Farrell, after a lifetime of service, decorated her room with nothing but the photos and hand-me-downs of the family she had served. "Her mind is like a family album," Woolf writes in the unpublished second draft of her sketch "The Cook," usefully edited in these pages by Susan Dick (127). Biddy Brien, a thinly disguised Sophie, is given no inner life or working-class consciousness but considerable power to annoy, achieved by claiming and exaggerating the genteel standards of a previous generation of employers. As Dick astutely points out, Woolf's criteria in revising the story seem to have included a desire to remove as far as possible her own naggingly class-ridden perspective, the voice of "the bemused mistress" (133). Dick further speculates that Woolf's formal goal of experimenting with a narrative prose that was all style and no character may have been encouraged by its association with servants who, having given their life over to others, putatively had no character of their own.

Like Dick, whom she credits appropriately, Wilson wants to connect servants with innovations in literary form. Where Woolf is concerned, it's not so much mops and desks as doors and doorways that seize her imagination. Borrowing from Rosner the figure of the threshold, she lays out a brilliant hypothesis suggesting that servants are formally present in Woolf's use of parenthetical asides: "Woolf physically separates what is contained within the parentheses from what surrounds them, and in so doing creates a series of narrative thresholds which the reader must cross" (50). This entails "writing servant labor into the structure of the novel" (54). Snobbery passes, but form is forever.

The chapter on Stein offers repetition as a resonant formal parallel to Woolf's parenthesis. While emphasizing the distinctive racial or ethnic foreignness of young women in service in the United States, it also makes a daring argumentative move. The fact that a woman serving someone else's family cannot have a family of her own (as was the case for the two servants Woolf knew best) might be expected to register as a sign of unequal opportunity and social injustice. But if domesticity signifies compulsory heteronormativity, then the servant's alienation from it can be re-coded as something positive. Wilson finds ample evidence in Stein of a queer ethic. Downplaying the much-discussed "Melanctha" in favor of the other two stories in *Three Lives*, which have been neglected in part because (like Woolf's "The Cook") they feature submissive, utterly accepting characters, Wilson delicately raises the question of whether servitude looks better when the idealized and presumably preferred alternative—marriage, a home of one's own, children of one's own—comes to be seen as socially destructive. Is there a sense in which servants benefit from silently embodying the writer's queer transvaluation of values? Or is the new anti-domestic framework merely a backhanded excuse for telling them they are better off than they might have felt they were?

Queerness as ethic and aesthetic is also central to Wilson's reading of Larsen's *Passing*—more central than the maid who crosses thresholds and picks up broken crockery or than Larsen's use of the dash, a formal habit that Wilson again tries to map onto the servant presence via its effect of marking interruption and ambivalence in the mistress. In the reading of Rhys's *Wide Sargasso Sea*, on the other hand, the theme of queerness disappears, replaced by a new interest in the alienated sense of the home produced by servant voices (the acquisition of voice representing a kind of progress over the silence of servants in Woolf) and a return to the book's initial focus on thresholds and spatiality. By ending the chapter with a reflection on Grace Poole, Wilson anchors her neatly phrased conclusion: "the woman in the attic is not alone, though she may appear to be" (125).

In her conclusion, Wilson suggests that gender changes everything. It's not just that women writers are different, but women servants do different things than male servants for fiction, just as they do different things in the household. This point is well taken though it doesn't really answer the question that seems to underlie the project as a whole: to what extent does common gender override class difference?

—Bruce Robbins, *Columbia University*

Works Cited

Dick, Susan. "Virginia Woolf's 'The Cook.'" *Woolf Studies Annual* 3 (1997): 122-142.

Light, Alison. *Mrs. Woolf and the Servants: An Intimate History of Domestic Life in Bloomsbury*. London: Bloomsbury Press, 2008.

Virginia Woolf and Neuropsychiatry. Maxwell Bennett (Dordrecht: Springer, 2013) ix + 214pp.

At the age of fifty-nine, on the threshold of spring, as cinders and ash choked London's air and Europe careened towards a second world war, Virginia Woolf decided that she could not endure another battle with the emotional demons she had fought since childhood. The note on the mantel stated it clearly: "I feel certain that I am going mad again: I feel we cant [sic] go through another of those terrible times. And I shant recover this time. ..." (*L6* 481). Unable to concentrate and distressed by internal voices she could not quiet, Woolf committed suicide. Her emotional turmoil and death is the subject of *Virginia Woolf and Neuropsychiatry*, written by neuroscientist Maxwell Bennett, the founding Director of the Brain and Mind Research Institute at the University of Sydney.

In this short but tightly-packed series of essays Bennett enters interdisciplinary territory, an open landscape begging for development. Although my roots are in psychology, I too have taken excursions through the byways of literature and neuroscience. I enjoy lingering in an area, getting to know its unique qualities, people, history, and theory, but I am most interested in the intersections between disciplines, those places where minds meet to enrich one another's understanding. Bennett seems to enjoy the same kind of itinerary. *Virginia Woolf and Neuropsychiatry* is divided into three sections that travel across clinical psychology, "the circumstances and familial burdens that promote severe depression" via the literary trail of Woolf's "novels, plays, critical reviews, autobiographical sketches and diaries," and through the recondite provinces of brain networks, neurochemistry, epigenetics, and psychopharmacology (ix). While the general reader is invited to tour the first and last sections of the book, Bennett reserves the middle passage for "neuropsychiatric cognoscenti." I would add neophyte adventurers too, those who enjoy an intellectual challenge and do not mind getting lost.

In chapter three, the last stop before the most arduous section of the book, readers are offered a neuroanatomical tour. Early in the trek, Bennett clarifies a misunderstanding that has been a sore spot in the relationship between literary scholars and neuroscientists—a breach that has led some to dismiss any role that the brain has in our beliefs, desires, fears, or happiness. The problem, Bennett illuminates, is the popular press notion of specificity—that a particular feeling, thought, or behavior corresponds to an exact target in the brain. As scientist Gary Marcus says, "no single spot of the brain maps to hatred." Neuroscientists now look for patterns of responses across the whole brain.

Another tension between literary and scientific seekers is the specter of biological reductionism. Some dread that the natural processes of the brain, the electronic transmission of nerves or chemicals that float about its folds and crevasses, will shrink our very being to a single organ. Where is the role for unique experience, whether it is mundane or transcendent? How can we make decisions that are uniquely our own if everything can be explained by the electrochemistry of a single organ? Bennett's approach to the effects of stress, anxiety, depression, and sexual abuse on the brain's development might encourage the leery to reconsider. Here he highlights the role of individual experience, how it prunes synaptic connections, and invigorates or diminishes cortical anatomy. The result? No two brains are ever alike, and we are free to be our idiosyncratic selves.

Happily, chapter three was written for the uninitiated, those who may not understand the many ways the brain is divided into functional sections or what a neuron looks like. However, words like cortex—the sheath of neural tissue that envelops the brain—or amygdala—the almond shaped cluster of nuclei located deep inside the brain, the center of emotional processing—have no explanation. We need distinct diagrams, such as a clearly delineated graphic of the brain rather than an orange mass of folds covered in faint purple letters. Even if readers match the letter to its part in the figure notes, it is likely that many newcomers will not recognize the sections.

But these excursions through neuroscience are only part of the trip. The heart of the journey is the text about Woolf. It is here that Bennett leads us astray. The problems appear immediately, in the second paragraph of the preface where Bennett states that Sigmund Freud treated Woolf's depression. Later in the book he conjectures that Freud talked to Woolf about sexual abuse and in that conversation Freud questioned its impact on her emotional health (44). In fact, Woolf only met Freud once, on January 28, 1939. Freud and his family had recently fled Nazi persecution in Austria to 20 Maresfield Gardens in Hampstead. Woolf and her husband, Leonard, visited Freud, one of their eminent Hogarth Press authors, for tea. He was dying. In Woolf's diary she describes him as a man "with a monkey's light eyes, paralysed spasmodic movements, inarticulate: but alert" (*D5* 202). Talk was "difficult" said Woolf. Jaw cancer made Freud labor through conversation. There is no mention of incest in Woolf's notes about the occasion. Instead, she recounts concern about the advancing European war, the one that exiled him. Their visit and her diary entry end with the conflict, for as they departed Freud "took up the stand [sic] What are you going to do? The English—war" (*D5* 202).

The inaccuracies continue and sloppy fact-checking diminishes the verity of Bennett's arguments. In chapter one, for instance, the first part of Woolf's essay

"On Being Ill" is camouflaged as a diary entry. Innuendo fashioned from fragments of fact is offered as complete truth. Information is collated and presented to prove Bennett's point, leaving the reader adrift in conjecture. Two examples stand out.

The first is Bennett's insistence that Woolf's stepbrothers, Gerald and George, sexually abused her *continuously* from childhood through adolescence. The concern is not whether any abuse took place. Woolf is explicit in *Sketch of the Past* about Gerald's hand wandering around her "private parts," but the where, when, and how of George's molestations are less precise (*MOB* 69). While the evidence of exploitation is strong, says biographer Hermione Lee, it is "ambiguous enough, to open the way for conflicting psychobiographical interpretations which draw quite different shapes of Virginia Woolf's interior life" (Lee 156).

The corollary to this uninterrupted malevolence, and the second occasion in which certainty wears the emperor's new clothes, is Bennett's discussion of the risk factors for suicide. He cites sexual and physical abuse as the top contenders. True, both burdens leave victims vulnerable to suicide. However, mental illness, cited as a critical risk factor by the National Institutes of Mental Health, is absent from Bennett's list, despite his statement that Woolf was likely "predisposed to manic-depressive disorder because of a familial inheritance from her father…" (29). Why not let mental illness share top billing? Perhaps it did not match Bennett's itinerary. He seems determined to reach his destination—the crossroads where suicidal ideation, unremitting sexual abuse, and neurophysiological change meet and lead the victim to suicide. That crucial markers are missing on this trail to suicide appears moot to Bennett.

These omissions are disappointing. Bennett is a guest in the literary world, yet he treats his hosts with less respect than his hometown companions. Well trained in the methods of scientific inquiry and accustomed to the process of peer review, Bennett knows that meticulous data is the foundation of any reliable analysis. He is well aware that crude approximations yield poor statistical output that cannot be trusted. Scholars in the humanities care just as much about accuracy and accountability. They would be right to set him straight about the house rules—treat your hosts as you would yourself. Some may even be reluctant to take another excursion with him. Still, I would try again, ready to detour if necessary.

—Michele Wick, *Smith College*

Works Cited

Lee, Hermione. *Virginia Woolf*. New York: Vintage Books, 1996.
Marcus, Gary. "The Problem with the Neuroscience Backlash." *The New Yorker*. 19 June 2013. Web. September 2013.
National Institute of Mental Health. http://www.nimh.nih.gov/health/publications/suicide-in-the-us-statistics-and-prevention/index.shtml. Web. September 2013.
Woolf, Virginia. *Moments of Being*. Jeanne Schulkind, ed. San Diego: Harcourt, 1985.

Mapping the Modern Mind: Virginia Woolf's Parodic Approach to the Art of Fiction in Jacob's Room. Lindy van Rooyen (Hamburg: Diplomica Verlag, 2012) 119 pp.

Lindy van Rooyen's monograph is derived from her master's degree thesis and, as the title indicates, is purportedly based solely on *Jacob's Room* and the theme of parody. The volume itself begins on what is a disturbing note from the perspective of Woolfians for the author's very first assertion is that "Virginia Woolf is not a popular writer" (3). Just for the record, Woolf actually was a popular writer in the conventional sense during her own lifetime, and certainly has achieved not only significant status as a major literary figure but, as Brenda Silver has noted in *Virginia Woolf Icon*, has attained wide recognition as a cultural emblem. Mark Hussey notes in *Virginia Woolf A to Z* that *The Years* (1931) "was a popular success" and "[i]n the United States it became a best-seller, leading to a 1937 *Time* magazine cover for Woolf" (391). Similarly, *Flush* (1933) "was selected by the Book Society in England for October 1933, and by the American Book-of-the-Month club for September as an alternate selection" (Hussey 89).

In fact, van Rooyen doesn't even seem to be aware of existing recent scholarship on *Jacob's Room*. Though she has a robust bibliography, she lists only four titles that specifically name *Jacob's Room*. One is Barry Morgenstern's 1972 "The Self-Conscious Narrator in *Jacob's Room*," another is Judy Little's 1981 "*Jacob's Room* as Comedy: Woolf's Parodic Bildungsroman," and the remaining two are Sue Roe's 1992 introduction to the Penguin edition of the novel and my own 2008 introduction to the Harcourt edition. Of course, while there is an abundance of scholarship on *Jacob's Room*, including the free online access to the *Selected Papers* from the annual conferences on Virginia Woolf published by Clemson University Digital Press (2001-present) and the *Virginia Woolf Miscellany* (Spring 2003-present), it is possible that van Rooyen didn't have extensive opportunities to use databases requiring subscriptions and perhaps did not have access to fee-free online publications.

The book title suggests that van Rooyen will focus on humorous aspects of the novel, but she does not achieve a sustained argument. Of the six references she makes to what she terms the "golden thread" of parody, allegedly highlighting satire in the novel, none develop into detailed discussions of comical elements in the novel. One of the few instances where humor in the novel is actually apparent is van Rooyen's comparison of *Jacob's Room* to H. G. Wells's *Joan and Peter* (1918), a novel in which a guardian is very invested in choosing the right university for his young wards; in her comparison, van Rooyen highlights the absence of any such oversight in Jacob Flanders's life, remarking that

> Contrarily, in *Jacob's Room* (if the matter was duly considered in the kitchen *at all* by Mrs. Flanders and Captain Barfoot) the reasons for this important decision are left to the reader's imagination. In fact it is baldly stated with mock logic at the end of the 'parentage' chapters I & II that "Jacob, *therefore*, went up to Cambridge in October, 1906." (87; van Rooyen's italics)

Though the quotation above is quite lucid and amusing, generally the writing style and the structure of the volume are both very awkward and uneven throughout, with too many concepts jostling against each other and an overall sense of confusion, especially since a number of the most interesting ideas are mentioned only once or never actually fleshed out.

The author's opening overview of modernism is an example of this disorderly argument, which is continually interrupted by references to the numerically organized framework of the essay. Reviews of *Jacob's Room* at the time of the novel's publication are blurred into seemingly random references to Woolf's family history, her early education, and the context of Bloomsbury culture. For instance, the final sentence of the section numbered 3.2, titled "The Sceptical Sensibility of Virginia Stephen," states (in an oddly repetitive style) that "The Bloomsbury Group is sometimes given the credit of representing an English aesthetic movement analogous to the Aesthetic Movement, and thus it is necessary to deal briefly with their influence on Woolf's work" (29). However, instead of addressing this influence,[1] the very next section (numbered 3.3 and

---

[1] The topic is referenced only once more when the author makes a very strained claim that "the dramatic scenes constructed by Woolf incorporate into the tapestry of *Jacob's*

titled "The Hogarth Press and the Conception of *Jacob's Room*") heads off in a totally different direction as van Rooyen quotes a passage from Woolf's diary written the day after her thirty-eighth birthday and then adds an undated passage from a subsequent diary entry in which Woolf avers that she doesn't care about being "popular" (29). van Rooyen then returns to the question of Woolf's public standing and popularity, asserting, "She was not popular; yet she clung to her vision with tremendous tenacity" (29) and argues that Woolf was able to do so "because she and her husband literally crafted her fiction themselves in the basement of their home, which was to become the Hogarth Press" (29). In the next paragraph, van Rooyen again stresses Woolf's lack of fame at "The mature age of 37" and lists a number of early Hogarth Press publications (29).

In the following section, 3.4, titled "Bloomsbury and the Cambridge Apostles," the author travels back in time to 1904, writes about Woolf's essays "Old Bloomsbury" and "On Not Knowing Greek," and eventually aligns some elements of *Jacob's Room* with Thoby Stephen's experiences at university. As one can tell from this summary, no framework anchors the author's argumentation. Instead, the essay is more like Woolf's "incessant shower of innumerable atoms," but, "as they fall," the atoms remain disappointingly random and fail to "shape themselves into the life of Monday or Tuesday" ("Modern Fiction" 106).

While there are definitely intriguing flickers of insight in the essay—for instance, the author's occasional references to Woolf's rhetorical technique in *Jacob's Room* or her alignment of the novel with the biographical techniques of Lytton Strachey—there is no sense of progressive development, logic, or sequence. To wit, the essay seems almost entirely random; each paragraph is potentially a surprise with no guarantee whether the newly launched topic will be explored in any depth or whether it will simply be abandoned. Thus, the author briefly invokes the homoerotics of the Cambridge Apostles, stating that in *Jacob's Room* there is an "erotic tenor of the friendship between Jacob Flanders and two 'apostles,' Bonamy and Simeon in particular" (32). However, neither character at any later point in the argument is linked to homosexual relations that Jacob may have had, nor are there substantive references. Further, there is no evidence of research on the sexual practices of the Apostles during Thoby Stephen's years at

---

Room the various opinions aired in Jacob's Forum, including (by means of literary allusion) the academic debate of the Aesthetic Movement by means of a subtle allusion to Henry James's *Golden Bowl*" (45). Elsewhere, the author defines the novel as an "aesthetic 'room' for discussion on the nature of fictional form" and suggests that "*Jacob's Room* is utilised as a writer's (i.e. Woolf's) forum in which various points of view are analysed, including the *central question* lingering on the minds of the author, the gallery of characters and the protagonist respectively: 'Who is *Jacob Flanders*?'" (4-5).

Cambridge (for instance, there is no reference to Julie Anne Taddeo's important essay, "Plato's Apostles: Edwardian Cambridge and the 'New Style of Love'").

The essay is also plagued by peculiarities. One of the most irritating factors, aside from the confusingly numbered sections, is that van Rooyen uses title case for such invented terms as "Jacob's Forum" (5), "the Lantern Symbol" (46), and "the Moonlight Sonata Vignette" (90) to tag segments of the novel. Even more annoying, however, is that the publisher apparently employs neither copyeditors nor proofreaders and the document is a hot mess riddled with bizarre punctuation errors.

Jacob's Room, now more than ninety years in print, has always been regarded as a calculatedly fragmented narrative. It is sad that, rather than bringing fresh insights to bear on the novel, *Mapping the Modern Mind* instead unintentionally mirrors and distorts the novel's own disjointedness and incoherence and becomes itself a parody, a caricature of Woolf's novelistic experimentation and her purposeful rambling.

—Vara Neverow, *Southern Connecticut State University*

Works Cited

Hussey, Mark. *Virginia Woolf A to Z: The Essential Reference to Her Life and Writings*. New York: Oxford UP, 1995.

Silver, Brenda. *Virginia Woolf Icon*. Chicago: U of Chicago P, 1999.

Taddeo, Julie Anne. "Plato's Apostles: Edwardian Cambridge and the 'New Style of Love.'" *Journal of the History of Sexuality* 8.2 (Oct. 1997): 196-228.

van Rooyen, Lindy. "Mapping the Modern Mind: Virginia Woolf's Parodic Approach to the Art of Fiction in Jacob's Room." MA thesis. Hamburg University, 2012.

Woolf, Virginia. "Modern Fiction." *Collected Essays*. Vol. 2. New York: Harcourt, Brace and World, 1967. 103-10.

Virginia Woolf and the Materiality of Theory: Sex, Animal, Life. Derek Ryan (Edinburgh UP, 2013) vii + 221 pp.

In recent years, modernist studies has privileged historicist approaches and sidelined the poststructuralist readings that reached their apogee in the '80s and early '90s. While acknowledging the limitations of deconstructive analyses and affirming the critical turn towards deep archival engagement, Derek Ryan revitalizes theoretical approaches to reading modernist literature in *Virginia Woolf and the Materiality of Theory*. Specifically, Ryan considers Woolf's oeuvre in relationship to current critical debates that have advanced robust theories of materiality. As Ryan argues, Woolf's writings anticipate the "new materialisms" of contemporary theory, as they unfailingly foreground the multifaceted entanglements of "human and nonhuman, embodiment and environment, culture and nature, life and matter" (3). By examining Woolf's theorization of materiality and materialization of theory, Ryan argues, we might not only contribute to contemporary theoretical conversations, but also underscore the indebtedness of contemporary theory to modernist literature.

The interventions of *Virginia Woolf and the Materiality of Theory* are threefold. First, Ryan shows how Woolf elaborates and extends theoretical concepts ranging from Karen Barad's "agential realism" to Rosi Braidotti's "nomadic subject" to Jane Bennett's "vital materialism." The common influence upon these theorists and the prevailing interpretative framework of Ryan's study is Deleuzian, however. As Ryan explores how Woolf anticipates Deleuzian ideas in imaginative writing, he further highlights how Woolf's writing was actually generative of concepts such as "becoming" and "haecceity," drawing attention to Deleuze's frequent citations of Woolf. Second, Ryan strives to discredit the perceived opposition between historical and theoretical literary readings. While certainly Ryan's analysis of Woolf's theory of materiality would seem complementary to historicist approaches, Ryan fails to deliver fully on this second promise, as historical contexts remain somewhat underdeveloped in this study. Put differently, Ryan much more successfully demonstrates Woolf's theorization of materiality than the materialization of Woolf's theory. Still, in foregrounding Woolf's engagement with the nonhuman world and eschewing the human-centered analyses more prominent in Woolf scholarship—the third major aim of the study—Ryan contributes rich and timely readings.

The first chapter of the book elegantly troubles the distinction between "the cultural" and "the material," articulating the foundational theoretical intervention that subsequent chapters will elaborate with greater complexity. The unencumbered approach to this chapter is particularly gratifying, and throws into greater relief Ryan's intimate familiarity with Woolf's work. Beginning with the 1927 essay, "The New Biography," in which "granite" and "rainbow" appear to stand for the constituent and somewhat irreconcilable elements of truth and fiction, Ryan proceeds to carry out a "creative cartography" of Woolf's disparate usages of these terms across the expanse of her writings. While critics have argued that Woolf ultimately dismantles the strict opposition between "truth" and "fiction" that "The New Biography" would appear to present, Ryan usefully highlights how Woolf more foundationally destabilizes the meanings of "granite" and "rainbow" themselves. If Woolf's conceptualization of biography ultimately disrupts the binary of "truth" and "fiction," this is because Woolf configures granite-like fact and hard granite itself as changeable, while she casts rainbow-like fictions and rainbows themselves as material phenomena. To invoke Ryan's memorable phrasing, when Woolf is digging granite, she is simultaneously chasing rainbows.

In the second and third chapters, Ryan turns to questions of sexual difference and desire. Chapter two considers Woolf's theory of androgyny in *A Room of One's Own* alongside Rosi Braidotti's nomadic model of sexual difference. Like Braidotti, Ryan argues, Woolf emphasizes the differences between women and the differences within women. Yet in Ryan's assessment, Woolf's imagining of the androgynous subject ultimately extends Braidotti's concept of the nomadic subject, as Woolf challenges the fundamental difference between women and men, which Braidotti conversely maintains. In making this argument, however, Ryan fails to observe that Braidotti's emphasis upon this "first level" of sexual difference is bound up with her attention to embodiment. Thus if Woolf's stretches Braidotti's thinking as Ryan describes, she might simultaneously be said to slacken her engagement with the materiality of the body. Without addressing this difficulty, Ryan proceeds to invoke Deleuze and Guattari's notion of "becoming minoritarian" to read *To the Lighthouse* as a contestation of molar identities. Here, Ryan argues that Woolf's representation of "tri-subjectivities" disputes the primacy of the Oedipal triangle to show the productive formation of characters in relationship to nonhuman entities and environments. While Woolf's affirmation of molecular existence over molar identity is convincingly argued, at times Ryan's textual readings strain to conflate Deleuzian tropes and Woolfian representations: to take one example, Ryan ascribes a rhizomatic meaning to the lawn shared by Lily Briscoe and Mr. Carmichael, ironically contradicting a rhizomatic reading practice through a somewhat flattening application of theory. The third chapter, by contrast, advances a much more nuanced reading of *Orlando*. Beyond destabilizing sexual identity, Ryan argues, *Orlando* presents a Braidottian model of desire as an embodied material reality. Further, the representation of sexual desire in Orlando exceeds human subjects and entangles the nonhuman world. Accordingly, Ryan attends to representations of nonhuman objects that mediate desire, such as the rings that Shelmerdine and Orlando exchange, as well as the molecular nature of historical events. Whereas other critics have argued that Woolf disputes sexology's reduction of lesbian desire to bodily hardwiring in *Orlando*, Ryan refreshingly highlights how Woolf configures sexuality as materially embodied and materiality as something more creative than constraining. In fact, what is "queer" about Orlando, in Ryan's analysis, is precisely the qualitative and generative multiplicity of human and nonhuman bodies.

The fourth and fifth chapters of the book push beyond the purview of human objects of analysis. The fourth chapter engages the question of the animal in *Flush*, but arguably, Ryan fails to consider the specificity of animal life both in itself and in Woolf's representation of it. Sidelining the critical debate over the potentials and pitfalls of anthropocentrism, Ryan argues that Woolf is centrally preoccupied with molecular entanglements across species' lines in *Flush*, not "Oedipal animals" in their "molar form." Yet Ryan's disputation of the statist or psychoanalytic human subject leaves little room for reflection on the ethical subject, whether human or non-human, and thus Ryan's brief meditation on the representation of animal suffering in *Flush* falls flat. Of course, this is not a necessary consequence of the contestation of "the human," as recent work in animal studies scholarship would attest. Interestingly, Ryan even acknowledges Donna Haraway's well-known indictment of Deleuze and Guattari's theory of becoming-animal for its indifference to actual animals. However, Ryan never provides a satisfying rebuttal to Haraway, oddly accusing Haraway of an ad hominem attack in advancing as much: "If Haraway is engaged in a mud dance with her dogs, the problem, perhaps, is that she is also throwing mud" (152). In treating the question of the animal, in particular, Ryan might have benefitted from less loyalty to the Deleuzian paradigm and deeper engagement with conversations in critical animal studies. In the fifth chapter, Ryan argues that *The Waves* advances something like Karen Barad's idea of "agential realism," which posits that agency belongs neither to subjects nor objects but rather emerges within natural-cultural intra-actions. Ryan further suggests that Woolf anticipates Jane Bennett's "vital materialism" in showing how even nonliving matter and inanimate objects are constitutive of Deleuzian haecceities: creative events formed of non-subjective affects. In elaborating the arguments of this chapter, Ryan situates Woolf's writings in relationship to twentieth century developments in quantum physics. Although in so doing he borrows heavily from existing Woolf scholarship on the topic, Ryan thereby more centrally engages the materialization of Woolf's theory here than anywhere else in the book. This chapter often fails to register the material heterogeneity that Ryan ostensibly espouses, however. Interestingly, Ryan actually raises this theoretical difficulty: how does one dismantle hierarchies of being while maintaining the heterogeneity of existence? This is an exceedingly rich question, and one that

Ryan might have productively engaged in a more sustained and unsettled manner, both in relationship to animal life and in relationship to non-living matter, rather than confidently resolving by turning to Deleuzian ideas of univocity, with which he closes his discussion.

Virginia Woolf and the Materiality of Theory demonstrates an impressive command of contemporary theories of materiality as well as an intimate knowledge of Woolf's novels and essays. At times, however, Ryan privileges the explication of the former over the exploration of the latter. Although Ryan claims to eschew an "application" of theory to Woolf, many of Ryan's literary readings give the impression of an overreliance on existing theoretical frameworks, which Woolf might complicate more than Ryan allows. Perhaps the specificity of Woolf's theorization of materiality might have been better illuminated by attending more concertedly to the material forms of language, or, put differently, to Woolf's stylization of theorization. One of the questions this book provocatively raises, but leaves unanswered, is how the theorization of materiality or the materialization of theory is indebted to modernism qua modernism. Still, Ryan's *rapprochement* between contemporary theory and modernist studies is a welcome interruption of critical trends that would dispense with theory altogether.

—Annie Dwyer, *University of Washington*

Virginia Woolf's Late Cultural Criticism: The Genesis of The Years, Three Guineas *and* Between the Acts. Alice Wood. (London: Bloomsbury Academic P, 2013) i + 187pp.

In *Virginia Woolf's Late Cultural Criticism*, Alice Wood takes us into the archive to consider Woolf's complex position as feminist and social critic over the span of her career. As in many considerations of late modernism, Wood uses the language of a "turn" or shift in works produced in the decade leading up to World War II—language which has characterized studies as diverse as Samuel Hynes's *The Auden Generation* (1977) and Jed Esty's *A Shrinking Island* (2003). Wood assumes that Woolf's political engagement in later works such as *Three Guineas* (1938) is a clear extension of earlier feminist theories in *A Room of One's Own* (1929). Even if Woolf occasionally thought of figures such as T. S. Eliot as "building sand castles" in the heyday of high modernism, such an experimental method is certainly integral to the vision of her own Judith Shakespeare (*D5* 340).

Wood's book is a refreshing take on Woolf's political consciousness, one which assumes that the narrative experimentation of *Jacob's Room* (1922) and *Mrs. Dalloway* (1925) is a necessary bridge into the seemingly more realist and socially engaged family epic of *The Years* (1937). Much like Gillian Beer's and Grace Radin's foundational readings of the later Woolf, Wood's book also builds on the idea that something in Woolf's work is constantly evolving and engaged with not simply looking back to the pivotal moment of 1910 with a colder eye, but also considering how the history of English imperialist-militarism would strike her audience in the late 1930s.

At first glance, there does appear to be a significant gap between the privileged view of feminism suggested at the end of *A Room of One's Own*—which is dependent on an inheritance of £500 and a solitude few women in Britain could afford then or now—to Woolf's insistence in a May 1940 speech to the Brighton Workers' Education Association that "literature is common ground" that must be trespassed by "commoners and outsiders like ourselves" (*E6* 278). As feminist readers, we are in the uncomfortable position of trying to reconcile how Woolf could present such a populist call to take to the libraries and topple the "Leaning Tower" of patriarchal academia, but then privately describe her audience in a letter to Vita Sackville-West as "200 betwixt and betweens—you know how they stare and stick and wont [sic] argue. Well that's over" (*E6* 279).

Wood suggests a *rapprochement* between these two seemingly separate phases of Woolf's feminism through genetic criticism. In Wood's skillful readings, genetic criticism helps us to consider the *avant-textes* (or "pre-texts") of late modernism (2). Her focus is largely on unpublished works by Woolf such as scrapbooks and manuscript drafts, as well as letters, diaries, lectures, and other materials. These are works that are themselves always "betwixt and between" public consumption and private musings. Wood gives us a significant consideration of Woolf-in-process, an approach which complicates the hyphen between the novel-essay of *The Pargiters* to suggest that, although the political aims of *The Years* and *Three Guineas* ultimately took different forms, the writing processes between the two were inextricable.

Wood rightfully questions why there have been so few genetic readings of Woolf's manuscripts. She suggests that it is out of the fear that we might become "trapped within theoretical discussions of the documental remnants of Woolf's oeuvre and unable to debate the aesthetic and political implications of her works as a whole" (20-21). My sense is that this reluctance might also come from something closer to Woolf's own suspicion of literary holding spaces, with her very personal understanding of libraries being inaccessible spaces for even the "daughters of educated men." We have to wonder if genetic criticism—and the time for travel, often to multiple archives, that it requires—is itself a privilege fewer of us in the leaning tower can now afford.

Fortunately, books such as Wood's are instrumental in bringing this material to a wider audience. And we can see a compelling energy in genetic criticism that goes beyond pure manuscript study. As Wood suggests, genetic criticism assumes that the "*avant-textes*" of the published versions are "porous objects" which can easily absorb their "social and cultural surroundings during production in a manner that allows future generations to recapture the past through reading them…" (20). Woolf's fictional pasts are themselves notoriously allusive; most characters who attempt to pin down history in the scuttle of the present often find themselves trapped in almost prehistoric environs, as does the "batty" Lucy Swithin in *Between the Acts* (1941).

Wood's reading of *The Years* recovers this novel from perhaps an overly-assured feminist reading to suggest that the novel's subversive power exists in its popular form of the family epic. Texts such as Woolf's "research scrapbook" and her essays written for *Good Housekeeping* in 1931 are also key pieces for understanding the populist dimension of *The Years*. Especially helpful are Wood's readings of holographs from *The Pargiters* manuscripts, currently housed in the Berg Collection at the New York Public Library. Wood includes an extensive excerpt from the holographs that would become the "1907" and "1910" chapters in *The Years*. The temporal gap that we see between these two sections suggests that Woolf deliberately "directed her readers' attention to the changing experience and socio-political position of women within contemporary Britain" (58), a change which locates a generative feminist moment in the same period when Woolf famously suggested that "human nature changed."

Wood's chapter on *Three Guineas* provides a helpful consideration of Woolf's methodology in collecting research for her feminist-pacifist polemic. As Wood notes, the scrapbooks of newspaper articles that Woolf collected between 1931 and 1937 appear to not have any chronological order to them; rather, it seems that "Woolf hoarded material and then sat down to sustained periods of research" (75). The image of Woolf "hoarding" material suggests that "Woolf turned her attention out from British sexual politics to contemplate international politics long before her published writings evidenced this shift" (75). Wood also provides a glimpse into Woolf's notes for a drama entitled "The Burning of the Vote: A Comedy," the format of which suggests a "shift from a document-based to a performance-based text" when we consider it against the drafting of *Three Guineas* (84). By pairing this text with a reading of Elvira's refusal to accept the vote in the fourth notebook of *The Pargiters* (written in 1933), Wood convincingly argues that Woolf's pacifism in *Three Guineas* emerged from a long consideration of the costs, as well as the rights, of political engagement.

Wood reads Woolf's final novel as "ask[ing] what future there can be for English village life and for England as a whole in the midst of European conflict" (113). Here, I wonder how we might construct a genetic understanding of the Woolf archive that is invested in the question of process, but perhaps with a particular eye for *rupture* within historical and literary processes. Wood's genetic readings of *Between the Acts* give significant weight to the culture of anxiety fostered by an event such as the Blitz and Woolf's own grim preparation for a German invasion of Rodmell. Ultimately, though, this reading suggests that Woolf's political position remained largely unaltered under the weight of such national anxieties; *Between the Acts* provides a "tempering of her pacifist arguments," but an extended commitment to this stance, nonetheless (106). Wood suggests we see a pacifist commitment particularly through the figure of Giles Oliver, who demonstrates "how England's perceived civilized values, propagated by its patriarchal, bourgeois society, are upheld by barbarism" (129).

But perhaps what we see in the object of Giles's violence—the grotesque body of the snake choking on a toad—is a rupture within political and literary process. For life and death to become entwined—as they have in the uncanny image of the snake-toad—is a challenge to the very notion of stasis, stability and even peace; it also suggests something is awry in the organic life and history of England. Wood's genetic readings allow for Woolf as *late* modernist to occupy a position that is alive to the political investments of high modernist literature while remaining wary of art that is purely subservient to binary systems of citizenship and political collectivity.

Cailin Copan-Kelly, *University of Texas, San Antonio*

How Should One Read a Marriage?: Private Writings, Public Readings, and Leonard and Virginia Woolf. Drew Patrick Shannon. Bloomsbury Heritage Series 55. (London: Cecil Woolf, 2012) 51 pp.

Virginia Woolf: Walking in the Footsteps of Michel de Montaigne (with 8 illustrations). Judith Allen. Bloomsbury Heritage Series 63. (London: Cecil Woolf, 2012) 24 pp.

The Best of Blogging Woolf, Five Years On. Paula Maggio. Bloomsbury Heritage Series 64. (London: Cecil Woolf, 2012) 36 pp.

Virginia Woolf's Likes and Dislikes. Paula Maggio, ed. Bloomsbury Heritage Series 65. (London: Cecil Woolf, 2012) 54 pp.

Virginia Woolf and the Spanish Civil War: Texts, Contexts, and Women's Narratives. Lolly Ockerstrom. Bloomsbury Heritage Series 66. (London: Cecil Woolf, 2012) 35 pp.

Virginia Woolf as "Cubist Writer" (with 8 illustrations). Sarah Latham Phillips. Bloomsbury Heritage Series 68. (London: Cecil Woolf, 2012) 43 pp.

The primary goals of the Bloomsbury Heritage Series are twofold: a devotion to the life, works, and times of the Bloomsbury group, and a celebration of independent publishing in the spirit of Leonard and Virginia Woolf's Hogarth Press. Published by Leonard Woolf's nephew, Cecil Woolf, and under the general editorship of his wife, Jean Moorcroft Wilson, the monographs frequently and unsurprisingly demonstrate close, personal ties to the Woolfs and other members of the Bloomsbury Group; multiple volumes in this selection alone were solicited by Cecil Woolf himself. The series is self-defined as both authoritative and introductory, targeting both general readers and academics. This wide-ranging approach results in a wide range of topics, from emerging scholarship, to meditations on more obscure Bloomsbury connections, to reprintings of works by both major and minor figures tied in some way to the iconic group. As a result of the series' vast scope, it occupies a refreshing, if perplexing, niche in the sprawling fields of Woolf Studies and Bloomsburiana. But perhaps niche is the wrong word for a series that strives to be everything to everyone, at least in one volume or another. I like to think of the pamphlets as being more in the spirit of the Hogarth Essays, which enabled the publication of new work, particularly in the form of short essays by figures such as T. S. Eliot, E. M. Forster, Roger

Fry, Gertrude Stein, and Leonard and Virginia Woolf themselves. Despite this heritage, the inconsistency of the series' offerings—in genre, in length, in focus—results in a collection of volumes that is sometimes charming, often enlightening, but frequently sloppy. Yet even the proliferation of errors conveys a sense of urgency to the proceedings, as if the publishers cannot keep up with the demand for new Bloomsbury-inspired publications, or the number of new discoveries that are forever being made.[1]

The six monographs that are the subject of this review represent a range of approaches, and provide a clear example of the diversity of offerings of this series, for better or for worse. While monographs such as Lolly Ockerstrom's exemplify the more traditionally academic end of the spectrum, the majority of the volumes in this (admittedly limited) selection are more a presentation of potential topics for further exploration, frequently taking the form of a literature review. On the popular consumption end of the spectrum are two booklets by Paula Maggio taken directly from entries on the *Blogging Woolf* website (bloggingwoolf.wordpress.com), an online resource started by Maggio with the goal of "meld[ing] the personal and academic approach to Woolf, while providing a way to document her growing iconic popularity within a public forum that encourages feedback." *Blogging Woolf* is comprised of blog entries by Maggio and regular and guest contributors who maintain an exhaustive collection of news about Woolf and the Bloomsbury Group, event listings, compilations of Google "sightings" of Woolf, and details about new Woolf-related books and research. More collection than curation, this cataloguing approach makes no attempt to synthesize its findings into any kind of focused, cohesive argument.

The two volumes by Paula Maggio, *The Best of Blogging Woolf, Five Years On*, and *Virginia Woolf's Likes and Dislikes*, both derive from *Blogging Woolf*—the former comprised solely of excerpts from the website organized into four broad categories (Virginia Woolf in the Twenty-First Century, Woolf in the Real World, Woolf Reading and Woolf Writing, and Woolf as Iconic Commodity), and the latter initially begun as an attempt to use the site to crowdsource the publication. In her introduction to *The Best of Blogging Woolf* Maggio writes that "[a]ll participants need to have in common is access to the necessary technology, a willingness to

---

[1] It is hard to tell whether the frequent typographical errors are the fault of the writer, the publisher, or both, though I have noticed in my reading of more than a dozen of these monographs that there tend to be many more errors in those volumes written by amateur scholars, as opposed to those by professional academics. In addition to your run-of-the-mill typos and missing words, the most egregious error I found was probably the attribution of the copyright of No. 63 to Sarah Latham Phillips (who wrote No. 67), though it was actually written by Judith Allen. Another pamphlet had been printed with the wrong volume number, but had been corrected with a sticker.

use it, and an interest in Woolf" (6). The third requirement is a given for readers of the Bloomsbury Heritage series, and in the case of this odd compilation, Cecil Woolf seems concerned with making sure no amount of unwillingness to engage new technologies will prevent access to the "dizzying pace" of Woolf as "Internet phenomenon" (5). How else to explain the irony of printing out blog posts?[2] Much of *The Best of Blogging Woolf* has to do with attempting to organize and make sense of large quantities of data—something the non-blog-related monographs do as well, but more on that later. The task of tracking Woolf-related information on the Internet, Maggio explains, has grown daunting: equating Google hits with popularity, Maggio shares that between 2007 and 2012, "the number of hits on Woolf's name has grown exponentially, by more than fifty percent" (5). Maggio interprets the "dizzying" rise in Woolf's popularity on the Internet as a fitting expression of Woolf's "philosophy of democratic inclusiveness" (5).[3] She parses the consumption of Woolf into "interest" versus "education," "public and popular" versus "academic," and argues that her site successfully makes room for both approaches to Woolf and her work. In some ways, Maggio's focus on the democratization of Woolf studies connects to current discussions in academia about the value of and need for such phenomena as MOOCS and open access journals. Yet the presentation of blog posts in fixed form seems clunky and quaint compared to the possibilities of tagging and live updating available in the original blog format. This pamphlet was dated before it even made it to publication, which seems to undermine the goals of the original website.

Maggio's second contribution, *Virginia Woolf's Likes and Dislikes*, was begun at the behest of Cecil Woolf, who contacted Maggio in the hopes that she would be able to harness the enthusiastic readership of *Blogging Woolf* to crowdsource enough examples to fill a volume. However, when less than a handful of readers responded, Maggio conducted a key word search of the *Virginia Woolf* CD-ROM, which contains Woolf's diaries, letters, *A Passionate Apprentice*, and *A Writer's Diary*. Maggio freely admits that her method is not exhaustive, nor is it capable of "sifting out the more nuanced phrases Woolf used to express her preferences as

---

[2] In a reverse irony, in order to obtain a catalog of Bloomsbury Heritage monographs, or to place an order for one or more monographs, one must contact Cecil Woolf Publishers directly by writing, calling, or emailing (unless one happens to be lucky enough to visit Monk's House, where you can purchase select volumes in the gift shop). The Bloomsbury Heritage series has no web presence save through sites such as *Blogging Woolf*, which perhaps explains the publisher's seeking partnerships with such sites.

[3] Much like Wikipedia, Maggio's version of democratized information is presented anonymously. Though she acknowledges "loyal" contributors to her blog such as Alice Lowe, Vara Neverow, Suzanne Bellamy, and Patricia Laurence, no author information is given for any of the forty-two posts collected in this pamphlet.

well as her aversions";[4] like most contributions to the Bloomsbury Heritage series, this volume serves as a starting point, not a conclusion. As with the previous Maggio contribution, this pamphlet highlights both the limitations of manual data collection and the possibilities for the application of digital humanities work to vast amounts of data. Imagine if she had been able to write a custom program to search, collect, and collate her information—including the most subtly nuanced of phrases—instead of manually searching for literal "likes" and "dislikes." As for the likes and dislikes themselves, they are organized in a *Tender Buttons*-esque manner that emphasizes Woolf's preference for the everyday and the ordinary: People, Places, Things, and Abbreviations. Each of these categories is broken down further into a proliferation of subcategories that are often as vague as they are useful. Maggio notes Woolf's "ability to hold two opposing ideas in her mind," observing that this search uncovered both contradictions and consistencies that highlight Woolf's ability "to see beyond the surface meaning...to a transcendent reality" developed in her literary style, but the link to the literary here is weak and entirely implicit when there at all.

Woolf's deep connection to sixteenth-century essayist Michel de Montaigne is the subject of Judith Allen's *Virginia Woolf: Walking in the Footsteps of Michel de Montaigne*. Interestingly, Montaigne does not appear in Maggio's list of "likes," though Allen observes that Woolf's "veneration...is clearly evident in her diary entries, letters, reading notes, as well as her own essays and novels" (8). Allen's volume opens with a discussion of Woolf's letter to Ethel Smyth describing her overwhelming joy after the first of three visits to Montaigne's Tower in France. Woolf's delight at seeing "the very door he opened...the steps... the 3 windows; writing table, chair, view, vine, dogs, everything precisely as it was" echoes the enchanted reverence Woolfians often express when they visit Monk's House, and Allen here places Woolf's admiring mode of cultural critique in the context of the "rather intense relationship" that Woolf had with Montaigne's *Essays* (7). Supplemented with eight color photographs that illustrate Woolf's experience while visiting Montaigne's Tower and the statue of Montaigne at the Sorbonne, Allen's study reveals "the depth of [Woolf's] connection" to Montaigne, inventor of the "essay," a mode of writing which allowed Woolf to express the "inextricable connections" between her aesthetics and her politics (8). Allen traces Woolf's "exceptionally intricate narrative and rhetorical strategies" (multiple perspectives, varied voices, repetition, contradiction, equivocation) to

---

[4] Maggio searched for very literal expressions of taste, such as "like," "dislike," "love," "hate," "loathe," and despise." As she states, her compilation is about collecting existing data, not undertaking new research; she "did not look for new revelations when compiling notes for this work," instead relying on Anne Olivier Bell, Nigel Nicolson and Joanne Trautmann's notes, and Mark Hussey's reference guide, *Virginia Woolf A to Z* (5).

Montaigne, and argues that one can draw connections from other authors Woolf admired—Laurence Sterne, for example—to Montaigne. Here, Allen adds depth to Maggio's observation in *Likes and Dislikes* that Woolf held many contradictory views by arguing that such evident contradictions are an essential quality of the "essayistic" mode in its refusal of generic limitations. Allen also contends that such apparent contradictions are actually an expression of both Woolf's and Montaigne's "pervasive interest in the complex problems associated with reading and writing…and, ultimately, with the inadequacies of language" (10). In this way, Allen sees both Montaigne and Woolf as dialogians in the tradition of Bakhtin; their struggle with multiple voices in "their many acts of interpretation" is a struggle "to make language their own…; no unitary voice of certainty prevails" (12). Allen presents compelling juxtapositions of Montaigne, Bakhtin, and Woolf's ideas concerning the relationship between reader and writer, ultimately concluding that they "all share the dialogic aspect of this complicated process" (13). To support this conclusion, she offers in the second half of her study readings of a number of Woolf's essays, including her 1924 essay "Montaigne." Like Maggio, Allen cites Woolf's conviction about the inherent democracy of language, and effectively demonstrates that Woolf found in Montaigne a true literary "soul mate," both of them admiring the genre of the essay for its inherent resistance to "all attempts to constrain it" (20). Allen's volume is a "distillation" of two previously published versions of this study. Those wishing to read further on the subject can consult Allen's 2010 monograph, *Virginia Woolf and the Politics of Language*.

 If the Bloomsbury Heritage series provides a space for the collection of current, previously published Woolf scholarship, it also provides an important space for what Drew Patrick Shannon, in his study *How Should One Read a Marriage? Private Writings, Public Readings, and Leonard and Virginia Woolf*, refers to as "mainstream criticism—writing for the Woolfian 'common reader'" (7). Shannon laments the fact that Woolfian literary criticism that manages to be both "personal *and* learned, individual *and* universal" has given way to "lackluster, flat, impersonal theoretical prose," explaining that he cannot approach the subject of the Woolfs' marriage on any level except the personal. Shannon is thus the first to highlight the subjectivity of his topic (we are only capable of evaluating others' relationships through the lens of our own experience, he maintains), and his own investment in this particular relationship (he describes his imagination coming alive as he steps into Monk's House and sees the famous couple sitting beside the fire). It is clear throughout that his interpretation of this marriage is one based on "tremendous love and respect" (11). Yet his study functions as a candid and affectionate literature review that seeks above all else to let the voices of the central participants rise above the "unwieldy series of competing narratives" that have marked the evolution of representations of this famous marriage in the public consciousness. Shannon's survey of the Woolfs' marriage is structured in part after Regina Marler's *Bloomsbury Pie*, which provides a chronology of Virginia Woolf's posthumous reputation, and he examines primary sources, biographies, critical works, and select fiction in order to trace the ever-shifting public narratives about both Virginia and Leonard, while also attempting to "correct" readings of the Woolfs that have no basis in evidence. In this way, Shannon achieves the mainstream criticism he aims for—evaluating sources with a scholarly exactness while appealing to the common reader.

Shannon's eminently readable survey is both fascinating and passionate. He divides his examination into four sections: primary materials; critical (and not-so-critical) biographies; so-called "psychobiographies"; and fictional representations of Leonard and Virginia. One of his objectives is clearly to arm the "common" reader with the tools confidently to identify and reject biased accounts of the Woolfs, pointing out wherever he can that a particular author omitted clear evidence that did not fit a particular agenda. Shannon takes pains to highlight the ways in which so many of the treatments of the Woolfs' marriage are "remarkably skewed" as a result of their inattention to research (his account of the genre of "psychobiography" as it pertains to Virginia is justifiably scathing at times) (36). What emerges from Shannon's survey is that, if one is not irresponsibly selective in the use of available sources, a more positive view of the Woolfs prevails. Ultimately, Shannon succeeds in maintaining a balance between the scholarly and the mainstream, offering up his hope that "curious readers might investigate the Woolfs' marriage for themselves" (47).

Sarah Latham Phillips's *Virginia Woolf as 'Cubist Writer,'* a survey of the possible connections between Woolf's writing style and the ideas manifest in Cubism, is a less successfully authoritative introduction than Allen's or Shannon's. The problem is not that the connection she suggests is not compelling, but that she does not provide any clear or direct evidence to support her case. Phillips's essay is divided into four sections: an introduction to Cubism; two sections that connect selected Woolf novels and short stories to the artistic aims of Cubism; and a final section that examines Woolf and Cubist painters' shared interest in the ordinary. Phillips's introduction to Cubism is pitched so low that it probably will not be useful to anyone familiar with Cubism, and she neglects to fully define her terms. This results in a general overview lacking specific footholds. There are a number of descriptive terms that Phillips associates with Cubism—and thus with Woolf's "Cubist" narratives—but she relies on sheer repetition, without ever fully defining or illustrating these terms. The most frequent descriptor is "fragments," which Phillips invokes dozens of times, sometimes multiple times within a single sentence, assuming that her reader will know what Cubist "fragmentation" looks like in a given passage. Her analyses consist primarily of lengthy passages that she has labeled as "fragmented," "rhythmic," or "geometric"; the geometric shapes readily apparent in the Cubist paintings Phillips includes in her essay are less clear in the examples she offers from Woolf's writing. In a section on "The Mark on the Wall," for example, she writes that there are "slanting, geometrical angles," and "interrogational angles," but never ties these descriptive terms to the text by helping the reader locate these angles in the quoted passages. The reader is left to guess what Phillips is referring to.

Following her overview of Cubism in the first section, Phillips makes a somewhat bewildering attempt to place Woolf "in the context of Modernism," and in the second section references what she terms Woolf's "first two Modernist novels," *Jacob's Room* and *Mrs. Dalloway*, only describing modernism as a narrative style that "eludes representation" (7, 6, 13). She does not explain in any more depth her criteria for how to tell which works of Woolf's are Cubist/modernist, thus her framing argument remains vague and unhelpful. Phillips's analysis of paintings by Picasso, Braque, and Vanessa Bell is clear and well supported, but she never treats Woolf's texts with the same level of specificity, nor manages to persuasively connect the two art forms. Phillips's most compelling link between Cubism and Woolfian narrative is her explanation that *Jacob's Room* operates on a principle of negative or empty space, much as Cubism is "concerned with a different use of space on the canvas" (28). Yet this promising point is embedded within the section on Woolf and the Cubists' preference for ordinary subjects, not in the section on Woolf's prose, so it is not adequately developed. In the end, Phillips's essay is itself a collage of fragments, but this reader failed in her attempt to reconstruct them in any discernible order.

The final monograph in this selection, Lolly Ockerstrom's *Virginia Woolf and the Spanish Civil War: Texts, Contexts, and Women's Narratives*, is the most "traditional" offering in terms of scholarship, and it is also the least overtly connected to Woolf, title notwithstanding. Ockerstrom assumes a familiarity with Woolf's *Three Guineas*, and merely frames her essay with Woolf's essay, as opposed to returning repeatedly to *Three Guineas* as an obligatory focal point. This is not a failing; on the contrary, I left the essay feeling as though I could return to *Three Guineas* with a greater understanding of Woolf's project. This is the mark of an expertly executed introduction. Ockerstrom introduces the literary and historical context of *Three Guineas* located within the writing and activities of Anglo-American women in the Spanish Civil War. Like Shannon's survey, Ockerstrom's is comprised of many small pieces, and everything, from her section titles to her textual analysis, is clear, accessible, and persuasive. In her survey she: presents political and social contexts for *Three Guineas*; surveys ways in which women participated in the Spanish Civil War as combatants, nurses, and writers; separates the primary texts into a section on journalism (Josephine Herbst,

Nancy Cunard, Martha Gellhorn, Muriel Rukeyser) and a section on fiction, poetry, and activism (Sylvia Townsend Warner, Muriel Rukeyser, and Genevieve Taggard); and finishes with a section on war and memoir (Gamel Woolsey and Kate O'Brien), with sections treating each of Woolsey's and O'Brien's memoirs in greater detail. The overall effect—and a point to which Ockerstrom returns throughout—is to understand Woolf's essay as engaging with the Spanish Civil War on a more general level, as she performs "a deep and measured analysis of the causes of war" (34). There is a distance between *Three Guineas* and the actual experience of war, but Ockerstrom does not criticize this. On the contrary, she argues that Woolf's essay is enriched when read in concert with the "much wider range of writers and activists" who were deeply engaged in this *specific* war (34). Woolf's *Three Guineas* both is and is not "about" the Spanish Civil War, but placed in this context it can better provide "an important window on events and philosophy of the late 1930s," even as it is still a timely and relevant analysis of "patriarchal social systems that maintain a culture of war" (5). A tangential but essential point that underlies Ockerstrom's analysis is that most people can name male writers involved in the Spanish Civil War (W. H. Auden, John Dos Passos, T.S. Eliot, Ernest Hemingway, George Orwell) but that most of the women (noted above) are minor or forgotten figures. Ockerstrom pointedly notes that the invisibility and obscurity of most of these women "underscores Woolf's argument in *Three Guineas* that women were invisible in matters of war and policy development" (7).[5]

Ockerstrom's discussion of this array of female writers of the Spanish Civil War is not easily summarized, and that is both high praise and a recommendation that the reader experience their writing for themselves, under Ockerstrom's guidance. She points out that the works of the female authors she surveys here would have been among the accounts Woolf was reading as she was writing *Three Guineas*, and makes the related point that, though Woolf had access to visual images of the war, she chose to describe war in writing, not through the use of images, further emphasizing the importance and value of these women's written experience. She also presents some interesting finds, such as a number of examples pulled from articles in magazines such as *Women's Day* (13). In this way, the women's writing surveyed forms a "complex interweaving of the webs of war and domesticity," while "providing much-needed commentary specifically on the daily details of war in Spain" that dovetails nicely with Woolf's "important and thorough critique of the root causes of war" (33). Taken together, Shannon, Allen, and Ockerstrom's volumes exemplify the contributions of the Bloomsbury Heritage series at its best: freed from the constraints and conventions of more staid academic writing and venues, each author is empowered to introduce his or

---

[5] Nancy Cunard's war pamphlet *Authors Take Sides*, was reprinted in 2001 by Cecil Woolf.

her subject to a wide audience, and write about it with a palpable affection that is so often stripped from more theoretical approaches. This set of recent volumes from the Bloomsbury Heritage series is also, as I mentioned in my discussion of Maggio, representative of the larger project at stake here, namely accessibility. Are their offerings inconsistent? Certainly, as I and other reviewers have noted. Yet Cecil Woolf's production of a series for the "common," or "mainstream" reader contributes to current debates in the wider discipline of literary studies, and even higher education more broadly, about accessibility and the role of the digital humanities in the evolution of our discipline. In this way, the Bloomsbury Heritage series is very timely indeed.

—Sarah Terry, *Oglethorpe University*

Modernism, Feminism, and the Culture of Boredom. Allison Pease (New York: Cambridge UP, 2012) xiii + 159pp.

The Modernist Party. Ed. Kate McLoughlin (Edinburgh: Edinburgh UP, 2013) viii + 232pp.

At first glance, the topics of these two studies—parties and boredom—might seem to refer to two opposing phenomena of modern life; one usually signifies an exciting, collective event and the other often describes the dullness of solitary, everyday time. But of course, as Woolf's work reminds us and as Allison Pease discusses, people certainly get bored at parties. Such a feeling can underscore the superficiality of social interactions and the dullness of other people—or of the bored person herself, who may be so vacuous or so jaded that she is incapable of taking interest in anything. As this example suggests, considerations of boredom and the party can return us to long-standing critical conversations about the nature of the modern self and its relationship to others, and both of the volumes reviewed here address such issues extensively. In addition, these two volumes exemplify more recent, overlapping strands of modernist studies that re-examine often marginalized and feminized phenomena, including "minor" feelings (such as boredom and irritation), ephemeral pastimes (for instance, parties and social dance), as well as ideas and practices of the everyday. It is unsurprising, then, that there are chapters on Woolf in both books, as studies of Woolf and Bloomsbury have long been attuned to all of these important concerns. In that sense, these volumes attest to the continued centrality of Woolf to established and emerging topics in modernist studies.

Kate McLoughlin's edited collection, *The Modernist Party*, features essays by an excellent group of accomplished scholars—or "Guests," as McLoughlin dubs them. McLoughlin's "Introduction: A Welcome from the Host" draws upon Plato's *Symposium*, Immanuel Kant's ideal dinner party (combining "good living" and "good morals"), and Mikhail Bakhtin's theory of the carnivalesque to illuminate various facets of the party in modernism. McLoughlin suggests that the modernist corollary to Kant's ideal dinner party is a gathering that "provides inspiration, food for thought and a model for creativity" and "is often a forum for testing the relationship of the individual to other people, exploring the nature of the self and critiquing the state" (2). This model exists in tension with destructive and more chaotic alternatives, which may reflect the trauma of catastrophic loss. This tension is explored in Nathan Waddell's chapter on Ford Madox Ford's post-war depictions of pre-war festivities as well as in Jean-Michel Rabaté's essay on "The Dead" and *Finnegans Wake*, which also deftly takes up the intriguing relationship between social and political parties. Despite this nod to death and destruction, the volume maintains a spirit of fun, such as in McLoughlin's description of the table of contents as "The Menu." McLoughlin's introduction highlights the various and overlapping topics of conversation pursued in subsequent chapters, many of which connect the party to current critical discussions about the aesthetic, philosophical, or cultural dimensions of modernist literature. These topics include the party as a form of publicity (as illustrated by Alex Goody's analysis of Gertrude Stein's life and work), the party as an art work and the work of art as a party (which Bryony Randall, Morag Shiach, and David Ellison address in their chapters on Woolf, Huxley, and Proust, respectively), and the party as a realm of intersubjectivity and of ontological crisis (as discussed by McLoughlin in a chapter on "The Love Song of J. Alfred Prufrock," by Angela Smith in her analysis of a number of Katherine Mansfield's short stories, and by Margot Norris in her essay on *Women in Love*).

As this summary suggests, most of the chapters focus on a single, canonical modernist writer. This is happily not the case, however, in Joanne Winning's "'Ezra through the open door': The Parties of Natalie Barney, Adrienne Monnier and Sylvia Beach as Lesbian Modernist Cultural Production." Winning's chapter contributes to existing studies of modernist networks and spaces by analyzing the salon and the bookshop as festive sites for modernist creative work undertaken by those marginalized by their gender or sexuality. In describing the bookshop as a party space, Winning follows Monnier and Beach in de-emphasizing the role of commercial transaction in their business ventures, a move that at once opens up fresh insights about the importance of lesbian modernist space and brackets issues of class and economics (though not cultural capital). Indeed, although Winning conceives the bookstore as a party space, and other contributors discuss the labor of hosting and attending parties, the volume includes little consideration of the party as a site for paid work for those who might not otherwise be invited. A key exception is the chapter by Margo Natalie Crawford, "The Interracial Party of Modernist Primitivism and the Black 'After-Party,'" which also offers one of the volume's few engagements with racialized concepts and experiences. In one of the book's strongest chapters, Crawford brilliantly imagines the "after-party" as a site in which to perceive what she refers to as a state of "controlled abandon" in which African-American artists, individuals, and characters might inhabit and exceed or reclaim modes of seemingly primitivist joy and ecstasy (168). Crawford's essay presents an important challenge to accounts of the Harlem or "New Negro" Renaissance as defying or capitulating to (and hence as defined by) white fantasies about African Americans.

Bryony Randall's wide-ranging chapter on Woolf, entitled "Virginia Woolf's Idea of the Party," makes an intriguing conceptual move by presenting the party—and more specifically Woolf's idea of "party consciousness"—as a critical methodology. While acknowledging that Woolf's diaries, letters, and autobiographical writings often describe parties as detrimental to her work, Randall attends to Woolfian depictions of fragmented and "inconsecutive conversations" at parties to argue that "one productive way of seeing the relationship between [Woolf's] texts is as that between guests at a party" (96). Randall's model celebrates non-hierarchical interactions and heteroglossia, which offers a useful alternative to once-dominant New Critical accounts of a writer's *oeuvre* in terms of a clear aesthetic, intellectual, and even ethical trajectory. The chapter's clarity and accessibility are typical of the volume as a whole, which makes this well-coordinated volume especially useful for pedagogical purposes.

Allison Pease's slim monograph *Modernism, Feminism, and the Culture of Boredom* is also admirably accessible. It draws upon work such as Randall's *Modernism, Daily Time and Everyday Life* in its examination of the gendered nature and implications of the "cultural phenomenon" called boredom (1). Pease writes, "[b]oredom has no essential character; it functions as a stance toward, or a gauge of, not only what is valued and meaningful, but also one's access to that meaning and value at any given point in time. Boredom thus emerges as an important register of British women's experiences as they become increasingly aware of their lack of access to what is valued in their society" (3). Those values, as Pease maintains, are largely dictated by liberal individualism, and she demonstrates many of the ways that middle-class modernist women writers and feminists use boredom to negotiate and critique such values. The relationships amongst boredom, fiction, and individualism are at the heart of the book, and Pease stresses that boredom is an experience through which the subject is estranged from the defining terms of modern selfhood and of the novel: "individuality, agency, action, self-knowledge, and desire" (vii). While acknowledging that bored male characters populate modernist texts, Pease contends that middle- and upper-class women's boredom maintains particular narrative force in British modernist texts (as "impetus, antagonist, and climax" [120]) and has a distinct structure as the product of a culture which enshrined liberal individualism yet generally blocked women from succeeding fully according to individualism's terms.

Pease's introduction traces influential philosophical, political, scientific, and medical conceptions of boredom, from its ancient antecedents to its eighteenth century emergence through its divergence from more elevated and often masculinized concepts like ennui and nihilism. The subsequent chapter focuses on boredom in a group of male modernist writers whose works are not very formally experimental but who span highbrow/middlebrow/lowbrow divisions, including Arnold Bennett, H. G. Wells, D. H. Lawrence, E. M. Forster and the popular but now little-known author Robert Hichens. Pease connects these writers' relative lack of narrative innovation to their depiction of how the "public problem" of middle and upper-class women's boredom could be resolved (socially and narratively) through women's participation in sexually satisfying relationships (7). This claim sets the stage for the next two chapters, each analyzing a more experimental work by a modernist woman writer: May Sinclair's intriguing but relatively neglected novel *Mary Oliver* and Dorothy Richardson's *Pilgrimage*. Pease contends that in *Mary Oliver* Sinclair imagines that the bored woman might resist repressive social forces by, paradoxically, sublimating her own desires, a process that gives rise to discontinuous moments of "quasi-mystical ecstatic vision" that stand outside of conventional, narrative time (58). Richardson's depiction of Miriam Henderson's stream of consciousness is of course even more unconventional, and Pease persuasively argues that boredom, defined as "the frustration of meaning," is a central preoccupation, narrative technique, and impact of the novel. She shows that—as in Sinclair's and Woolf's texts—boredom is punctuated by moments of "transcendent wonder and self-connection" (Pease 99). Yet Pease argues that neither Sinclair nor Richardson imagine ways that a woman "can be an individual within the social real," nor do they grapple with "the value of the individual" in the first place (99). Pease observes, however, that such questions are addressed by *The Voyage Out*, which is the focus of her culminating chapter. That novel, in Pease's reading, depicts and deploys boredom to displace individualism as the predominant way of understanding and knowing the self and others. Rachel Vinrace's boredom thus suggests her inability to understand herself as an individual, while the novel's shifting mode of attention refuses to confirm the individual as the locus of knowledge and meaning. While Pease's assertions that Woolf and other modernist women writers confront and critique modern individualism are familiar, her sustained analysis of boredom in the novel is engaging and offers a clear if perhaps too narrow argumentative arc.

In addition to books on the everyday by Randall, Laurie Langbauer, and Liesl Olson, Pease's argument builds upon or echoes recent work in affect studies and scholarship that examines the relationship between modernity and boredom, including work by Patricia Spacks, Elizabeth Goodstein, Patrice Petro, and Sara Crangle (although, oddly, Pease does not cite Crangle's award-winning article on Woolf and boredom or her book). But whereas Goodstein stresses that boredom becomes nearly universal in modernity and argues that this is evidence of a widespread "democratization of skepticism," Pease focuses predominantly on boredom as described or experienced by middle- and upper-class women (Goodstein 10). This approach reflects Pease's interest in the form of boredom produced by women's increased access to education and limited opportunities for the sorts of social, economic, or political achievements celebrated in a capitalist, liberal individualist framework. Her discussion of Miriam Henderson's work as a dental assistant in *Pilgrimage*, for example, demonstrates that, for educated women, labor may be a further source of, rather than a solution to, boredom. This illuminating analysis of the boredom at work, however, opens up further questions about the economic and class dynamics of Pease's analysis, which she does not fully address. What is at stake in imagining boredom to be less common or less visible amongst less educated and privileged working women? Might we, for example, further investigate the implications of Woolf's depictions of working and lower class women as bored (as in the case of Florinda in *Jacob's Room*) or possibly incapable of boredom (as perhaps is the case of women such as Mrs. McNab and Mrs. Bast who undertake potentially boring tasks)? In particular, given Pease's focus on *The Voyage Out*, one might wonder what to make of the pivotal scene in which Rachel visits the native village and discovers women performing apparently monotonous and repetitive work in a place that she imagines is unchanged and unchanging. Does this scene draw attention to Rachel's inability to imagine that racialized others might experience boredom as she does, even as the episode makes her feel "very cold and melancholy" (*VO* 269)? Or might we read this as the novel's failure to do so? Either way, this failure (or attempt) suggests further dimensions or limitations to what Pease argues is the novel's challenge to individualism and its efforts to imagine other forms of being and knowing.

As with *The Modernist Party*, Pease's study would be even richer if it engaged more extensively with issues of race, class, empire, and economics. This is especially true if we are to heed Pease's call in her "Conclusion" to return to questions about how women's writing responds to patriarchy while incorporating newer critical concerns. Pease acknowledges an "anxiety in feminist criticism" about continuing to interpret women's writing "as simply a response to patriarchy," but insists that, however outdated such a reading might seem, "modernist women's narratives of women's boredom *do* revolt against the authority of tradition, they *do* register a very real 'sex war' that was occurring during the years they were written, and they *do* acknowledge woman's erasure, absence, and dispossession" (121-122). Pease's book convincingly demonstrates these assertions. But while Pease draws upon some recent work in affect studies, the long legacies of intersectional analyses or of postcolonial theory within feminist criticism, and in particular their impact on feminist conceptions of the self, are not readily apparent, despite Pease's focus on British women's identity formation. Though clear, Pease's argument about women and boredom would be even more powerful and persuasive if she pursued further the important question that she poses at the beginning of her study: "whose boredom and whose modernism?" (1). In taking up this question, Pease reminds us how much feminist theory still has to teach us about modernism.

—Elizabeth M. Sheehan, *Oregon State University*

Works Cited

Crangle, Sara. *Prosaic Desires: Modernist Knowledge, Boredom, Laughter, and Anticipation*. Edinburgh: Edinburgh UP, 2010.

——"The Time Being: On Woolf and Boredom." *Modern Fiction Studies* 54.2 (Summer 2008): 209-232.

Goodstein, Elizabeth. *Experience Without Qualities: Boredom and Modernity*. Stanford: Stanford UP, 2005.

Langbauer, Laurie. *Novels of Everyday Life: The Series in English Fiction 1850-1930*. Ithaca: Cornell UP, 1999.

Olson, Liesl. *Modernism and the Ordinary*. Oxford: Oxford UP, 2009.

Petro, Patrice. *Aftershocks of the New: Feminism and Film History*. New Brunswick: Rutgers UP, 2002.

Randall, Bryony. *Modernism, Daily Time and Everyday Life*. Cambridge: Cambridge UP, 2007.

Spacks, Patricia Meyer. *Boredom: The Literary History of a State of Mind*. Chicago: U of Chicago P, 1995.

Woolf, Virginia. *The Voyage Out*. 1915. London: Penguin, 1992.

Communal Modernisms: Teaching Twentieth-Century Literature and Culture in the Twenty-First-Century Classroom. Emily M. Hinnov, Laurel Harris, and Lauren Rosenblum, eds. (New York: Palgrave Macmillan, 2013) 216pp.

Communal Modernisms offers generative discussions of modernist women writers' texts, and the assignments and courses one can design around them. The contributors to this volume provide rich readings of work by authors such as Jessie Redmon Fauset, Djuna Barnes, Sylvia Townsend Warner, and Virginia Woolf, and suggest how to best bring the texts to life in the classroom. In the editors' introduction, Emily M. Hinnov, Laurel Harris, and Lauren Rosenblum invoke the history pageant in Woolf's final novel, *Between the Acts*, which, the editors posit, offers an alternative (multivocal, participatory) historiographic model. In addition, they write that for Woolf, like Walter Benjamin, "the seemingly small, vibrantly lived, personal moments are actually what make up the larger (antifascist) narrative of human history" (2). These concepts of history inform their use of the term "communal modernisms," which—in contrast to "Monolithic Masculine Modernism"—incorporates a range of other writers, media, and aesthetic forms to contextualize the creation of modernist texts (3). Several of the chapters suggest pairing literature with works from other media, like photography, films, periodicals, advertisements, and painting.

Every chapter ends with a section devoted to a lesson plan. Each author approached this section differently, and the variety provokes creativity on the part of the reader. Some authors outline assignments; others provide discussion topics; others write out a script of questions, assignments, or classroom activities. The lesson plans range from formally organized plans with learning objectives, assessment, and sample assignments, to a narrative reflection on teaching the text. A few of the chapters engage with digital pedagogy to foster collaboration and community among students. In "Visual Pleasure and the Female Gaze: 'Inter-Active' Cinema in the Film Writing of HD and Dorothy Richardson," Laurel Harris describes how students create a cinematic critical community as they share reviews on a course blog. Emily Wojcik's "Editing *Children of the Sun*: Jesse Redmon Fauset, Little Magazines, and the Cultivation of the New Negro" similarly describes possible assignments involving a periodical studies-inspired course blog or Facebook page. Many of the contributors note the availability of relevant archival materials online, including through the Modernist Journals Project, the Library of Congress, and YouTube.

The chapters in the first section focus on points of contact between literary texts and film, photography, and advertisements. Emily M. Hinnov's chapter pairs *To the Lighthouse* with Gertrude Käsebier's photography, linking them through the rubric of maternal longing. Illustrated with photographs by Käsebier and images from Leslie Stephen's album, including photos by Henry H. Cameron of Julia Stephen with Virginia, and Gabriel Loppé of Julia Stephen, Hinnov outlines her strategies for introducing undergraduates to modernist visual culture. She contextualizes the images and literature with the Victorian trope of the "Angel of the House," Barthes's *Camera Lucida*, and feminist theories of the visual. Laurel Harris contributes a chapter that compares the film criticism of H. D. and Dorothy Richardson in the magazine *Close Up*. When teaching H. D. and Richardson's early twentieth century visual criticism, Harris asks her undergraduates to compare their theories to those of 1970s feminist film critics. Harris notes, "H. D.'s and Richardson's writings on film simultaneously complicate and corroborate Laura Mulvey's argument about the 'male gaze'" (45). Lauren M. Rosenblum's chapter reads Nella Larsen's *Quicksand* (1928) in conversation with magazine culture of the era. Rosenblum highlights advertisements in *The Messenger*, *Harper's Bazaar*, *Vogue*, and *The Crisis*, and links the commodity culture promoted in mass media to Larsen's presentation of Helga's subjectivity through the objects that she owns and wears. These chapters provide specific examples of photographs, films, and magazines that instructors can bring to the classroom to enhance our teaching of modernism.

The second section of *Communal Modernisms* focuses on politics, and like the previous chapters, links modernist literature with photography, magazine culture, and advertisements. Kristen Bartholomew Ortega reevaluates Lola Ridge's 1918 long poem *The Ghetto*, commonly characterized as "political poetry," as a modernist long poem. Ortega leads her students to interrogate the definitions of "realist" and "modernist," bringing Ridge's poem into conversation with Jacob Riis's tenement photos. Wojcik writes on Fauset's role in shaping black literary culture as the literary editor of *The Crisis* and the children's magazine *The Brownies' Book*. The chapter highlights poems by Fauset, Georgia Douglas, and James Weldon Johnson, and focuses on several contributions from Langston Hughes as precursors to his more mature work. In keeping with the theme of "communal modernisms," she writes, "Helping [students] to see a poet like Hughes in the context of magazine culture establishes a deeper understanding of the ways that popular culture influences high culture and, ultimately, history" (89). Judy Suh's "Jean Rhys's *Voyage in the Dark*: Community, Race, and Empire" describes her approach to teaching the novel's form. Suh also points out the descriptions of the advertisements that hang in Anna's rented room, and the historical connections between British imperialism and advertising aesthetics, which resonates with Rosenblum's reading of *Quicksand* in the first section. The connections across chapters begin to suggest themes around which one could organize a syllabus or a section of a course.

The authors in the final section, "Reinvention within Communal Modernisms," more explicitly suggest grouping literary texts around particular themes, literary concepts, and genres. Robin Hackett's chapter pairs *The Pargiters* with Eve Kosofsky Sedgwick's *Dialogue on Love*, noting that this pairing could fit into a course on the writing process, women writers, feminist theory, or traditions of women's writing. At the end of the chapter, Hackett suggests fourteen thematic groupings of work by Woolf and other authors, including *Three Guineas* (1929) and Tsitsi Dangarembga's *Nervous Conditions* (1988) to discuss links between imperialism and patriarchy, war, and motherhood; and *The Waves* (1931) and Mulk Raj Anand's *Coolie* (1936) to discuss gender and empire, the position of white women in the British Empire, and social stratification (186-187). Rita Kondrith's chapter suggests teaching Sylvia Townsend Warner's epic poem *Opus 7* (1931) with texts by Rebecca West, Katherine Mansfield, and Woolf that depict "the traumatized female non-combatant" from World War I (113). Noreen O'Connor suggests teaching the utopian modernism of Warner's *Lolly Willowes, or The Loving Huntsman* (1926) after "more 'traditional' and 'alienated experimental modernist narratives such as *Nightwood*, *Mrs. Dalloway*, and *Voyage in the Dark*," to recognize the generic particularity of Warner's novel (142). Vicki Tromanhauser argues that the presence of animals in Elizabeth Bowen's *The Last September* (1929) is "irrepressibly visible, so firmly connected in the cultural imagination is Ireland with the animal" (150). She suggests teaching the novel alongside Charles Darwin's *The Descent of Man*, Dix Harwood's *Love For Animals and How it Developed in Great Britain*, *Punch* cartoons, and Jonathan Swift's "A Modest Proposal." When Bonnie Roos teaches Djuna Barnes's *Nightwood*, she similarly assembles a range of contextual material, including Henri Rousseau's painting *The Dream* [Le rêve], historical information about U.S. involvement in the League of Nations, and the first three books of Genesis in the Bible, in order to position her students as detectives who must identify clues about what the novel says about its historical moment. Roos provides examples of the discussion and writing prompts that guide her students to interpret the text with knowledge of its cultural allusions and historical context, empowering her students to investigate difficult texts. She reflects, "My goal is limited to helping them recognize that modernist texts are a puzzle, to give them tools to recognize the clues when they see them, to model methods of thinking about the works, and to encourage them to be responsible for seeking out the answers for themselves" (170).

The editors position *Communal Modernisms* as an "answer to Woolf's call for a more ethical version of higher education" (7). The collection neither advocates the "Rags. Petrol. Matches" approach to transforming educational institutions that Woolf's narrator puts forth in *Three Guineas*, nor does it dwell on the feminist and social justice problems around higher education's increasing reliance on contingent labor and student debt in the twenty-first century classroom. Nonetheless, *Communal Modernisms* promotes pedagogy that empowers students to read modernist culture as well as their own. As the editors put it, they depart from the idea of students as "customers" buying training for the "real world" (7). Jane Marcus's afterword connects our ethical positions as teachers to a much larger field of surveillance and war culture.

Marcus writes, "One way to heal the wounds we sustain from living and teaching in a war culture is to build a peace culture in our profession and in our universities, starting with our classrooms" (189). She cites Nancy Cunard's long poem *Parallax* (1925), which poses the question, "contemporaries, what have you done?" and turns the question to us (qtd. 198). This query is an apt ending to a book on what we do in our classrooms. Many of the chapters describe practices that aim to help students to connect modernist women's projects with the political concerns of our own day. The concept of communal modernism offers a way not only to present women modernist writers in conversation with mass culture, history, and each other, but also to rethink our classrooms as collective spaces in which students practice skills of critical analysis and cooperation. The volume is a valuable contribution for instructors committed to teaching modernist women writers, as well as those looking for inspiration as they design a new course, revise a syllabus, write an assignment, or reflect on their pedagogical goals in the classroom.

—Anne Donlon, *The Graduate Center, City University of New York*

Virginia Woolf and the Natural World: Selected Papers from the Twentieth Annual International Conference on Virginia Woolf. Ed. Kristin Czarnecki and Carrie Rohman (Clemson: Clemson U Digital P, 2011) xii + 246.

From the rhythm of the waves at the St. Ives of her childhood to *Mrs. Dalloway*'s "voice of an ancient spring spouting from the earth" near Regent's Park Tube to the horrors of *Between the Act*'s toad-choked snake, Woolf's works continually harvest structure, setting, and metaphor from the natural world, which in turn has provided fertile pickings for Woolf scholars. Building upon research by Gillian Beer, Jane Goldman, Julia Briggs, Emily Dalgarno, James Naremore, and many others, this volume of selected papers from the 2010 Woolf conference is a valuable cross-section of such scholarship: it ranges from macrocosmic explorations of time, the primordial, the post-human, determinism and the natural order, pastoralism, ecofeminism, and natural violence, to smaller expeditions into botany, the body, weather, distinct topographies and terrains, specific species, and outdoor activities such as walking and swimming.

Editors Kristin Czarnecki and Carrie Rohman have successfully corralled these varied topics into loose order, and the keynote essays by Bonnie Kime Scott, Diana Swanson, and Elisa Kay Sparks all provide ample insights. Scott's opening essay traverses much ground, providing a laudably concise survey of the past three or so decades of scholarship on Woolf and the natural world, as well as a critical exploration of various ecofeminist readings of Woolf and her own incisive analyses of the introspective practice of sea-gazing, the rapid-fire poetics of natural experience, and broader motifs including the overarching quest for unity (Scott's assessment—"that the cosmic order [...] just as often seems to offer cosmic indifference, not consolation"—resonates clearly).

Meanwhile, Swanson's keynote serves as an ecocritical and ecofeminist rallying cry, demanding a less hubristic appreciation of humankind's place in the wider natural world and positioning Woolf as an advocate for non-androcentric and non-anthropocentric worldviews. Beginning with a striking and productive comparison between Woolf's and Ursula LeGuin's theories of women and writing, Swanson argues that Woolf's non-androcentric worldviews are inherently less concerned with ownership, dominance, and individual ego. Her paper is of most value and originality, however, when it moves away from non-male perspectives into non-human ones: Swanson beautifully analyzes and celebrates Woolf's attempts to write from the perspective of the non-human organisms with whom we share a planet.

Multiple formats are housed within this volume, including a number of useful compendia and encyclopedias such as Elisa Kay Sparks's fascinating compilation of Woolf's botanical references. Beginning with Woolf's early horticultural heritage, Sparks describes Woolf's lifelong horticultural influences (chiefly Leslie Stephen, Violet Dickinson, and, of course, Vita Sackville-West), and then collects and analyzes Woolf's botanical references work-by-work. Sparks could have dwelled for a bit longer, perhaps, on Sackville-West's impact, and it was cruel to tease readers with a suggestion that further work could be done on Woolf's use of vegetables as comic relief from the earnestness of flowers, but overall Sparks concisely demonstrates the centrality of botanical images within Woolf's work and provides a useful introduction to the handful of other essays that explore Woolf's horticultural side. She also neatly explicates flowers' triple function as "literal natural organisms, as artificial renderings of the natural, and as figurative strategies"—perhaps a useful summation of all living organisms referenced by Woolf.

An equine encyclopedia yields similar insights: in "Taking Her Fences," Beth Rigel Daugherty presents a largely uninterpreted compendium of Woolf's horse references which make for surprisingly engrossing reading. After Daugherty introduces Woolf's repeated use of "taking her fences" as a steeplechase metaphor for the labors and course of writing, she leaves us to gallop on our own through a diverse field of equine references. Woolf's horses function variously as historical markers; as metaphors for organicism, for outdated pastoralisms, for patriarchy, or, especially if wild, for social freedoms and unfettered adventurousness; and as indications of Woolf's gentility and country lifestyle—she was a regular spectator at the local races and shows a connoisseur's eye for equine beauty and sport.

Daugherty is honest about the limitations of her list: it is a curated, incomplete selection, and she has exempted the essays, as well as any terms beyond "horse" and "pony," from her search. Had the search been more expansive, Daugherty would have found other references which round out and complicate the portrait— for instance, in a 1941 letter to Ethel Smyth, Woolf writes that the city is "my only patriotism: save one vision in Warwickshire one spring when we were driving back from Ireland and I saw a stallion being led, under the may and the beeches, along a grass ride; and I thought that is England" (*L6* 460)

Whereas some contributors address flora and fauna, others tackle natural phenomena. Verita Sriratana interprets Woolf's references to weather in *The Years* as both deliberate means of transitioning the narrative smoothly between eras, and as boasting "transformative power and impact on place" more broadly. Sriratana's concept of weather-as-transition-device is engaging but the examples given seem tenuous. The essay also occasionally confuses weather with climate and season, and suggests that weather's uncertainty and "paradox" exacerbated Woolf's frustration with *The Years*' composition, which seems unlikely given that, at least in text, weather is fixed. However, Sriratana's research holds much promise: the function of weather (and of climate and season) in Woolf's novels certainly will sustain further investigations, particularly because Woolf's meteorological descriptions not only establish place, mood, and narrative structure, but also often deflate situational expectations and rhetoric, instead playing up absurdity, futility, and fragmentation. (For example, Woolf's diary entry of 6 September 1939 laments war's creative suffocation and thuggery and then ends with an ironic comment about perfect summer weather [*D5* 235].)

As with many conferences and their resulting compendia, there are a few essays in this book which bear little relation to its overarching theme. The editors have inserted these as bookends: Cecil Woolf's charming memoir about his aunt and uncle opens the collection, and two papers about Leonard Woolf close it. Cecil Woolf's essay—set largely in rural landscapes but not dwelling upon them—provides a warm descriptive reminder of the Woolfs' busy, everyday lives, as well as a caution to anyone to eager to paint Virginia Woolf as dominated by her depression: he speaks of her humor and liveliness, and reminds us that the coroner assessed her death not as a culmination of decades of illness but as a topical response to the "general beastliness" of war. In general, this essay's inclusion is a constructive reminder not only that there are personal unknowns about Woolf which will always remain thus, but also that there are quotidian aspects of her life that scholarship can and perhaps should leave alone.

Conversely, scholarship is less developed around Leonard Woolf, a fact which this volume acknowledges and briefly mitigates. Wayne Chapman productively demonstrates the utility of Clemson University's digital resources in his essay linking Leonard Woolf, Yeats, and Oswald Spengler. And Luke Reader's paper about Leonard Woolf's radio pedagogy of the 1930s and 1940s is a lucid summary of Leonard Woolf's efforts to broaden the BBC's programming in order to create a better informed public and thereby strengthen Britain's—and the empire's—democratic capacity to self-govern. While Reader's essay does not greatly expand the boundaries of Leonard Woolf scholarship, it is useful to scholars of Virginia who may not be familiar with this aspect of Leonard's output. It could, however, have better situated Leonard within wider conversations about social reforms, public education, and the democratizing potential of radio technology (no mention was made of Orwell, the Third Programme, the respective educational mandates of BBC Directors-General Reith and Haley, and other relevant topics such as Mass Observation and the Beveridge reforms). Reader's paper also discusses facets of Leonard's intellectual stance that could fruitfully be linked back to Virginia—for example, the kind of shuttered, safe cultural consolidation which Leonard argues the BBC is practicing is satirized throughout *Between the Acts*—and, with more effort, to the collection's natural themes. There are, after all, intersections between Leonard's visions of a more democratic post-war Britain; Virginia's wartime jabs at a brave, new, technologically-enhanced future ("Each flat with its refrigerator, in the crannied wall. [...] all liberated; made whole..." [*BTA* 213]); and Virginia's evocations of primordial and post-human futures.

There are many other contributions to this volume which deserve (and cannot here receive) extensive comment and commendation. Vara Neverow elegantly explores motifs of horses and foxes in *Jacob's Room*; Diane Gillespie draws a fascinating link between Virginia Woolf and ornithologist W. H. Hudson; and Jane Goldman speculates intriguingly about canine sources for *A Room of One's Own*, chiefly drawing upon Albrecht Dürer and James Thomson. Alice Lowe provides a delectable taster of food and dining in Woolf's work; Rebecca McNeer examines swimming and diving as metaphors for writing; Jane

Lilienfeld's intelligent pairing of *Mrs. Dalloway* with Willa Cather's *One of Ours*, and Rachel Zlatkin's eloquent discussion of the natural world, citizenship, and post-war disillusionment in *Mrs. Dalloway*, both interrogate the use of natural and pastoral conceits as the foundation for patriotism. Other scholars delve into *Flush*, geological time and narrative structure, aging, "Lappin and Lapinova," Woolf as would-be mountaineer, and many similarly engaging interrogations of Woolf's natural world.

Despite this breadth of material, *Virginia Woolf and the Natural World* is still far from comprehensive. Nevertheless, it represents a worthwhile addition to an already well-established category of Woolf scholarship, ultimately providing an intelligent, diverse, and often delightful expedition into Woolf's gardens, wastelands, and wildernesses.

—Kris Anderson, *Independent Scholar*

Charleston Bulletin Supplements. Virginia Woolf and Quentin Bell. Edited and with an introduction by Claudia Olk (London: The British Library, 2013) ix + 134 pp.

British Library publications opt for sobriety. Confronted with the rollicking humor which Virginia Woolf and Quentin Bell packed into the *Charleston Bulletin Supplements*, they almost lost their nerve. But not quite. They found a designer prepared to produce the neat, background wallpaper for the dust-jacket to tame the vigorous crudities in the drawing and design by Quentin Bell shown on the front and back. And, perversely, they chose for the format of the book, a size and shape which bears no relation to the actual Supplements. This means that full page reproductions are merely a quarter their actual size, and are bordered with too much white. The result is nevertheless an exquisite production, wholly at odds with its content, for most of the stories here recounted take place at Charleston, aptly described by David Bradshaw in the preface, as "a slapstick realm of hilarious upheavals, sudden explosions, zany mishaps, and paint-bespattered foggy-mindedness." John Betjeman would have praised Charleston for its absence of "ghastly good taste."

The Charleston Bulletin was an in-house newspaper, founded in the summer 1923 when the fifteen-year-old Julian Bell, together with his brother Quentin, two years his junior, decided to entertain the residents with a daily record of the goings-on at Charleston. It was typed before breakfast, with abundant typos, and ornamented with drawings by Quentin. As Charleston was then chiefly a holiday home, the newspaper continued fitfully, until 1927, by which time this rag was mostly written as well as illustrated by Quentin. In addition he had become aware that the *New Statesman and Nation*, of which his uncle Leonard Woolf was then literary editor, gained prestige and popularity by bringing out occasional supplements on a particular topic. In the spirit of rivalry, Quentin decided to do the same and the first one, detailing the mishaps and absurdities that had punctuated his mother Vanessa Bell's life, was both written and illustrated by him.

Thereafter, needing assistance, he turned to his Aunt Virginia. She was said to know a thing or two about writing, Quentin recollected, though at the time he was largely unaware of this as he had tried, but failed, to read to the end of her short story *Kew Gardens*. However, from then on each Supplement was the product of collaboration, as he and Virginia sparked off each other, and the wit, irony and fanciful exaggeration of each issue became more potent. Claudia Olk, who deftly introduces these Supplements, raises the issue as to whether the written account or the picture came first. The answer, in most cases, is surely that the drawing came first, for it has a centrality on the page, leaving the text to squeeze into the margins and sometimes duck the overspill of the illustration. A more interesting question is whether or not any of the drawings are by Virginia. She certainly drew when young, for some of her early drawings were retained by Violet Dickinson and bound by her into the two volumes she had made of typed copies of Virginia's early letters. Later, in 1915, in the middle of one of her most severe breakdowns, Woolf scribbled drawings on page after page in a book of Frances Cornford's poems. This question regarding the authorship of the drawings is, however, impossible to answer from this British Library publication alone, as it only includes selected pages from these Supplements, and in too many places offers the reader merely a typescript of Virginia Woolf's words.

An instance of this occurs in "The Life and Death of a Studio." Olk dates this "[1924?]" but it relates to the decision in 1925 to fill in a courtyard at Charleston with a large new studio, based on plans drawn up by Roger Fry. In August that year workmen descended on Charleston, demolished an old studio and created a great deal of rubble, much of which went into the making of garden paths. All this work stimulated Quentin Bell's draftsmanship to new heights. But this gem of a narrative is broken up and made incomplete by the publisher's decision not to illustrate four of its pages. Any reader who enjoys the medium of comics will recognize how frustrating this is.

Yet there are plentiful treasures inside this book, making it not only a delightful object to acquire as a gift for others, but also an essential publication for the shelves of Bloomsbury scholars. It is fascinating to discover how much familiar history is triggered in the reader's memory by such compact scenes as, say, the Thurber-like drawing of a dinner party at 46 Gordon Square. My favorite is the busy illustration titled "Arrival at 46 Gordon Square" which appears in "The Messiah," a narrative based on the life of Clive Bell. It details the mass of objects he brought with him, after his marriage to Vanessa Stephen: among other things, cases of wine, piles of pictures, a bicycle, guns, as well as carts and vans, one piled high with books, all filling the road outside the house. "This is a bald and timid statement," writes Woolf in her accompanying text, "of what actually occurred when the newly married arrived at their house. Vans, crates, wagons lorries, cabs, hansom & growler, balloons, captive and escaped, motors, hired and borrowed, sacks, peddlars [sic], packing cases, Pickfords, Carter Pattersons, perambulators – in short anything on wheels or trotters bowled up to 46 & deposited, heaped, piled, stacked in short dumped down & piled up what was the material foundation of years upon years of miscellaneous family bliss. The door was burst open by the impact of a cast of the Venus de Milo: which disclosed an old woman, & a serried file of the familiar Beetle, commonly, but erroneously styled, Black."

—Frances Spalding, *Newcastle University*

Haptic Modernism: Touch and the Tactile in Modernist Writing. Abbie Garrington (Edinburgh: Edinburgh UP, 2013) viii + 208pp.

Abbie Garrington's thorough study of touch and the tactile in modernist texts, particularly in reference to the human hand, offers close readings of "the haptic" in four major modernist figures—James Joyce, Virginia Woolf, Dorothy Richardson, and D. H. Lawrence. Her introduction, which analyzes Sinclair Lewis's *Babbitt* in intense detail, will quickly dispel any doubts that modernist authors showed "an unprecedented level of interest in what we can more colloquially call simply 'touch and the tactile'" (17).

Garrington sees the modernist literary era as "a kind of 'hinge point' in the multi-stranded history of the haptic," a moment when eighteenth- and nineteenth-century theories of perception converged and pointed toward "the role of touch for the perceiving subject" in the next centuries (17). As Garrington shows, scientific and technological transformations—such as X-ray technology, the automobile, and cinema—that also transformed perceptions of touch, kinaesthesis, and proprioception "(the body's sense of its orientation in space)," influenced modernists as diverse as George Bernard Shaw and Aldous Huxley (16). These new technologies developed in conjunction with an interest in philosophies "concerned with the connection between human sense perception and aesthetics" (22). Even World War I, a persistent marker of the modernist turn, is relevant to the haptic in "the impact of trench warfare on the tactile responses of participants" (34). Less well-known historical events include the upper-class fad for X-raying hands in late nineteenth-century New York so that women could "compete with one another regarding the delicacy of their structure" (96). Garrington's study of the tactile also considers turn-of-the-century understandings of mental illness, particularly schizophrenia, which often manifests in "cutaneous hallucinations such as formication or crawling skin" (25).

Indeed, *Haptic Modernism*'s reach is impressive. Firmly grounded in modernism, Garrington nonetheless creates a genealogy of the tactile in literature as she gathers haptic references in Ovid, the New Testament (Doubting Thomas's insistence on touching Jesus to verify His resurrection), Shakespeare, and Bram Stoker. Garrington even admits to the potential for losing focus with such a wide embrace: "Trouble comes from the capaciousness of the project—as a book about everything, can we be sure that we are tackling a book about touch?" (49). But part of the pleasure in reading Garrington's analysis is seeing how far the haptic pervades the work of Joyce, Woolf, and Lawrence, among others. And, indeed, by the end of her study, it seems that hands and touching are as central to literary modernism as its classic demarcations of World War I, Freudian psychology, and technologies of transportation.

In reading *Haptic Modernism*, Woolf scholars will find themselves more attuned to her pervasive focus on touch. Interestingly, the chapter devoted to "Virginia Woolf, Hapticity and the Human Hand," examines *The Years* (1937), which Garrington aptly calls "a bridesmaid of a book, rarely the centre of attention in a critical assessment of Woolf's work" (119). The chapter opens with a discussion of Woolf's brief dabble in palmistry in 1935 at Aldous Huxley's house where Dr. Charlotte Wolff analyzed Woolf's palm. In her treatise, *Studies in Hand-Reading* (1936), Wolff wrote, "Virginia Woolf's rectangular palm is divided into two by the Head-line which runs right across the hand and ends in a fork. It is the Head-line of a philosopher" (qtd. in Garrington 115). Unsurprisingly, according to a letter by Woolf, Leonard Woolf thought hand-reading was "humbug" (qtd. in Garrington 118). Woolf herself was skeptical, but nonetheless fascinated enough that, as Garrington notes, the subject "occupies her mind and her work at this time," especially *The Years* (119).

Woolf's preoccupation with hands as interpretable texts does more than merely influence her writing of *The Years*, according to Garrington. She argues for the centrality of the haptic in *The Years* alongside the novel's concern with the passage of time:

> *The Years* is a peculiarly gestural novel; one which chooses repeatedly to alight upon the use of the hands—and ongoing registration of manual action well beyond a simple reading of the manners and the manicures of the day. Woolf is engaged throughout her writing with the flow of time and its fraying effects upon personhood and identity. Through meeting Wolff under the lamp, she found a means of illustrating those concerns via the mobilisation of the human hand, as a place where history and heredity are ingrained in skin inscriptions, and as an organ that is superseded in its attempts to know and to control by time's ceaseless flow. (119)

Garrington notes in *The Years* a preoccupation with how the body registers and records movement and time, particularly in experiencing new technologies of travel, such as the motorcar: "The rhythmic representation of travel, and the multiple 'I,' are often found when Woolf tackles the transport experience" (121). Since the body records its experience of the world, it also becomes a readable text, most notably, through gesture, and thus "*The Years* may be read in part as an attempt to find a language for the daily drama of the body" (124). In this way, while *The Years* "appears at first a retrogressive move" by an author who has primarily been celebrated as a stylistic innovator, Garrington argues that Woolf's seemingly conventional novel is shaped "at the deepest level" by the Wolffian "science" of hand-reading (123, 126). Garrington argues that "it is through the hand that we as readers are, despite our position on the outside of characters' mental spheres, given an insight into their thoughts and personalities. Further, such manual evidence is made use of by other characters; everyone is at the hand-reading game" (126).

Reading for the tactile in modernism opens up investigations into "understanding the touch-transforming social and historical contexts out of which those writings emerge" (50). The intersection of science and gender ideologies of the era, the transformation of "the human understanding of what is and is not available to the touch," thus become a revealing backdrop for *Haptic Modernism*'s reading of the skin border in Joyce's *Ulysses* (97). Titled "James Joyce's Epidermic Adventures," Garrington's chapter on Joyce opens with a discussion of masturbation, most notably in the "Nausicaa" episode of *Ulysses*, and links manual pleasures in Joyce to "the caressing gaze of the viewer" of sculpture (76). X-rays also find reference in Joyce: "Ideas of exposure haunt the newspaper reports of Röntgen's efforts, seguing into Bloomian fantasies of stripped outfits, flayed or burst skin and crumbled flesh" (95). It can sometimes be difficult to follow the associative links that Garrington makes (Stephen's name "Dedalus" connects to ancient Greece, which "leads us back once more in the direction of sculpture, the hand-crafted replication of human form, and thence to the look which contains the imagined grasp" [76]), but otherwise Garrington persuasively supports her readings with close textual analysis and extra-textual evidence, such as letters and diaries.

A very brief chapter (only 12 pages, compared to 41 pages on Joyce) on Dorothy Richardson focuses on "her prescient phenomenology of film spectatorship" (142). Woolf gets mention here, too, for her "concept of the licking eye" in her 1926 essay "The Cinema" (144). A slightly longer chapter on Lawrence looks closely at his novel *St. Mawr* (1925) and his short story "The Blind Man" (1922) to "consider the way in which Lawrence mobilises touch to argue for the place and potency of the knowing hand in what he reads as a predominantly visual culture" (156). The closing chapter, "Horrible Haptics," tantalizingly skims a compendium of the proto-horror texts that span the modernist era, such as Wilkie Collins's *Poor Miss Finch* (1875), Bram Stoker's *The Jewel of Seven Stars* (1904), and Maurice Renard's *The Hands of Orlac* (1920), all of which feature severed or mangled hands. It's not exactly clear what we are to make of hands that take on lives of their own as a concluding gesture, so to speak, of *Haptic Modernism*, but the notion that the part of the body most associated with touch might gain autonomy apart from the self that usually controls it produces "an unnerving sense of both body and agency gone awry" (173).

In its wide reach and detailed analysis, Garrington's *Haptic Modernism* is impressive and certainly deepens our understanding of modernist literature's preoccupation with the constituting qualities of perception. Garrington not only makes an important contribution to studies of phenomenology and the body but also to their intersection with modernism.

—Justine Dymond, *Springfield College*

The Boundaries of the Literary Archive: Reclamation and Representation. Ed. Carrie Smith and Lisa Stead (Burlington: Ashgate, 2013) xi + 210pp.

As its title suggests, Carrie Smith and Lisa Stead's expansive collection defines and questions the contours of the "literary archive." In her introduction, Stead cites Paul Voss and Marta Werner's understanding of "the archive" as "both a physical site—an institutional site—a conceptual space whose boundaries are forever changing" (2). As readers turn the pages of Virginia Woolf's *To the*

Lighthouse notebook using *Woolf Online*, for instance, they might imagine viewing the original artifact in the reading room or Woolf herself holding the notebook, collecting her thoughts as she envisions Lily Briscoe before her painting. As more archival materials become digitally available, *The Boundaries of the Literary Archive* provides an indispensable resource, responding to and complicating what the introduction refers to as the "spate of current works [that] testify to the increasing interest in the archive-as-subject into the 2000s" (1). Reflecting the perspectives of scholars and archivists, this volume inspires readers to return to primary sources, invigorating their research and teaching with new questions and materials.

The volume's first section, "Theorizing the Archive," examines the complex relationship of material artifacts to creativity. Taking William Wordsworth's *Prelude* as a case study, Wim Van Mierlo observes in "The Archaeology of the Manuscript: Towards a Modern Palaeography" that "[r]ecognizing the disjointed nature of the manuscript gives us a better sense of the mind in creation" (26). He concludes that pursuing archival research, scholars need to "come to terms with the manuscripts' inner logic, how they function within their creative process, and how they reflect and contribute to the manuscript culture of their time" (27). While critics have a tendency to cite writers' reading to confirm their own suspicions, Iain Bailey wants critics to address Samuel Beckett's "reading notes" in a fashion "where the whole function of the manuscripts is not so much to shoulder a burden of proof about intertextuality or influence, but to show composition as work in progress" (31, 32). In order to do so, there should be a more rigorous interpretation of "the intersections between *exogenesis*, a subcategory of genetic criticism with a methodological focus on compositional processes, and *intertextuality*, a term which covers a dense set of theoretical propositions concerning the relationships between texts" (32). In "Original Order, Added Value? Archival Theory and the Douglas Coupland Fonds," Jennifer Douglas addresses the inherent complications in the attempt to preserve and study materials as authors have left them. There are various ways of approaching an archive, and as Douglas notes, "[a]rchivists have pointed to the fact that a body of records may be used or maintained in a number of different orders over the course of its active life and . . . we must instead consider that there are multiple or 'parallel' original orders that need to be respected and represented through arrangement and description" (51).

The second section, "Reclamation and Representation," considers the ways that archival materials can shape writers' reputations. In "Untrustworthy Reproductions and Doctored Archives: Undoing the Sins of a Victorian Biographer," Isabelle Cosgrave argues that Amelia Opie's biographer altered and misquoted original documents to present Opie in a more conservative light. Fran Baker reconstructs Charles Dickens's role in editing Elizabeth Gaskell's story,

"The Crooked Branch" (1859). Baker discovers that this case study "also reveals Gaskell's increasing professionalism as an author throughout the 1850s and her attitude to short stories as a quick, convenient and lucrative form of writing" (75). In "Lost Property: John Galsworthy and the Search for 'That Stuffed Shirt,'" Simon Barker argues that Galsworthy's reputation suffered from a remark that Woolf supposedly made. Barker reports that "according to David Holloway (1968: 1), [Woolf] recorded in her diary of 1933 her thankfulness that 'that stuffed shirt' had died" (91). Barker corrects this error, noting that in her diary Woolf "simply reported 'that stark man lies dead'" (91-2). Subsequently, the BBC production of *The Forsyte Saga* in 1967 helped to provide a new audience for Galsworthy (92). In the final contribution to this segment, "Poetry and Personality: The Private Papers and Public Image of Elizabeth Jennings," Jane Dowson argues that because Jennings is primarily known as a Catholic poet, critics have not investigated her biography in the same fashion as they have with Sylvia Plath. Dowson sought "material that would help establish Jennings' significance to twentieth-century English poetry. I also wanted to enhance the human interest that might heighten her public profile and anticipated that the papers relating to Jennings's breakdown might be the most valuable in dispelling myths of the merely quiet poet" (106). Dowson was primarily seeking to revive interest in Jennings, but there may be more to consider regarding her influence at midcentury on poetry and publishing. While Dowson does not note it, Plath reported in 1960 that she had "met the popular British Oxford graduate—poetess, Elizabeth Jennings, a Catholic, who reads for a London publishing house and lives in a convent while here, returning to her rooms in Oxford on weekends to write (she has three volumes out). We got along very well" (Plath 369). Plath was observing Jennings and in Plath's *New Poets of England and America* (1962) anthology at Smith College, the corner of Jennings's poem "Teresa of Avila" remains turned down.

The collection's penultimate section, "Boundaries," shifts the focus from literature to its intersections with visual art and film. Carrie Smith in "Illustration and Ekphrasis: The Working Drafts of Ted Hughes's *Cave Birds*" analyzes the manuscripts of *Cave Birds: An Alchemical Cave Drama* (1978) that Hughes placed in the University of Exeter's archives, a collection which "reveals the nature of [Leonard] Baskin's and Ted Hughes's collaboration—one that foregrounds the tension between poetry and visual art built into the creation of the book" (123). Smith argues that the composition of this volume revises our sense of ekphrasis, presenting "a collaborative process which passes back and forth between two living artists . . . This intensifies the tension at the heart of ekphrasis—the power struggle between the two arts and methods of composition, as each writes back to the other" (129). Also drawing on Exeter's collections, in "Letter Writing, Cinemagoing, and Archive Ephemera," Lisa Stead reads women's letters in British film fan magazines "to explore an interactive female audience in early twentieth-century Britain" (140). She proposes that "this kind of archive involves embarking on an investigation that takes the researcher . . . into the material culture that both surrounds and constitutes film history" (141). Stead's research may inspire research with similar materials that contextualize Woolf's relationship to film and popular culture.

The volume's closing section, "Working in the Archive," leaves readers with the realities of researching and teaching with primary sources. Sara S. Hodson, in "To Reveal or Conceal: Privacy and Confidentiality in the Papers of Contemporary Authors," deals with protecting the interests of collections' authors or their estates. As she clarifies, "two ethics—access versus privacy—stand in direct competition" (162). In "Teaching the Material Archive at Smith College," Karen V. Kukil introduces methods for teaching students to work critically with primary sources, particularly Woolf and Plath's correspondence. At Smith, students have the opportunity to shed new light on writers' exchanges and the shape they take. As Kukil demonstrates, the watermarks on the pages of Woolf and Lytton Strachey's correspondence at Smith underscore the ways that artifacts can shape meaning (178). In the volume's final essay, "'What will survive of us are manuscripts': Archives, Scholarship and Human Stories," Helen Taylor captures the commitment and skill needed to acquire rare materials:

> Archivists describe shuffling on hands and knees through filthy attics on the prowl for invaluable material someone has offered to a library, on the condition that their staff fetch it. This is a job requiring you to get down and dirty—both inside and outside the large holdings such as the British Library and the Bodleian—calling for considerable diplomacy, tact and low cunning. Furthermore, timing is all. (191-192)

Taylor concludes with the challenge and value of creating digital archives, inspiring a sense of the limitless projects and archives that could exist.

The Boundaries of the Literary Archive provides an exciting resource for Woolf scholars invested in understanding the complexity of her writing and the contexts informing it. The contributors' range of topics and approaches suggests just how many directions there are to pursue in future Woolf and modernist scholarship. The collection's subject also raises new questions regarding the geographical, physical, and digital boundaries that shape our engagement with Woolf's *oeuvre*.

—Amanda Golden, *Georgia Institute of Technology*

Works Cited

Hall, Donald and Robert Pack, eds. *New Poets of England and America*. Cleveland: The World Publishing Company, 1962. Library of Sylvia Plath. Mortimer Rare Book Room, Smith College, Northampton, MA.

Plath, Sylvia. *Letters Home*. 1975. Ed. Aurelia Schober Plath. London: Faber and Faber, 1999.

Woolf Online. www.woolfonline.com. Accessed 1 January 2014.

Virginia Woolf, Life and London: Bloomsbury and Beyond. Jean Moorcroft Wilson (London: Cecil Woolf, 2011 rev. edition) 256pp.

The Cambridge Companion to the Literature of London. Lawrence Manley, ed. (Cambridge: Cambridge University Press, 2011) xviii + 297pp.

"I like this London life in early summer – the street sauntering and square haunting," Virginia Woolf wrote in her diary in April 1925 (*D3* 11). *Virginia Woolf, Life and London: Bloomsbury and Beyond* is a welcome reissue of Jean Moorcroft Wilson's 1987 guidebook to the role of the city in Woolf's life and writing, revised in order to provide up-to-date visitor information for Woolf's houses, as well as to acknowledge relevant literary studies published since its first. For those readers coming to it for the first time, *Life and London* is split into three main sections, the first discussing Woolf's relationship to the different houses in which she lived and worked, from childhood until she and Leonard finally moved to Rodmell in 1940, the second the role of London and the symbolism of its landscape and landmarks in her writing, and the third taking the reader on a tour of some of the key sites of "Woolf's London." It is here that the book assumes the role of the guidebook proper. Three walks are suggested in areas that Woolf herself enjoyed walking—Bloomsbury, Hampstead, and the City—while a further four imaginatively recreate walks taken by characters within the novels: Clarissa's famous walk from Westminster to Regent's Park in *Mrs. Dalloway* is of course the first, but also included are Helen and Ridley Ambrose's walk from Temple Bar to the docks at Wapping in *The Voyage Out*, Ralph Denham's along the Victoria Embankment in *Night and Day*, and Martin and Sally Pargiter's from St. Paul's to Hyde Park and Kensington Gardens in *The Years*. A further chapter offers recommendations for visiting places outside of London associated with Woolf's life and writing, including Talland House in Cornwall, and Asham, Monk's

House and Charleston in Sussex. This is where most of the updated information is included. Both the architectural illustrations of Woolf's residences by Leonard McDermid, faithfully recreated from life or photographs but in each of which the London pavement evocatively shimmers as if with sunshine on fresh rain, and the delightful maps and line drawings by Tamsin Hickson that accompany the walking guides, are retained.

As a combination of biography, literary criticism and walking guide, all of which integrate with and illuminate each other, Wilson's book still surprises with the detail and breadth of its engagement with Woolf's literary London. Carefully researched and packed with wonderful quotations from Woolf's oeuvre, yet light and engaging in tone, it adeptly straddles both the scholarly and more popular readership, offering what remains one of the most informative and accessible introductions to the significance of London for and in Woolf's work. The references remain minimal, which may be frustrating for some readers, and it is perhaps a pity that they were not added in full to the revised version (the payoff is a book that can fit comfortably in the hand of the would-be Woolfian street-saunterer). What particularly marks Wilson's account is her sensitivity to Woolf's personal, psychological and aesthetic response to London, such as the nuances she identifies in Woolf's emotional and symbolic engagement with different spaces on the London map (between the vitality of the city center and the oppressiveness of the suburbs, the peace and intellectual stimulation of bohemian Bloomsbury and the social respectability and demands of Victorian Kensington, the exclusivity of Bond Street compared with the gaudy dynamism of Oxford Street, the seriousness and purpose of the City, the mental escape of Regent's Park, and the emotional intensity symbolized by the Thames, and so on), and her recognition of the powerful importance to Woolf of its history and prehistoric past. Wilson argues forcefully that the vitality of life that Woolf found in London was crucial to her ability to function as an artist, marshalling much evidence from Woolf's diaries and letters to do so. "Contrary to what Leonard had always maintained," she observes, "London was good for Virginia precisely because it kept her attached to the surface of life" (121). The social demands of London, visitors and dinner parties, and the constant proximity of life beyond the individual mind, Wilson suggests, meant that Woolf "could not linger in those queer regions of the mind which fascinated and appalled her" (121). Perhaps the most striking example is Woolf's diary entry for the 28th of June 1923, while living in what she was increasingly regarding as enforced seclusion in Richmond, in which she writes dejectedly of "sit[ting] down baffled and depressed to face a life spent, mute and mitigated, in the suburbs […] I'm tied, imprisoned, inhibited ... For ever to be suburban" (*D*2 250). By comparison, one year later in May 1924, after she had persuaded Leonard to return to London and they had moved to Tavistock Square,

Woolf declares with obvious elation that "London is enchanting," continuing, "One of these days I will write about London, & how it takes up the private life & carries it on, without any effort. Faces passing lift up my mind; prevent it from settling, as it does in the stillness at Rodmell" (*D2* 301-2).

Her next novel, *Mrs. Dalloway*, published in 1925, would be her most passionate celebration of the city, opening with Clarissa's delighted plunge into the sunlit June streets, following her own period of illness and seclusion. She was still articulating the importance of the city as the necessary stimulus for her creative process in 1928, writing on the 31st of May that "London itself perpetually attracts, stimulates, gives me a play and a story and a poem without any trouble, save that of moving my legs through the streets" (*D3* 186). As Wilson notes, walking in London was essential to Woolf's conception of herself as a writer, something she explained in her essay "Street-Haunting" (1927). Venturing out into the crowd under the subterfuge of buying a pencil, Woolf's narrative persona is afforded an escape from the enclosure of the self, and the opportunity to enter imaginatively into multiple other lives, forming characters and giving expression, as she would put it in *A Room of One's Own*, to "the accumulation of unrecorded life" passing in its teeming streets: "Into each of these lives one could penetrate a little way, far enough to give oneself the illusion that one is not tethered to a single mind, but can put on briefly for a few minutes the bodies and minds of others" (*DM* 35). Walking in London, seeing its people and monuments, imagining their lives and picturing its history, was the material with which Woolf's pencil worked.

Woolf is just one of the many writers who feature in *The Cambridge Companion to the Literature of London*, edited by Lawrence Manley, which contains fourteen essays by leading literary, art history and cultural studies scholars on the literary representation of London from the medieval period to the present day, informed by theories and methods drawn not only from literary analysis but also social and urban studies, historical studies and psychogeography, among others. In common with the broader Cambridge Companion series, and as the chapter titles indicate—Images of London in medieval English literature, London and the early modern stage, London and the early modern book, London and poetry to 1750, Staging London in the restoration and eighteenth century, London and narration in the long eighteenth century, London and nineteenth-century poetry, London in the Victorian novel, London and Victorian visual culture, London in poetry since 1900, London and modern prose 1900-1950, Immigration and postwar London literature, Writing London in the twenty-first century, Inner London—this is intended as a survey collection, and as such covers a wide range of periods and writers, with necessarily brief consideration of each. Moreover, the five-and-a-half-page "chronology" of key historical events and literary texts of the city from 1045 to 2007 can only hope to be representative, as the inclusion of only one Dickens novel (*Bleak House*) and one Woolf novel (*Mrs. Dalloway*) indicates. That said, the Companions have set a standard for the recent profusion of scholarly introductions, and the individual essays here offer new research and insightful arguments that are far from mere summaries of accepted readings and ideas.

Woolf readers will be most interested in Leo Mellor's essay on London in prose in the first half of the twentieth century. Faced with the essential unknowability of the ever-expanding modern metropolis, Mellor argues, writers sought "literary forms that were analogous to maps, or could incorporate characters' encounters with vistas or directions" (207). While this still included the traditional narrative model of the *flâneur* as walker, observer and "reader" of the city, Mellor suggests that the perspective of the pedestrian was "complemented and counterpointed" by the new vistas offered by the aerial view from the airplane, and the subterranean space of the London Underground. Drawing upon less familiar examples of Woolf's urban writing—including her essay "Flying Over London" (published in 1950)—he offers a concise but stimulating discussion of not only what he describes as Woolf's "perambulatory" mode of urban observation, but also her use of these new spatial perspectives of modernity in her representation of characters' experiences of, on the one hand, tube travel, and on the other, the vista of the city as seen from the air. Interestingly, however, given the context of the volume as a whole, Mellor pays little attention to the strong sense of London's history, and literary history, that also so charges Woolf's writing.

In his introduction, for example, Manley emphasizes that "[t]he urban environment in which (and in response to which) so much of English literature has been written has itself been constructed in many respects by its representation in that literature—by the ideas, images, and styles created by writers who have experienced or inhabited it" (2). Yet few of the subsequent essays really engage in detail with this intertextual aspect of London's identity, or the previous essays in the volume that set up London's literary history from the medieval period onwards. John Ball notes that the West Indian narrator of Sam Selvon's *The Lonely Londoners* (1956) enters enthusiastically into the *flâneur*-like roaming of "the storied city of Shakespeare and Dickens and Woolf" (227), and James Donald describes London as an "archive city [...] built of words, images, and stories" from literary texts from Chaucer to Zadie Smith, but much more might have been done to explore the palimpsestic nature of London's literary representation.

Woolf, of course, was highly conscious of the redolence of the London of Defoe, or Dr. Johnson, or Dickens, in her own experience of the city, and used the image of the city as seen through their eyes to capture the historical depth of London's landscape, as it could break into even the modern moment. Wilson indeed discusses the detailed depictions of the changing landscape of London in

Orlando from the seventeenth century, to the eighteenth, to the Victorian period, to the 1920s, as well as the ways in which many of her characters connect with the city's past: Bernard in *The Waves* for example, who senses the prehistoric remains far below the pavement under his feet, or the beggar-woman singing in Regent's Park in *Mrs. Dalloway*, whose song is an ancient one that reaches back through millions of years. The chapters in the *Cambridge Companion*, taken together, offer an invaluable guide to the experience of London as the setting and inspiration for literature over the course of this long history, and the ways in which literature in turn helped to create and interpret the London that is experienced. Wilson's study provides a fascinatingly detailed example of this dynamic between London and its imaginative representation in process.

—Deborah Longworth, *University of Birmingham*

Virginia Woolf and Classical Music: Politics, Aesthetics, Form. Emma Sutton (Edinburgh: Edinburgh University Press, 2013) vi + 171 pp.

Interest in the topic of Woolf and music, as Emma Sutton explains in her introduction, has undoubtedly grown during the last ten to fifteen years in Woolf scholarship. Indeed, it is surprising that no monograph on the subject has appeared until now, as Joyce E. Kelley's thorough documentation of Woolf critics who have discussed the word-music interchange demonstrates (her essay on the subject is in *The Edinburgh Companion to Virginia Woolf and the Arts*, 2010). Significantly, Sutton proves beyond a doubt that a book is warranted. Indeed, her project lays important historical and cultural groundwork, opening up new avenues for exploration in the process.

The book begins, however paradoxically, with a visual gesture: a stunning photograph of the Roger Fry/Arnold Dolmetsch spinet housed in The Courtauld Gallery, London. To my mind, this is an entirely fitting way to begin the book. Sutton's perceptive study of Fry's painting on the inside of the keyboard's lid is juxtaposed with the instrument itself (Dolmetsch was a leading figure in the Early Music revival, as both a performer and instrument–maker). Sutton employs the spinet to introduce the seemingly antithetical issues of history and contemporaneity: "The instrument, then, combines historical and avant-garde elements, most obviously encapsulated in the unexpected combination of an instrument popularized in the seventeenth century with contemporary decorative aesthetics" (2). This juxtaposition informs the study as a whole, which, she elaborates, has a twofold focus: "it considers the role and significance of music in Woolf's politics and in her aesthetics. It offers an account of classical music's ... place in the socio-political vision of Woolf's writing and in her formal experiments in prose" (5). Although no theorization of how Sutton reads literature and music together is elaborated, the introduction is chock full of new archival findings and excellent historical and biographical materials. Sutton's investigation of Leonard Woolf's cash accounts to discern record and music journal purchases, scrupulous scanning of the letters (published and unpublished) and the catalogue for the *Library of Leonard and Virginia Woolf*, as well as then-contemporary concert programs, all combine to provide the reader with a new sense of the music the Woolfs most likely heard before 1939—the lamentably late start date of Leonard's "Diary of Music Listened To." Additionally, Sutton's comprehensive survey of both Leonard and Virginia Woolf's diaries illustrates the extensive concert-going practices that Woolf enjoyed over her entire career. The introduction, therefore, leaves the reader with little doubt that music was of vital and sustained significance for Woolf's writing and life.

Significantly, the introduction also clarifies Sutton's concern to continue the trend in musicology, begun by Susan McClary, Lawrence Kramer, Phillip Brett, and others, to understand music as imbued with political import. As she argues, "attending to the political significance of Woolf's uses of music concerns not only the diegetic representations of music in the fiction but also the politics of form itself" (19). Somewhat weaker, or at least slighter, where the latter is concerned, Sutton's ability to tease out the political implications of "'the outside world' in Woolf's writing" (19), is estimable and perhaps her most valuable contribution to Woolf Studies. Indeed, any cross-disciplinary study with music should attempt to attend to the seminal shifts that have occurred in New Musicology, and Sutton certainly accomplishes her task on this front. In chapter 3, for example, Sutton's discussion of the nationalist rhetoric that informs the discourse of the English Musical Renaissance and her reading of Woolf's resistance to said rhetoric in *The Voyage Out*, *Jacob's Room,* and *Mrs. Dalloway* is highly illuminating.

In this chapter, however, Sutton also returns to the personage who looms very large over the entire book: Richard Wagner (and his operas). Indeed, time and again, Sutton will demonstrate that Woolf's primary musico-literary influence is the operatic oeuvre of Wagner (the link forms the primary material for chapters 1, the beginning of 2, and the bulk of 3, 5, and 6). Perhaps this is not a surprise given Sutton's 2002 *Aubrey Beardsley and British Wagnerism in the 1890s*. But, despite the title of the first chapter, "On Not Writing Opera" (based on a simultaneously published essay in Phyllis Weliver and Katherine Ellis's collection, *Words and Notes in the Long Nineteenth Century*, 2013, "Fiction as Musical Critique: Virginia Woolf, *The Voyage Out* and the Case of Wagner"), the reader has to wait until chapter 5, which is the most critical of Wagner's anti-Semitism, to get a thoroughly nuanced understanding of what Sutton considers to be Woolf's critique of his operatic plots and libretti. In other words, much more time is spent in the book proving that Woolf is in Wagner's "debt" than in demonstrating how her anti-fascist politics, for example, also inform her musically-infused innovations. But the fifth chapter, which focuses on Kitty's attendance at *Siegfried* in *The Years*, does make headway in this regard, and admittedly, it is decidedly difficult terrain. I suspect we will get more of Woolf's critical stance on Wagner in Sutton's forthcoming article, "Flying Dutchman, Wandering Jews: Romantic Opera, Anti-Semitism and Jewish Mourning in *Mrs. Dalloway*," in Adriana Varga's essay collection, *Virginia Woolf and Music*.

All the more surprising, then, that in the final chapter, Sutton returns to Wagner, but not as convincingly, to Woolf's dissatisfaction with his methods. Instead, she reads *The Waves* as primarily Woolf's version of the *Ring* cycle. Numerous and compelling correspondences in "character" and plot are listed, a pattern that begins in the opening chapter and comes back throughout the book, but further exploration of the effect of the associations on Woolf's writing practices, or even the historico-cultural import for the novel, is warranted. Similarities and likenesses to opera are successfully sought by Sutton, to show the many "intermittent parallels between Wagner's characters and Woolf's" (148), but less so, the differences or exciting diversions that Woolf produces. And in the summary statements to the chapter, Woolf's reverence for Wagner is again confirmed, almost despite her departures: "for all that the novel persistently undermines the totalizing aspirations of the *Ring*, the conclusion—like the opening—of Woolf's novel draws heavily, and surely admiringly, on Wagner's work" (149).

The first book to pronounce the arrival of a new subject area is often tasked with the necessary, but not always pleasurable, duty of justification. It might be this impetus that leads Sutton to provide admirable (but almost overwhelmingly copious) proof of likenesses and indebtedness, but also, ultimately, to say less about music and more about words (another issue that haunts the study as a whole). When Wagner is not the focus—as in chapter 4, which examines the fugue and Ludwig van Beethoven—other operatic composers come in to complete the picture, such as Rhoda's experience of the "arrow into the note, 'Ah'" (*TW* 122), which Sutton perceptively links to Gioachino Rossini's *Wilhelm Tell* and Jacques Offenbach's *Tales of Hoffman*. Perhaps because of the pervasiveness of opera in the book, Sutton seems to be inadvertently led away from the properties of music, which does not necessarily need to be the case. There are some notable exceptions: the Beethoven chapter, which superbly explores the implications of homoeroticism and heroism in the musical allusions from *Mrs. Dalloway*, and the summary thoughts from chapter 1 where Sutton compares Wagner's ending for

Tristan und Isolde with *The Voyage Out* to discuss the structural implications. But the correspondences that are made with Wagner and other operatic writers are, by and large, those of plot and character, the products of the verbal component of opera—tied to music, certainly, but not music in and of itself.

Overall, Sutton has produced a lucidly-written, comprehensively researched, and thoroughly astute study of Woolf and classical music; it is a welcome addition to Woolf scholarship.

—Elicia Clements, *York University*

Shell Shock and the Modernist Imagination: The Death Drive in Post-World War I British Fiction. Wyatt Bonikowski (Burlington, VT; Farnham, UK: Ashgate, 2013) viii + 192 pp.

"The emergence of shell shock during the First World War brought about a dramatic shift in the way we understand the effects of war," Wyatt Bonikowski's highly readable study begins. And, in producing the shell-shocked soldier "as a historical and a literary figure," this shift raised "the problem of the effects of war on the mind" (1). Through readings of post-war fiction by Ford Madox Ford, Rebecca West, and Virginia Woolf as well as of the writings of psychoanalysts and military psychiatrists, Bonikowski teases out some of the intriguing complexities embodied in the returning shell-shocked soldier, who not only brought his war experience back to the home front but also encountered the challenges of wartime traumas experienced by civilians, especially women. "Return" did not always mean soldiers going home after fighting in the trenches. As Bonikowski notes in a rewarding discussion of West's *The Return of the Soldier*, it could also refer to soldiers being sent back into action once their wounds had been mended or their psychological disorders cured. In their attempts to grapple with the returning shell-shocked soldier, Bonikwoski argues, modern authors employed new literary methods in order to reshape and refigure material that otherwise would have eluded literary representation.

The key to these literary variations on the central theme of traumatic wartime, according to Bonikowski, is Freud's theory of the death drive. Manifesting itself in wartime experience and in writing about that experience, he contends, the death drive provided authors with the ultimate challenge because, "resistant to representation and communication, [it] reveal[ed] itself only indirectly, through silence, disruption, or figuration" (172). Put this way, the death drive seems to confer theoretical coherence on the study as a whole while suggesting an array of epistemological and expressive complications. That the book doesn't always display such coherence is the result of a failure to integrate the theoretical material as fully as it might be into the central chapters on war fiction. Those chapters usually move along under their own steam. Each, to be sure, includes cross-references to Freud, often to quite illuminating effect, as in the discussion of the interplay of external and internal stimuli in Ford's treatment of sexual passion, but such moments, characterized as offering a "striking resemblance to Freud's descriptions" (66), function less as integral parts of a larger analytical whole than as elaborations or clarifications of insights yielded by close reading of the literary text. Even if pursued more consistently, moreover, the emphasis on the death drive would still pose problems. To present the death drive as the central psychological phenomenon that "reveals itself" in the war and in war writing is to imply that experimental modernism's encounters with wartime trauma are underwritten by a fairly simple form of realism. Attentive to the complex relations between fact and fantasy in the work of Freud and Lacan, on whose theories of trauma he relies for his understanding of "the real," Bonikowski seems less interested in exploring an analogous sense of complication in the relations between literature, history, and psychoanalysis.

The highlight of the book is the chapter on Ford. Bonikowski offers a stimulating account of how the interlocking "transports" of war and traumatic sexuality at work in *Parade's End* (1924-1928) engender a "wartime impressionism" that disrupts Ford's earlier notions of memory and representation. Using a strategically limited definition of Ford's pre-war impressionism as an aesthetic of visualization, Bonikowski shows how Ford combined a new understanding of the impression as a "material inscription" with his insight into the "divisions of the mind at war" (65) to dramatize "a crisis of meaning aligned with a historical shift from a stable social order to one of unpredictable mobility and insecurity" (67). The central section of this chapter, "Tea-trays and Tietjens: Impressionism in the Key of T," which investigates how Ford's fiction links the traumas of war and sexuality to "the broader problem of what it means to write a novel about the traumatic effects of war" (75), is a real treat. So, too, is the next section, which specifies more clearly *how* Ford connects wartime with sexual trauma. Here, Bonikowski works out in compelling detail how the fiction's narrative repetitions generate effects of "static restlessness, a kind of moving-in-place" (91). These effects, he shows, raise important questions about "bringing a narrative of the First World War to a close, especially one whose narrative motivation has been the seemingly unstoppable forces of war and sexual passion" (87).

The last full-length chapter turns to Virginia Woolf—specifically, Septimus Warren Smith, the shell-shocked soldier of *Mrs. Dalloway*. Taking the title for this chapter from Clarissa Dalloway's thought on hearing of Septimus's suicide that "Death was an attempt to communicate," Bonikowski considers the problem of what Clarissa gleans from the story of Septimus's demise and of the "relationship between these two characters, between a mad soldier and a society woman, a suicide and a party hostess" (134). These are old chestnuts, but Bonikowski brings new insight to an already busy critical conversation, especially when considering the passage in which Septimus thinks he hears the birds speaking to him in Greek. Taking his cue from Woolf's contemporaneous essay "On Not Knowing Greek," Bonikowski suggests that her reference to Greek (a language Septimus doesn't understand) allows her to "represent the mind of Septimus from within" and thus "to speak about the unspeakability of madness" (140). Woolf, Bonikowski argues, seeks "to make the experience of madness readable, not simply to describe it but rather to represent its intensity and disorder through a particular use of language" (140). In Woolf's view, the "power of Greek words derives in part from the fact that they come to us broken, cut off from their origins" (143). Such indirectness and fragmentariness, Bonikowski suggests, enable her to make "a narrative out of the seductive allure of death and the dangerous leap of poetic intensity, both in Septimus's mad desire for communication and in Clarissa Dalloway's attempt to grasp the meaning of his suicide" (145).

Extending this discussion to consider the "internal logic, and even beauty" of Septimus's madness, Bonikowski observes that this figure of the returning soldier "insists on a meaning beyond the conventions and frameworks of Woolf's time and our own" (147). In explicating this meaning, he offers the provocative claim that Woolf places "death at the center of the novel—not so that it may be mourned but [...] so that it may be enjoyed" (146). Derived from his reading of Freud on the death drive, this account of *Mrs. Dalloway* as a work of "aesthetic sublimation" that "shows how a novel, by organizing itself around death, might sustain the pleasures of life" (173) may cede too much authority to Clarissa's response to the news of Septimus's death; it suppresses the possibility of meeting her response with irony (at the expense, for instance, of her upper-class presumption that she could know how Septimus felt). Bonikoswki argues persuasively that Mrs. Dalloway subverts ideas of proportion associated—in a disproportionately vehement passage in the middle of the novel—with Sir William Bradshaw, but in that case it is illogical to argue that Clarissa's response, "given its placement in the novel, is the right reading" (150). Conversely, when he does raise the possibility of seeing Clarissa ironically as a devotee of "senseless" party-giving, Bonikowski suggests that Woolf "tempts the reader to judge Clarissa the way those close to her, Richard and Peter in particular, do" (150-151), an unlikely reading unless you agree that Woolf is encouraging us to cozy up to the dull and conventional (Richard Dalloway) or the creepy and unhinged (Peter Walsh). When he claims that "One might say that she [Clarissa] perseveres in her senselessness to the point of a certain kind of madness" (151), Bonikowski is forcing the point; by using safety-commas to speak of "Septimus's 'choice' of madness," he signals that he, too, feels this. It's hard to make the case that Septimus is mad but that he chooses madness; rather than trying to grant him such extravagant agency, it would make more sense to say simply that he dramatizes the problem of agency in fictional character.

Nothing ventured, nothing gained. You don't have to buy all of Bonikowski's arguments in order to find his chapters on Ford, West, and Woolf well worth reading. While his approach to the shell-shocked soldier as "a literary figure" tends to emphasize plot, character, and theme over formal or stylistic device, he has new and interesting things to say about a good topic. At its best, this is a book that offers compelling evidence in support of its twin claims that the returning soldier "presented a problem of representation and memorialization" (2) and that this problem was often aggravated by symptoms of repetition that resisted conventional narrative forms and even language itself.

—Adam Parkes, *University of Georgia*

Notes on Contributors

David Bradshaw is Professor of English Literature at Oxford University and a Fellow of Worcester College. In addition to editing various modernist novels, including *Mrs Dalloway*, *To the Lighthouse*, *The Waves*, and *The Years*, he has published numerous articles on modernist writing and culture and (co-)edited *The Hidden Huxley* (1994), *A Concise Companion to Modernism* (2003), *The Cambridge Companion to E.M. Forster* (2007), *A Companion to Modernist Literature and Culture* (2006) and *Prudes on the Prowl: Fiction and Obscenity in England, 1850 to the Present Day* (2013).

Clara Jones has recently completed a PhD on Virginia Woolf at Queen Mary University of London, where she teaches courses on Virginia Woolf and Feminism(s). She is currently working on a monograph, *Virginia Woolf: Ambivalent Activist*, which examines the details of Woolf's political activism and social participation with a number of organizations including the People's Suffrage Federation, the Women's Co-operative Guild and the National Federation of Women's Institutes.

Ella Ophir is Assistant Professor of English at the University of Saskatchewan. Her research and teaching focus on British and American modernism. She has published articles on Wallace Stevens, Laura Riding, Wyndham Lewis, James Agee, and Joseph Conrad. She is currently preparing a digital scholarly edition of *The Note Books of a Woman Alone* for release in 2015.

Rod C. Taylor is an Assistant Professor of Literature and Writing at Tennessee State University. His work in modernism concerns the reoccurring images of education in early twentieth-century literature.

• HENRY JAMES • WILLIAM FAULKNER • *THE GETTYSBURG ADDRESS* • NEW YORK SCHOOL POETS •

—linguae americanae—

ARIZONA QUARTERLY

American literature, culture, and
theory, four times a year

1 year $20
3 years $40

1731 E. Second St. • University of Arizona
Tucson, Arizona 85721-0014

—Return this ad for a free sample issue—

• WALT WHITMAN • DOS PASSOS' *MANHATTAN TRANSFER* • HERMAN MELVILLE • STEPHEN CRANE •

criticism

A Quarterly for Literature and the Arts
renée c. hoogland, editor

Criticism provides a forum for current scholarship on literature, media, music, and visual culture. A place for rigorous theoretical and critical debate as well as formal and methodological self-reflexivity and experimentation, *Criticism* aims to present contemporary thought at its most vital.

Subscriptions
- Institution: $179.00
- Individual: $64.00
- Student/Senior: $29.00

Back Issues
- Institution: $50.00
- Individual: $20.00

Recent and upcoming Special Issues:
- 56.3: Andy Warhol
- 56.2: Jack Smith Today
- 55.4: Melodrama

For more information, visit
digitalcommons.wayne.edu/criticism

Wayne State University Press
www.wsupress.wayne.edu
800-978-7323

Comparative Literature

The official journal of the American Comparative Literature Association

George E. Rowe, editor

The oldest journal in its field in the United States, *Comparative Literature* explores issues in literary history and theory. Drawing on a variety of theoretical and critical approaches, the journal represents a wide-ranging look at the intersections of national literatures, global literary trends, and theoretical discourse.

Subscribe today.
Online access and keyword and table-of-contents alerts are available with a print subscription (four issues each year).

Individuals: $40
Students: $28 (photocopy of valid student ID required)

To order, please visit **dukeupress.edu/complit**.
Postage applies for international customers.

Theorizing Breast Cancer: Narrative, Politics, Memory

Guest Editors Mary K. DeShazer & Anita Helle

Tulsa Studies in Women's Literature
Vol. 32, No. 2 / Vol. 33, No. 1
Fall 2013 / Spring 2014

Legacy
A Journal of American Women Writers

Edited by Jennifer S. Tuttle
Theresa Strouth Gaul and Nicole Tonkovich, Co-Editors

Legacy is the only journal to focus specifically on American women's writings from the seventeenth through the mid-twentieth century. Each issue's articles cover a wide range of topics: examinations of the works of individual authors; genre studies; analyses of race, ethnicity, gender, class, and sexualities in women's literature; and historical and material cultural issues pertinent to women's lives and literary works.

Coming in 2013: A special issue on "Women Writing Disability".

Legacy is the official journal of the Society for the Study of American Women Writers.

For subscriptions and back issues:
Visit **nebraskapress.unl.edu**
or call **402-472-8536**

> *Legacy* is available online
> on Project MUSE
> **bit.ly/LEG_MUSE**
> and
> JSTOR Current Scholarship
> **bit.ly/LEG_JSTOR**

 Follow us on Twitter @LegacyWmenWrite

UNIVERSITY OF NEBRASKA PRESS

Subscribe to film LITERATURE QUARTERLY

Literature/Film Quarterly is the longest-standing international journal in adaptation studies, a field of inquiry into the ways that films are adapted from literature, history and other films. The journal represents an exciting range of interdisciplinary approaches to understanding cinema, and, in addition, since its establishment in 1973, we have featured interviews with many revered directors, such as Frank Capra, Robert Altman, Terence Davies, Baz Luhrmann and Richard Linklater. Both intellectually stimulating and accessible, with subscriptions in over 30 countries, *Literature/Film Quarterly* is for film scholars and aficionados alike.

Subscriptions are available at just $35 for individuals.

FOR MORE INFORMATION:
Visit: www.salisbury.edu/lfq
E-mail: litfilmquart@salisbury.edu

Mississippi Quarterly
The Journal of Southern Cultures

Since 1948 the *Mississippi Quarterly* has published refereed articles on the life and culture of the South, past and present. Recent issues include essays on William Styron, Christine Wiltz, Arna Bontemps, Mary Lee Settle, Willie Morris, Lillian B Horace, Marsha Norman, Wendell Berry, and Forrest Carter. Recent special issues are devoted to Lewis Nordan, Faulkner and Labor, Lynching and American Culture, American Indian Literatures and Cultures in the South, the South in Film, and Southern Roots and Routes. The *Quarterly* is published by Mississippi State University's College of Arts and Sciences.

Subscriptions are $24 per year in the United States, $27 in Canada and Mexico, and $29 in all other countries. Back issues are available.

> *Mississippi Quarterly*
> P.O. Box 5272
> Mississippi State, MS 39762

missq.msstate.edu

Mosaic
a journal for the interdisciplinary study of literature

A matter of *lifedeath*
An international interdisciplinary conference

October 1-4, 2014

University of Manitoba
Winnipeg, Canada

Andrea Carlino
Françoise Dastur
David Palumbo-Liu
H. Peter Steeves
Elisabeth Weber

Forthcoming Publications

ROMANCE 47.2 (June 2014) This *Mosaic* special issue engages the rich history of the word *Romance*, with essays on "the Romantics," the roman, romantic fiction, Romanticism, the state of the love story in literature and film, and the figure of the "romantic."

Recent Publications

FEATURING: NICHOLAS ROYLE 47.1 (March 2014) Nicholas Royle is Professor of English at the University of Sussex. He is the author of numerous books, including *Veering* (2011) and the novel *Quilt* (2010). This issue will feature a "Crossings" interview with Professor Royle and new writing by him.

BLINDNESS 46.3 (Sep. 2013) This issue brings together critical and disability theories to address historical and contemporary studies and interpretations of blindness across various genres, as well as studies of, to use Samuel Weber's title words (in *Institution and Interpretation*), "The Blindness of the Seeing Eye."

Mosaic, a journal for the interdisciplinary study of literature
University of Manitoba
208 Tier Building
Winnipeg MB
R3T 2N2
Canada

Tel: 204-474-9763
Fax: 204-474-7584
mosaic@umanitoba.ca
www.umanitoba.ca/mosaic

Policy

Woolf **S**tudies **A**nnual invites articles on the work and life of Virginia Woolf and her milieu. The *Annual* intends to represent the breadth and eclecticism of critical approaches to Woolf, and particularly welcomes new perspectives and contexts of inquiry. Articles discussing relations between Woolf and other writers and artists are also welcome.

Articles are sent for review anonymously to a member of the Editorial Board and at least one other reader. Manuscripts should not be under consideration elsewhere or have been previously published. It is strongly advised that those submitting work to *WSA* be familiar with the journal's content. Among criteria on which evaluation of submissions depends are whether an article demonstrates familiarity with scholarship already published in the field, whether the article is written clearly and effectively, and whether it makes a genuine contribution to Woolf studies.

Preparation of Copy

1. Articles are typically between 25 and 30 pages, and do not exceed 8000 words. Inquiries about significantly shorter or longer submissions should be sent to the Editor at woolfstudiesannual@gmail.com.

2. A separate page should include the article's title, author's name, address, telephone & fax numbers, and e-mail address. The author's name and identifying references should not appear on the manuscript to preserve anonymity for our readers.

3. All submissions must include an abstract of no more than 250 words.

4. Manuscripts should be prepared according to most recent MLA style.

5. Submissions may be sent *either* by email to woolfstudiesannual@gmail.com *or* by mail to Mark Hussey, English Dept., Pace University, One Pace Plaza, New York NY 10038. For mailed submissions, please send **three** copies of the article and abstract.

6. Authors of accepted manuscripts are responsible for any necessary permissions fees and for securing any necessary permissions.

All editorial, review, and advertising inquiries should be addressed to woolfstudiesannual@gmail.com.

Inquiries concerning orders should be addressed to PaceUP@pace.edu.

Other Woolf titles available:

"The Hours": The British Museum Manuscript of Mrs. Dalloway, transcribed and edited by Helen M. Wussow (paper 2010).

Virginia Woolf, Jacob's Room: *The Holograph Draft.* Transcribed and edited by Edward L. Bishop (paper 2010)

Women in the Milieu of Leonard and Virginia Woolf: Peace, Politics and Education Ed. Wayne K. Chapman and Janet M. Manson (1998)

Virginia Woolf and Trauma: Embodied Texts Ed. Suzette Henke & David Eberly (2007)

Woolf Across Cultures Ed. Natalya Reinhold (2004)

Woolf Studies Annual 5 (1999)

Woolf Studies Annual 6 (2000): The *Three Guineas* Correspondence, edited by Anna Snaith

Woolf Studies Annual 7 (2001)

Woolf Studies Annual 8 (2002): The Fawcett Library Correspondence, edited by Merry Pawlowski

Woolf Studies Annual 9 (2003): *Virginia Woolf and Literary History Part 1*, edited by Jane Lilienfeld, Jeffrey Oxford, and Lisa Low

Woolf Studies Annual 10 (2004): *Virginia Woolf and Literary History Part 2*, edited by Jane Lilienfeld, Jeffrey Oxford, and Lisa Low

Woolf Studies Annual 11 (2005) - *Woolf Studies Annual 18* (2010)

Woolf Studies Annual 19 (2013): *Special Focus Virginia Woolf and Jews*, edited by Mark Hussey

Virginia Woolf and Communities: Selected Papers from the Eighth Annual Conference on Virginia Woolf edited by Jeanette McVicker and Laura Davis

Virginia Woolf Turning the Centuries: Selected Papers from the Ninth Annual Conference on Virginia Woolf edited by Ann Ardis and Bonnie Kime Scott

Virginia Woolf Out of Bounds: Selected Papers from the Tenth Annual Conference on Virginia Woolf edited by Jessica Berman and Jane Goldman

www.ingramcontent.com/pod-product-compliance
Lightning Source LLC
Chambersburg PA
CBHW061447300426
44114CB00014B/1869